IRISH PLACE NAMES

IRISH
PLACE NAMES

Deirdre *and*
Laurence Flanagan

GILL & MACMILLAN

Published in Ireland by
Gill & Macmillan Ltd
Goldenbridge
Dublin 8
with associated companies throughout the world
© Deirdre and Laurence Flanagan 1994
0 7171 2066 X
Print origination by
Seton Music Graphics Ltd, Bantry, Co. Cork
Printed by
ColourBooks Ltd, Dublin

A catalogue record for this book is available from the British Library.

3   5   4

for

Seán Mac Airt, Éamonn de hÓir
agus Heinrich Wagner

Tosach eolais imchomarc

CONTENTS

FOREWORD

Although she was born in Belfast Deirdre Morton spent most of her childhood in Donegal, in an Irish-speaking area. Here she acquired an awareness of the realities of Irish rural life, both its hardships and its joys, as well, of course, as the basis of her command of the Irish language. Her interest in Irish place-names was inspired by Seán Mac Airt, with whom she worked as a research assistant; it was encouraged by Heinrich Wagner, who succeeded Seán as Head of the Celtic Department of the Queen's University, Belfast, but enjoyed the title of Professor – a title which had been in abeyance for some time. She formed a deep and long-lasting friendship with Éamonn de hÓir, then Principal Officer of the Irish Place-Names Commission. To these three, therefore, we have dedicated this book.

It was from Deirdre that I learned everything I know about the non-material aspects of Irish culture: she filled the gap in my education that schools and domestic background had ignored. It was by her that I was introduced to Irish history – in its fullest sense; to Irish literature; to Irish mythology; to the Irish language; and, not least, to Irish place-names. In return, she was made aware of the contribution Irish archaeology could make to her own speciality.

Before her untimely death on 2 March 1984, Deirdre had talked of writing a book on Irish place-names. The present work is not that book, but a substitute for it – not a wholly unworthy one, I hope, in that its main purpose is to make available to as many people as possible some understanding of the nature of Irish place-names, in as accessible a form as possible. This was a purpose Deirdre held close to her heart.

Although I have drawn extensively on Deirdre's material, both published and unpublished, any omissions and errors are entirely my own responsibility: I apologise for them both to Deirdre and to our readers. It is appropriate that this book should be published exactly ten years after Deirdre's death.

In addition to being divided into four provinces and thirty-two counties, in their turn divided into baronies and parishes, all having names, Ireland is further divided into some 60,000 townlands, all of which again have names (though many of them, of course, share the same, fairly descriptive, name). Inside these townlands, the smallest official land-unit in the country, are many minor names, possibly averaging out at twenty to thirty per townland as recorded on the large-scale maps of the Ordnance Survey, although an intensive ground-survey has revealed as many as 800 minor names in a single townland in Co. Mayo. This amounts to an enormous number of place-names – running into many millions; to explain, or even merely to list, all of these in a single work would be impossible.

Contrary to popular belief, the vast majority of these names are fairly simple, describing natural features – mountains, hills, lakes, rocks, rivers, streams, swamps, forests, woods, inlets, etc. They all, however, reflect the impact of the natural environment on man, and of man, simply by observation, on the environment. The impact, and activities, of man, however, created another category of place-name: those describing the additions or alterations made by man to this natural environment. Thus we get names describing the use of the landscape by man: its division into fields for grazing stock or growing crops; the addition of various structures for human habitation, of structures for industrial purposes, of structures to facilitate passage through it, of structures to accommodate religious observance – be it pagan or Christian – and of structures to accommodate the dead – again pagan or Christian. Any of these, moreover, may contain a claim to a feature, natural or artificial, by a group of people or by an individual. This rich diversity creates problems in interpretation; it also creates an immense wealth of information about the land which has been so liberally bestowed with names.

Introduction

By and large the majority of the surviving products of this naming-process extend over at least 2,000 years. While the vast majority are *Irish*, in the linguistic sense, some, it has been claimed, of physical features such as mountains and principal rivers, 'are not Celtic at all and go back to a time long anterior to the Celtic invasion'. Even of those which are Irish some contain words that are long obsolete and are in consequence virtually unintelligible, even if an uncorrupted form survives, to any speaker of Modern Irish. It must be remembered, however, that place-names provide a great lexicon of the language, a great series of ostensive definitions (definitions created by 'literally' pointing out examples of the feature to be defined), in some cases waiting to be interpreted. Unfortunately, in many instances a feature that was all too evident 2,000 years ago may have by now changed out of all recognition: the trees may have been long since cut down (or died of elm-disease); the lake may have dried up; the site may have been built upon; the monument destroyed at any stage in the period since it was first named. Toponymists are no more immune to the destruction of sites and features than are archaeologists.

There are further problems to perplex the toponymist. If all the names survived in recognisable Irish forms their interpretation would be considerably simpler. Unfortunately this is not the case; a 'blanket of Anglicisation covers them, as a result of the English conquest, throughout a great part of the country'. Large numbers of names do exist in pre-conquest native writing. If the name in question can be identified with an existing name or a surviving feature it is a real help but this happy accident seldom occurs; many names that are preserved cannot now be attached to a place, many places (or surviving names) have no such pre-conquest written record.

In the vast majority of cases, therefore, the toponymist is faced with a process not totally dissimilar to that undertaken by an archaeologist excavating a site: a stratified array of information has to be constructed from all available sources, Irish and English. In an area that is still Irish-speaking, additional source-material may be forthcoming from locals; on the other hand, the more Anglicised the area, and the longer it has been so, the greater the likelihood of documentation, albeit in a form or forms that have suffered various degrees of corruption.

A salutary example of misconceptions arising from failure to follow this procedure arises in the interpretation by a recent writer of the name 'Legoneil', Co. Antrim, part of which is within the boundary of Belfast city (by whose officials it is spelled, for some unknown reason, 'Ligoniel'). The writer interprets the name as 'Hollow of the lime' but adds that another possible meaning is 'O'Neill's hollow'. A chronological listing of cited forms of the name – all, unfortunately, from documentation in English – indicates that, *pace* the *Ordnance Survey Name-Book*, the first interpretation is the only acceptable one.

1	Ballylagaile	*Calendar of Patent Rolls, James I*, 49a (1604)
2	Ballylagaile	*Inquisitions, Antrim* (1605)
3	Ballylagaile	*Calendar of Patent Rolls, James I*, 120a (1607)
4	Ballylaganyle	*Inquisitions, Ulster*, no. 7, James I (1621)
5	Ballylagaile	*Inquisitions, Ulster*, no. 7, James I (1621)
6	Ballylagayle	*Calendar of Patent Rolls, James I*, 523b (1621)
7	Lagainele	*Census* 1659
8	Ballylegaile *alias* Ballyleganile *alias* Legeneile	*Confirmation of Chichester Patent* 1669 (ex Young, R.M., *Old Belfast*)
9	Lag Uí Néill, 'Ó Néill's hollow'	*Ordnance Survey Name-Book*
10	Lag an Aoil	*Ainmneach Gaeilge na mBailte Poist*

The mineral in question is cretaceous limestone and despite their aberrant interpretation of the name the *Ordnance Survey Name-Book* records that '[The townland] abounds in limestone which is extensively quarried'; several disused quarries are marked within the townland on the large-scale Ordnance Survey map. It is difficult to say whether the forms such as 'Ballylagaile' represent a variant form, *lag aoil*, or are just scribal aberrations. It is unlikely that *baile* was ever part of the original name-composition: in the seventeenth century 'Bally-' was often prefixed to established names to indicate that they constituted recognised townland units. This is a fairly simple example of the desirability of listing documented forms of a name. Another, slightly more complex, case appears as an appendix below.

The overwhelming majority of the place-names considered in this book are the names of towns and townlands: that is, names for the most part referring to relatively small areas of land. Names of larger areas have a great contribution to make to the understanding of many aspects of Irish history – indeed without some understanding of them, much of early, and indeed medieval, history is difficult to follow.

Most of the territorial names are basically population-names, sept-names or kingdom-names. The evidence of these names can be used, in conjunction with formal documentation, to establish the location and extent of early kingdoms, both overkingdoms and petty kingdoms. Population-names and sept-names could be used in a transferred sense of the land ruled by the population or sept. The names of three of our provinces illustrate this: Laighin (Leinsterman/ Leinster) or, more formally, *Cúige Laighean* (literally 'The Fifth of the Leinstermen'); *Connacht* (Connaughtmen/Connaught) or *Cúige Chonnacht*, 'The Fifth of the Connaughtmen'; *Ulaidh* (Ulstermen/Ulster), or *Cúige Uladh*, 'The Fifth of the Ulstermen'. *Laighin* and *Ulaidh* are population-names, ruling populations in their respective 'fifths' in the protohistoric period. *Connacht* is a sept-name, the descendants of Conn, identified by our native medieval historians as Conn Céadchathach, 'Conn of the hundred battles', and assigned by them to the second century AD.

The transferred population-name was coextensive with the overlordship in question; the extent of the overlordship might vary from one period to another. The territorial-name *Ulaidh* was coterminous with the overlordship of the *Ulaidh*. The earliest documented *Ulaidh*, the old 'fifth' of the *Ulaidh*, extended, according to traditional definitions, from Drowse, which enters Donegal Bay, to Boyne. This was the protohistoric overlordship of the *Ulaidh*; this is the *Ulaidh* of the *Rúraíocht* (Ulster Cycle of Tales), the *Ulaidh* of King Conchobhar Mac Neasa, of the boy-hero Cú Chulainn. By the mid-fifth century, the beginning of the historical period, this overlordship of the *Ulaidh* was considerably diminished; the application of the territorial name had diminished accordingly. The *Ulaidh* were now reduced to about a third of their former kingdom: the area roughly commensurate with later Counties Antrim, Down and North Louth. It is to this reduced kingdom that the territorial name *Ulaidh* applies from the fifth and sixth centuries onwards. This was the *Ulaidh* that the Anglo-Normans took over when John de Courcy defeated the king of the *Ulaidh* in 1177 to assume to himself the title *Princeps Ultoniae*; this is what became some years later the Anglo-Norman Earldom of Ulster.

Domhnall (Mac Briáin) Ua Néill, king of Cineál Eoghain, is believed to have been the first of the O'Neill kings to call himself *Rí Uladh*, 'King of Ulaidh/Ulster', when, on sending his letter of Remonstrance to the pope in 1317, he signed it *Donaldus Oneill Rex Ultoniae*. With the decline of Anglo-Norman power to the east and the expansion of O'Neill overlordship and control, the title of *Rí Uladh* came to apply more and more to the O'Neill overking, so that eventually the term *Ulaidh* came to apply again to the full northern stretch. In the early seventeenth century the terms Ulster, Ultonia and Provincia Ultoniae were in use formally to indicate the full extent of the north with its nine counties. In view of the several applications of the name Ulaidh/Ulster throughout the ages, it is perhaps not surprising that the name Ulster should have more than one meaning today.

Three sons of Niall Naoighiallach ('Niall of the Nine Hostages'), Conall, Eoghan and Éanna, made swordland of the western portion of the old 'fifth' of Ulster and left their mark on district-names within Donegal. It was in the first half of the fifth century that they seized these lands and established kingdoms for themselves and their descendants. The Tír Chonaill ('Conall's Land') of this period was not the Tír Chonaill of the later medieval period; Conall's territory, or that of Conall Gulban, as he was called, was in the west of the modern county, and this was the kingdom held by his sept, Cineál Chonaill, in his wake. Eoghan gave his name to Inis Eoghain, 'Eoghan's peninsula', the modern Inishowen; this was the early Tír Eoghain, Tír Eoghain na hInse ('of the peninsula'), as it was called somewhat later. The third brother, Éanna, seized the fertile lands of the Laggan in east Donegal; his progeny, Cineál Éann, were of no great political significance but the name Tír Éanna was still applied to the area as late as the seventeenth century.

In the course of time the overlordships of Cineál Chonaill and Cineál Eoghain underwent considerable change and the reference of the associated kingdom-names changed accordingly. The northern sept, Cineál Eoghain, were the more adventurous of the two; no sooner were they firmly established in Aileach than they began to push eastward and south-eastward into the more profitable lands of Airghialla. By the ninth and tenth centuries they had control of most of mid-Ulster, they had established a new seat of kingship at Tulach Óg, 'Tullaghogue', Co. Tyrone, and had gained the lordship of the surrounding lands. With the consolidation of their new kingdom, this central location was more favourably positioned than the original home-kingdom in the far north; Tulach Óg eventually ousted Aileach as the headquarters of Cineál Eoghain. This was now the domestic kingdom of Cineál Eoghain, the pulse of the widespread overkingdom which they ruled. It was the new Tír Eoghain of the medieval period, the kingdom which at a later date provided the modern county-name, Tyrone.

As the kings of Cineál Eoghain turned their backs on their northern homeland, Cineál Chonaill grasped their opportunity. They succeeded in extending their sway into Tír Éanna and Inis Eoghain; the reference of the territorial name *Tír Chonaill* extended accordingly. *Cineál Eoghain* were never content to surrender their old patrimony and Aileach remained a bone of contention between them until the career of both dynasties came to an end in the early seventeenth century.

Inevitably in the course of 2,000 years, and after several major cultural innovations and invasions, there were important accretions to the basic stock of name-elements: the introduction of Christianity with its import of specialised terms for churches – *lann, ceall, domhnach*, etc.; the trading and raiding of the Vikings – who left a remarkably small legacy of place-names, and then mainly on the coast, since they probably cared little what names were on the monasteries they plundered and had even less mind to change them; the Anglo-Normans even, who although introducing new terms for special features – *gráinseach, pailís, briotás*, etc. – did little to impose their own names on the existing ones, probably for the very simple reason that the existing place-names were legally tied up with land-tenure.

When the lands were bestowed upon the new grantees they were apportioned in large units – a barony or several baronies – and the townlands within these units were listed. The townland-names were written down in the official documentation in Anglicised form as they sounded to the English court-scribes, so when the lands were leased to the new tenants the townlands were still known by their Irish names. Thus, because the Irish place-names were formally used in grants and leases, they became the official place-names of the country.

Two things in particular are worth noting in connection with the Anglicisation of the original Irish names: one is the way in which different Irish words are made to appear the same in the Anglicised form – for example, 'Bally' can cover *baile, béal átha, bealach*; the other is the way in which the same Irish word can be Anglicised in several different ways – as with *craobh*, Anglicised as both 'crew' and 'creeve', or *ceis*, Anglicised as 'kesh', 'kish' and 'cassagh'.

APPENDIX — GLENAVY, CO. ANTRIM

A more complicated example of the importance of compiling a chronological list of documented early forms has been constructed for Glenavy townland, Glenavy parish, Co. Antrim.

1	Láthrach Patricc	Gwynn, *The Book of Armagh*, I, p. 36 (ninth c.)
2	Lat(h)rach Pátraic	Mulchrone, *Bethu Phátraic*, p. 98 (ninth-c. text)
3	Lettir-phadruic	Colgan, *Trias Thaumaturga*, p. 147 (AD 1647)
4	o Lainn abhaich	Stokes, *Félire Óengusso* (notes), p. 240
5	o Lainn Abaich	Stokes, *Félire huí Gormáin* (gloss), p. 212
6	o Lainn abaich	O'Donovan, *Mart. Donegal*, p. 298
7	(airchindeach) Laindi Abhaic	*Book of Uí Maine* (facs.), fo 68a
8	(aircined) Lainne Abhaich	*Mac Firbis' Gen.*, p. 515
9	Lann Abhaich, Ecclesia	Colgan, *Trias Thaum.* p. 183 (AD 1647)
10	Llannavach	Archdall, *Mon. Hib.* (AD 1782)
11	Lennewy, ecclesia de	Papal Tax. 1306 (ex Reeves, *Eccl. Antiq.*)
12	Lenavy, ecclesia de	Terrier 1615
13	Lanaway, vicarium de	King's Books (AD 1616)
14	Lunavie, capella de	Ulster Visitation 1622
15	Lynavy	Regal Visitation 1634 (ex Groves's copy)
16	Glanawy, vicarium de	Visitation 1661
17	Clenough al' Linawey	*Inq. Ult.* (Down), no. 2, as I (AD 1605)
18	Cleonagh al' Lynawy	*Cal. Pat. Rolls*, Jas I, p. 146b (AD 1609)
19	Ballyglenaey	*Inq. Ult.*, no. 1, Car. I (AD 1625)
20	Ballylenany (recte -avy)	*Inq. Ult.*, no. 2, Car. II (AD 1661)
21	Glenavie (par., td)	*Census* 1659
22	Glennevey td Glanevey par.	Down Survey bar. map (bar. Massereene) (c. 1660)
23	Glenavey	Hearth Money Rolls (c. 1669)
24	Glanavie td Glanavy par.	Petty, *Hiberniae Delineatio* (c. 1680)
25	Glenavey (par., td)	Conway Estate Map 1729
26	Glanevy	Taylor & Skinner (1778)

27	Glenevey	Lendrick, Map of Antrim 1780
28	Glean Abhaic,	O.S. *Name Book*
	'Glen of the dwarf'	
29	glé-'nevi	Current local pronunciation
	Lann Abhaigh[1]	*Ainmneacha Gaeilge na mBailte Poist*, p. 96

Meaning 'Church/monastery of the dwarf'.

(Forms 1–20 are grouped, as far as possible, in chronological order, within the several ranges of source-material.)

The original form of Glenavy is attested in native sources nos. 4–9 and by the semi-Gaelic version in no. 10. The traditional explanation of the name *Lann Abhaigh* is given in source no. 2: *Luid i nDáil nAraithi íar suidiu . . . Ocus asbertai dano congabad dú itá Lat(h)rach Pátraic. Is and sin atá Daniel aingel & abhacc Pátraic.* ('After this he went into Dál Araidi . . . And he proposed moreover to take the place in which Láthrach Pátraic ['Patrick's site'] is [now]. Therein is Daniel [who is called from his purity] 'the angel' and [from his small size] 'Patrick's dwarf'.[2]) Here the compiler gives sufficient information to allow the reader to identify the site as Lann Abhaigh but avoids, apparently consciously, use of the anachronistic term *lann*. (*Lann*, Welsh *llan*, 'enclosure, monastic enclosure, church', does not occur in the Patrician context but belongs to the immediate post-Patrician phase.[3]) The name *Láthrach Pátraic* does not recur recognisably in later documentation[4] and may possibly have been consciously composed in order to bring *Lann Abhaigh* within the Patrician mission.

The sources of nos. 4–6 are locational glosses in the martyrology on Aedhá Mac Colca (6 November). The sources of nos. 7 and 8 refer to *Maelpátraig (mac Celen) .i. aircined Lainne Abhaich 7 secnab Bennchair* (Maelpátraig son of Celen .i. erenagh of Glenavy and vice-abbot of Bangor). The *Annals of the Four Masters* give the obit. of AD 927: *Maolpátraicc mac Celen, saccart 7 secnap Bennchair (décc).* At the dissolution of the monasteries the rectory of Glenavy, with its thirteen townlands, was found to be appropriate to the Abbey of Bangor (sources nos. 12, 17 and 18; the association obviously goes back at least to the early tenth century.

Lettir-phádruic (no. 3), with the same reference and in the same context as *Láthrach Pátraic* (nos. 1 and 2), may be an error for the latter on Colgan's part. But on the strength of Colgan's *Lettir-phádruic*, Reeves (*Eccl. Antiq.*, p. 237) and O'Laverty (*Down and Connor*, II, p. 303) suggest the equation of Glenavy with *Leitir Dal Araidhe*, a locational gloss in the Martyrologies on the three 'daughters' of Comhghall (22 January); the account in *Mart. Donegal*[5] is the most detailed:

Colma, Bogha, Laisri, tri derbhsethracha, acus tri hógha, do cloinn Comhgaill, mic Fianghalaigh, etc. Acus robta daltadha do Comhgall Bennchair iatt, acus i lLeitir Dal Araidhe ata . . . No gomad i cCamas Comhgaill no beittis.

Colma, Bogha, Laisri, three sisters, and three virgins of the sept of Comhgall, son of Fianghalach, etc. And they were disciples of Comhgall of Beannchar, and they are at Leitir Dal-Araidhe . . . Or they are at Camus-Comhgaill.[6]

The equation rests on rather slender evidence. The old Glenavy churchyard, which may have been the original church-site, was at 'an angle formed by the Glenavy and Pigeontown roads' (*Par. Sur.* II, p. 256). The term *leitir*, 'hill-slope', is not an obvious topographical definition of the site.

The corruption of *lann* to 'glen', which had clearly set in by 1625 (no. 19),[7] was no doubt accelerated by the presence of a physical glen. The alternative name Clenough/Cleonagh (nos. 17 and 18) does not survive recognisably and is too lightly documented to justify speculation on its original Irish form; it may be no more than a corrupt spelling form of *Lann Abhaigh* (or possibly *Lann Abhaic*) in its transitional Anglicised stage.

Notes

1. The modern Irish form of *Lann Abhaic*.
2. Translation from Stokes, *Tripartite Life of St Patrick*, I, pp. 163, 165.
3. cf. *Proc. 10th Congress Onom. Sciences*, Vienna, 1969, p. 283.
4. On the strength of this name-form, O'Laverty (*Down and Connor*, V, p. 140) identifies the church of Latrach in Dalebinu, granted to St Patrick's Abbey, Down *c.* 1183, with Glenavy; since Glenavy was appropriate to Bangor – an association of long standing – it is unlikely to have been included in a grant to the Abbey of Down.
5. O'Donovan, *Martyrology of Donegal*, pp. 24–5.
6. Near Coleraine.
7. Reeves (*op. cit.*, p. 47) notes that the earliest form with g he had observed was that in *Vis.* 1661. This is so in the ecclesiastical documentation which tends to use earlier source-lists; it is obvious from the civil documentation that the substitution of 'glen' for *lann* was part of the early-seventeenth-century Anglicisation of the name.

This 'case-history' indicates some of the difficulties involved in the process and some of the ways in which they may be overcome, particularly where the name in question occurs in early Irish documentation.

LIST OF MAPS

A

A

Abbey:	*See* MAINISTIR
ABHA/ABHAINN:	Is the common Irish word meaning 'river'; it is usually Anglicised as 'aw' or 'owen', though 'avon', the common Anglicised form of the same Celtic word in England, is sometimes used. The short form appears, appropriately enough, in Awbeg, in Cos Cork and Limerick, *Abha Bheag*, 'Little river', which appears as Avanbeg in Co. Wicklow, *Abhainn Bheag*, and as Owenbeg in Co. Sligo. For some curious reason the original Irish form, *Abhainn Mór*, 'Big river', is frequently Anglicised as 'Blackwater', which appears in Cos Cork and Tyrone, though 'Owenmore' and 'Avonmore' do often appear as well. Inevitably a number of places take their name from their siting on or proximity to a river: the most obvious examples are probably Bunnahowen and Bunowen, Co. Mayo, *Bun na hAbhann* and *Bun Abhann* respectively, both meaning 'Mouth of the river'. Ballinahowen, Co. Westmeath, *Buaile na hAbhann*, is 'Milking-place of the river', as is Ballynahown, Co. Galway, while Ballynahow, Co. Kerry is *Baile na hAbha*, 'Homestead of the river'. Drumderaown, Co. Cork appears to be *Droim 'dir dhá Abhainn*, 'Ridge between two rivers'.
ABHALL/UBHALL:	Means 'apple' and 'apple-tree' and has several different Anglicised forms. As a first element it appears as Oulart, in Cos Wexford and Kilkenny, which is the compound word *Abhall-Gort*, literally meaning 'Apple-field' or 'Orchard'. The form *Achadh Abhla*, 'Apple-field', also occurs, however, in Aghowle, Co. Limerick, Aghyowle, Co. Fermanagh and

Aghyowla, Co. Limerick. Oola, Co. Limerick, by some thought to represent *Úlla*, 'Hills', is thought by others to represent U*bhla*, 'Apple-trees'. It occurs, of course, in more complex formations such as Ballyhooly, Co. Cork, *Baile Átha* U*bhla*, 'Homestead of the ford of the apple-trees'.

ACHADH: Is the most widespread and least specific term for a 'field' and is very common as an initial element in place-names throughout the country. Unusually it appears without qualification as the name of a parish in Co. Carlow, Agha (the original qualification has been dropped). Very often it is qualified by terms descriptive of its size or shape, as in Aghada, Co. Cork, *Achadh Fada*, 'Long field'; Aghalane, Co. Fermanagh, *Achadh Leathan*, 'Broad field', or Aghamore, Co. Mayo, *Achadh Mór*, 'Big field'. Sometimes some feature of the field is described, as in Aghabog, Co. Monaghan, *Achadh Bog*, 'Soft field', or Aghabullogue, Co. Cork, *Achadh Bolg*, 'Field of the bulges', or, with a slightly different Anglicised form, Aughnacloy, Co. Tyrone, *Achadh na Cloiche*, 'Field of the stone'. A distinguishing mark might be referred to, as in Aghacashel, Co. Leitrim, *Achadh an Chaisil*, 'Field of the stone fort', or Aughnamullen, Co. Monaghan, *Achadh na Muileann*, 'Field of the mills'. There can be a reference to its use: Aghaboe, Co. Laois, *Achadh Bhó*, 'Field of the cow(s)', or Aghowle, Co. Wicklow, *Achadh Abhla*, 'Field of the apple-trees'. Very often, however, the qualifying element is a personal name, as in Achonry, Co. Sligo, *Achadh Conaire*, 'Conaire's field', or Aghadowey, Co. Derry, *Achadh Dubhthaigh*, 'Dubhthach's field'. It does not always appear as the initial element; sometimes an adjective precedes it, as in

Garvagh, Co. Derry, *Garbhachadh*, 'Rough field', or Ardagh, Cos Limerick and Longford, *Ardachadh*, 'High field', with a slight Anglicised variant in Ardaghy, Co. Monaghan.

Agha: *See* ACHADH

AILL: Like FAILL, which is a form more or less restricted to southern counties, means a cliff; one of its simplest expressions is to be found in Naul, Co. Dublin, *An Aill*, locally always known as 'The Naul' despite the fact that the 'n' of the definite article is an integral part of the Anglicised form. Without the article it appears as Aille, in Cos Clare and Mayo, and as Ayle, Co. Mayo, all of which represent *Aill* without qualification. It forms part of the name Allihies, Co. Cork, *Ailichí*, which is interpreted as 'Cliff-fields'. It appears also in Co. Cork in the name Doneraile, *Dún ar Aill*, 'Fort on the cliff', and in Waterford in Dunhill, *Dún Aill*, with the same meaning.

AIRD: A word meaning 'point' or 'promontory', is readily confused with *ard*, 'high' or 'height', the more so since both are usually Anglicised 'ard'. Two names illustrate this superbly: Ardglass, Co. Cork has been shown to represent *Ard Glas*, 'Grey/green height', while Ardglass, Co. Down, with identical spelling, represents *Aird Ghlais*, 'Grey/green point'. The term is particularly common – with a palpable indication of its meaning – in the form Ardmore, especially along the west coast, in Cos Mayo and Galway, *Aird Mhór*, 'Big point'; tautologically, as frequently happens with Irish terms for geophysical features, the English form is often 'Ardmore Point'. Similarly the Ards Peninsula in Co. Down is *Aird*, 'Promontory'. Other examples, both on the sea-coast and on the coasts of inland expanses of water, such as Lough Neagh, include Ardroe, Co. Galway, Aird Rua, 'Red point', and Arboe, Co. Tyrone, Aird Bó, 'Cow point'.

AIRNE/ARNA: Means a 'sloe' or 'sloe-tree', and occurs and recurs in the form of Killarney, not only in Co. Kerry but also in Cos Kilkenny, Roscommon and Wicklow, representing Cill Airne, 'Church of the sloe-tree'.

ÁIT: Basically means 'place' or 'site'; it normally occurs in place-names in combination with tí, meaning 'house'. Understandably enough this is usually followed by a personal name to indicate ownership of the house-site in question: examples of this construction include Attical, Co. Down, Áit Tí Chathail, 'Cathal's house-site', and Attymachugh, Co. Mayo, Áit Tí Mhic Aodha, 'MacHugh's house'. Sometimes the two terms are not quite so compounded: Attatantee, Co. Donegal is Áit an tSean Tighe, 'Site of the old house'.

AITEANN: Means 'gorse' or 'furze'. It appears as a qualifying element in quite a number of place-names in Ireland, since it is a very common plant in the Irish countryside. Coolattin is the name of places in Cos Limerick, Wexford and Wicklow: Cúl Aitinn is 'Hill of gorse'; Ballynahattina, Co. Galway, Ballynahatten, in Cos Down and Louth, and Ballinattin, Cos Tipperary and Waterford, are all Baile na Aitinn, 'Homestead of the gorse'.

ALT: Has been, somewhat confusingly, construed as meaning both 'mountain' and 'ravine'; in place-name contexts, however, it is usually translated as 'height', and its diminutive form Altán as 'little height', concurring with the suggestion in Cormac's Glossary that it is related to the Latin altus. In this sense the diminutive form appears in Altan, Co. Donegal, without qualification. It appears throughout the country as Altagowlan, Co. Roscommon, *Alt an Ghabhláin*, 'Height of the fork'; as Altavilla, Co. Limerick, *Alt a' Bhile*, 'Height of the sacred tree', and as Altinure, in Cos Derry and Cavan, *Alt an Iúir*, 'Height of the yew-tree'.

Alternative Names   There are a number of places in Ireland where the received English form has no connection with the Irish form. (This can be particularly confusing if you are travelling in an Irish-speaking area, where the signposts contain the Irish name, your map the English.) Examples of such non-correspondence occur all over the country. Clifden, Co. Galway, presumably an English name imported by John Darcy, who founded the town in about 1812, is known in Irish as *An Clochán*, 'The little stone'. Westport, Co. Mayo, a town laid out by James Wyatt in about 1780 and presumably named from nearby Westport House, is in Irish *Cathair na Mart*, 'Stone fort of the market'. The Norse-named Wexford and Waterford are, in Irish, *Loch Garman* and *Port Láirge*, while even Kells, Co. Meath, which might reasonably be expected to appear in Irish as *Na Cealla*, appears as *Ceanannas Mór*, but for a slightly different reason: the name 'Kells' is a corruption of Anglo-Norman *Kenlis*, which in turn is a corruption of the original Irish *Ceanannas*. Even 'Dublin' could be considered an alternative for the native Irish *Baile Átha Cliath*.

AN: Is the singular form of the definite article in Irish; it is normal practice, in citing Irish forms of unqualified, or simply qualified, place-names to include the definite article as part of the name. For example, the Irish form of

Carrick, Co. Donegal would be cited as *An Charraig*; the Irish form of Daingean, Co. Offaly would be cited as *An Daingean*; the Irish form of Dromard, Co. Sligo would be cited as *An Droim Ard*. This practice is not followed in this book on the ground that the absence of the article makes it easier for the non-Irish-speaker to associate the Irish form with the Anglicised form, especially in instances where the presence of the article causes lenition of the initial letter of the noun, as in Cabragh, Co. Dublin, *An Chabrach*, or Cahir, Co. Tipperary, *An Chathair*. The definite article is retained only where it, or at least its 'n', forms part of the Anglicised form of the name. There are quite a few instances of this. Naul, Co. Dublin, for example, is *An Aill*; Navan, Co. Armagh is *An Eamhain*; Navan, Co. Meath is *An Uaimh*; Neale, Co. Mayo is *An Éill*; Nenagh, Co. Tipperary is *An tAonach*; Nobber, Co. Meath is *An Obair*; and Nurney, Co. Carlow is *An Urnaí*. In all of these Anglicised names, and others besides, the initial letter is, in fact, the 'n' of the article.

Annagh: *See* EANACH

AONACH: Means 'fair' or 'assembly', and is probably best known for such assemblies as *Aonach Tailtean*, the great *Lughnasa* festival whose name is remembered in Teltown, Co. Meath, and also recorded in *Lag an Aonaigh*, 'Site of the assembly', near the town. As a place-name element it appears, now without qualification, in Nenagh, Co. Tipperary, *An Aonach*, 'The assembly' (another of those cases where the 'n' of the definite article has become part of the Anglicised form of the place-name); this was formerly known as *Aonach Urmhumhan*, 'The assembly of Ormond'. The term appears in a number of place-names, such as Monasteranenagh, Co. Limerick, *Mainistear an Aonaigh*, 'Monastery of the assembly', a Cistercian abbey founded in 1148 by Turlough O'Brien, King of Thomond, in thanksgiving for his victory over the Norse at nearby Rathmore. Similarly Dunineny, Co. Antrim, a promontory fort where Somhairle Buidhe Mac Donnell resided until his death in 1589, is *Dún an Aonaigh*, 'Fort of the assembly'.

ÁRAINN: Is a word construed as meaning 'ridge' and is virtually confined to Aranmore, Co. Donegal, *Árainn Mhór*, 'Large ridge', and the Aran Islands, Co. Galway, *Árainn* + 'Islands', 'Ridge (islands)'.

ARD: Is probably the most common term used in Irish place-names to signify 'height', or, as an adjectival prefix, 'high'. It occurs the length and breadth of the country. In some instances it can readily be confused with *aird*, 'point' – most cases of Ardmore, especially coastal examples, occurring in Cos Galway, Waterford, etc., having been shown to represent *Aird Mhór*, 'Big point', rather than *Ard Mór*, 'Big height'. In its adjectival sense, 'high', it occurs regularly: in Ardagh, Cos Limerick and Longford, as well as Ardaghy, Co. Monaghan, it represents *Ardachadh*, 'High field'; in Arless, Co. Laois, *Ardlios*, 'High fort'. As a noun it appears regularly as a first element: in Ardara, Co. Donegal, *Ard an Rátha*, 'Height of the fort', confusingly similar in its English form to Ardaragh, Co. Down, *Ard Darach*, 'Height abounding in oaks'. Terms denoting the vegetation associated with the height in question are quite common: Ardattin, Co. Carlow, *Ard Aitinn*, 'Height of the gorse'; Ardrahan, Co. Galway, *Ard Rathain*, 'Height of the ferns'; or Ardlougher, Co. Cavan, *Ard Luachra*, 'Height of the rushes'.

Sometimes a notable feature of the height is used to describe it, as in Ardfert, Co. Kerry, *Ard Fhearta*, 'Height of the grave', or Ardmillan, Co. Down, *Ard an Mhuilinn*, 'Height of the mill'. Very often a personal name is used: Ardgarvan, Co. Derry, *Ard Garbháin*, 'Garbhán's height', or Ardpatrick, Co. Limerick, *Ard Pádraig*, 'Pádraig's height'. Sometimes the qualifying element implies delusions of grandeur, as in Arderin, Cos Laois and Offaly, *Ard Éireann*, 'Éire's height', as if this were the highest point in the entire country, which at 527 m it assuredly is not! Sometimes the word is reduced in the English form of the place-name to 'art' or even 'ar': Articlave, Co. Derry is *Ard an Chléibh*, 'Height of the wattle', perhaps because osiers grew on or near it, or because a wicker causeway was close by. Armagh, Co. Armagh has been construed as referring to a mythical person: *Ard Macha*, the 'Height of Macha', of whom numerous stories are preserved, although it has been argued that the 'macha' is more likely to represent 'ground cleared for agriculture', or even 'plain'.

Ard: *See* ARD *or* AIRD

ÁTH(A): Means 'ford' and, where applicable, is a common element in Irish place-names, from the very beginning of recorded history or pseudo-history. It is, for example, the commonest initial place-name element among places named in *Táin Bó Cúalnge*, where *Áth Lúain* (modern Athlone, Co. Westmeath) and *Áth Troim* (modern Trim, Co. Meath) are two of the most easily identifiable modern places to be mentioned. In *Táin Bó Cúalnge*, however, there is a nice example of incidental *dinnseanchas*, for the change of name from *Áth Mór* to *Áth Lúain* is attributed to the fact that the Brown Bull left the loin (*lón*) of the White Bull there. In modern toponymy, though, the name is interpreted, less gorily, as meaning 'Luan's ford'. In the case of Trim, while in the English form the *Áth* has been dropped, in Irish it rejoices in the full title of *Baile Átha Troim*, 'Town of the ford of the elder-tree'. Other less spectacular *Áth*-names are to be found all over the country, most with quite simple descriptive qualifications, as in Athlacca, Co. Limerick, *Áth Leacach*, 'Ford of the flagstones', or Athleague, Co. Roscommon, *Áth Liag*, 'Ford of the stones', or even Athboy, Co. Meath, *Baile Átha Buí*, 'Town of the yellow ford'. With Athenry, Co. Galway, a slightly more exalted qualification is to be seen, *Béal Átha an Rí*, 'Ford of the kings'. Quite apart from its frequent connection with *béal*, 'mouth', *átha* sometimes occurs as a second element, as in Finnea, in Cos Cavan and Westmeath, *Fiodh an Átha*, 'Wood of the ford'. It also, of course, appears in the alternative Irish name for Dublin, *Baile Átha Cliath*, 'Town of the ford of the hurdle'.

Augh(a): *See* ACHADH

Aw: *See* ABHA

BÁD: Means simply 'boat' and occurs occasionally in place-names, but always as part of a compound name. The most obvious example is Donabate, Co. Dublin, *Dún an Bháid*, 'Fortress of the boat'. Others are Rinawade, Co. Dublin, *Rinn an Bháid*, 'Point of the boat', and Craigavad, Co. Down, *Creag an Bháda*, 'Rock of the boat'.

BÁDHÚN: Is usually accepted as being derived from *bó dhún*, meaning literally 'Cow-fortress', in the sense of a place intended to keep cattle safe from either rustlers (rustling was an old Irish pastime) or the wild beasts which were reasonably abundant; *bó-dhaingean* was also used. It is generally Anglicised as 'Bavan', 'Baun' or 'Bawn'; this last form has passed into the English language to describe the fortified enclosure built around or in front of a tower-house, the equivalent of the ward of a medieval castle. Examples of such bawns are numerous: at Audley's Castle, Co. Down, where a roughly rectangular bawn contains indications of the foundations of ancillary buildings; at Carrigaholt, Co. Clare or at Aughnanure, Co. Galway, where there are two. Bavan, Co. Donegal is an example of one common form of Anglicisation; Bawnboy, Co. Cavan, *Bádhún Buí*, 'Yellow bawn', of another. It has been suggested of a site at Tildarg, Co. Antrim, consisting of rectangular earthwork, 82 m by 53 m, with a rectangular house, that it was in fact literally a *bádhún*, a defended cattle enclosure, possibly dating from the thirteenth century.

BAILE: Is usually Anglicised as 'Bally', or 'Balli', and is by far the most common settlement term in Irish place-names. It is generally assumed to denote 'townland' or 'town' (the latter both in the nuclear sense and in the sense of 'townland') and is most reasonably translated in these terms: Ballynafeigh, *Baile na Faiche*, 'Townland of the green'; Ballinaspick, *Baile an Easpaig*, 'Townland of the bishop'; Ballinakill, *Baile na Coille*, 'Townland of the wood'. Despite its apparent simplicity there are aspects of *baile* as a place-name element that are enigmatic. Three main questions are posed: how far back can *baile* be traced in place-name composition? what was its original meaning? is its spread in place-names related to the emergence of the formalised townland-pattern?

It has been demonstrated that *baile*, as an element in the formation of place-names, is not documented until the middle of the twelfth century. The earliest examples occur in a charter relating to the monastery of Kells, *c*. AD 1150: *Baile Uí Uidrin* with the mill and land and *Baile Uí Comgain* with the land and mill (literally 'the place where the Ó hUidrin/Ó Comgain family was', i.e. their homestead). Monastic charters of the 1160s and 1170s have, in their enumeration of endowed lands, further instances of *baile* place-names, with no separate mention of attached lands, the place-name itself being sufficient to indicate the unit of land being endowed. In all of these instances *baile* is qualified by a family-group name (or possibly a surname), e.g. *bale ochianagain, bale meic marcaig, bali idubain*. This is the beginning of the monastic charter phase: it had not been the practice in Ireland before the middle of the twelfth century to record grants and land-transfers in writing. This practice seemingly began with the new monastic orders in the middle of the twelfth century and was formalised some decades later, in both civil and monastic contexts, by the Anglo-Normans. We do not have in Ireland, prior to AD 1150, documents of the same genre as those which provide us with our records of *baile*-names in the phase from 1150 to 1300 – monastic endowments, Anglo-Norman grants, leases, Pipe Rolls, etc. Therefore when we state that *baile*-names begin to be recorded in the mid-twelfth century we must see this in the context of the new class of document which begins at this time.

It is unresolved whether the absence of documentation on *baile*-names prior to 1150 necessarily indicates that only then did the word acquire the definitive meaning of 'homestead', and consequently the extended reference to the land attached to or associated with the homestead, i.e. a recognised, formally delimited unit of land. The word *baile* is well documented in Middle Irish (900–1200) composition, both metrical and in prose. It means 'place', both in the general sense and in a specified sense. The former is the commoner, e.g. *ro ordnestar Oengus macc Ailella isin bali sin*, 'he ordained Oengus son of Ailill in that place'. There are, however, occasional instances in Middle Irish of *baile* in a more definitive context: *i mbal Ruadain*, 'in Ruadan's place' (with reference to his monastery); *tánic isin mbaile leo*, 'he came into the place with them' (the reference being to the monastic unit of Clonmacnoise). Other instances which suggest that *baile* had already achieved its more definitive meaning before the mid-twelfth century are as follows:

(i) In a ninth-century dialogue poem between King Guaire and his hermit brother, Marbán, the hermit is extolling the delights of his chosen life:

> *Mét mo boiithe, bec nád bec,*
> *baile sétae sognath*

which the editor translates as: 'The size of my hut – small yet not small – a homestead with familiar paths'.

(ii) In Cormac's *Glossary* the term *ráth*, 'fort', is glossed *baile* – *baile* here obviously indicating a settlement-unit.

(iii) In *Tochmarc Emire* ('The Wooing of Emer') emissaries were sent to find a wife for Cú Chulainn *i nnách dunad i nnách prímbali i nHerind*, 'in any fort or superior *bali* ['homestead'] in Ireland'.

(iv) In *Annals of Ulster*, under the year AD 1011, *Slogad la Flaithbertach H Neill co Dun Echdach co ro loise in dun agus co ro bris a baile*, 'A hosting by Flaithbertach Ua Neill to Dun Echdach [Duneight, Co. Down], when he burned the *dún* ['fort'] and broke down its *baile*'. Whatever the specific meaning of *baile* here, its application is specific and not general: it clearly has reference to a settlement-unit.

The weight of the evidence, therefore, would point to the use of the term *baile* in the sense of a settlement-unit before the mid-twelfth century. The references cited above are to dwelling-units rather than to land-units; the extension in the application of *baile* – from its use of the dwelling-unit of a named family group to its use of the lands of the named family group – would be a natural development. The extended reference of the name of a defined feature, e.g. *dún*, 'fort', to the land adjoining the feature was well established by the twelfth century: a ninth-century example has been observed in the case of *Dún Cruithen*, 'Fort of the Cruithin', Duncrun, Co. Derry. All in all, despite the absence of documented *baile*-names there is enough to suggest that we look somewhat farther back than 1150 for the origin of our *baile*-unit.

It has been shown that the common use of *baile* was considerably accelerated by the Anglo-Norman use of Latin *villa* and English *tún*, 'town', qualified by the name of the feudal tenant: Nicholtown, Phylippestown, Punyertoun, Perestoun. *Baile* was regarded as the Irish equivalent of these terms and *baile*-named units emerged alongside the Anglo-Norman *toun*-named units. Anglo-Norman place-names were, for the most part, Gaelicised in the fourteenth and fifteenth centuries, hence Ballynichol, Ballyphilip, Ballyfounder and Ballyferis (all in the Ards Peninsula area of Co. Down). The incidence of *baile*-names is highest in areas of intensive Anglo-Norman settlement, as a comparison of Lecale and the Ards Peninsula, for example, with Cos Tyrone and Fermanagh indicates. This is not, however, due solely to the Gaelicisation of Anglo-Norman settlement terms, but also to the fact that in these areas *baile* came to be the commonest settlement term in the later medieval period. It came to be used in Gaelic place-names with qualifications which referred to aspects of the land in question: situation, as in Ballintlieve, Co. Down, *Baile an tSléibhe*, 'Mountain townland'; shape, as in Ballykeel, Co. Down, *Baile Caol*, 'Narrow townland'; quality, as in Ballybought, Co. Antrim, *Baile Bocht*, 'Poor townland' or Ballyginniff, Co. Antrim, *Baile Gainimh*, 'Sandy townland'; or association, as in Ballynageeragh, Co. Down, *Baile na gCaorach*, 'Townland of the sheep'. The qualification could refer also to a prominent feature of the area in question, either natural or artificial: Ballynure, Co. Antrim, *Baile an Iúir*, 'Townland of the yew'; Ballymagarry, Co. Antrim, *Baile mo Gharraí*, 'Townland of my garden'; Ballylumford, Co. Antrim, *Baile Longphoirt*, 'Townland of the

fort'; Ballylesson, Co. Down, Baile Leasáin,
'Townland of the fort'.

Whether these *baile*-names referred in their
original application primarily to a settlement-
unit (a homestead, a cluster of homesteads or
a small nuclear town) or primarily to the
townland-unit is problematic. In some cases
it certainly was to a farmstead, homestead or
nuclear town: Shanbally, *Seanbhaile* (a
reasonably common townland name), makes
better sense as 'Old homestead' than as 'Old
townland'; likewise, Ballynure, another
common name, *Baile an Iúir*, is more likely in
most instances to have been applied to
'Homestead of the yew-tree' than to
'Townland of the yew-tree'. References in the
Annals of Ulster in the year 1348 to the burning
of *Balie in Múta*, now Ballymote town and
townland in Co. Sligo, show that here the
original allusion was to a nuclear settlement.
The fact that in 1239 the *Annals of the Four
Masters* records the endowment of a *lethbhaile*,
half a *baile*, indicates convincingly that for a
considerable time before this endowment to
the Canons of Trinity Island in Lough Key,
baile had been established as a term for a unit
of land. In this context it is interesting to note
that *sráidbhaile*, 'street-town', is used in *Annals
of the Four Masters* of *Dún Dealgan*, Dundalk, Co.
Louth, as early as 1283. Even a cursory glance,
however, at the instances and acreages of the
townland name Ballybeg, *Baile Beag*, in the
Townland Index, reveals that it does apply, quite
literally, to a small townland. Similarly from
maps that show townland boundaries it can
be seen that many of the instances of
Ballykeel, *Baile Caol*, do manifestly apply to
'Narrow townlands'.

It seems, therefore, that *baile* in medieval
place-name usage could have primary reference

to a homestead, or to the lands of a kin-group (possibly as an extension of 'homestead'), to a nuclear settlement, i.e. a cluster of homesteads or dwellings, or a 'street town', or simply to a delimited land-unit.

In modern understanding and usage *baile* is commonly identified with the concept of 'townland' (the smallest territorial unit recognised in Ireland), despite the fact that *baile*-names do occur inside townlands as minor names, e.g. there is a Ballybrack, presumably *Baile Breac*, 'Speckled homestead', in Altdrumman townland, Co. Tyrone. This would seem merely to indicate that *baile* in some instances retained its meaning of 'homestead' while another name-formation assumed the role of townland name. In this book the standard translation is 'homestead', even in cases where the *baile*-name in question palpably now refers to a town, such as Ballymena, Co. Antrim, *Baile Meánach*, 'Middle homestead'. 'Bally' or 'Balli' as an Anglicisation can be deceptive: Ballinafad, Co. Sligo, for example, is *Béal an Átha Fada*, 'Mouth of the long ford', and Ballinalea, Co. Wicklow is *Buaile na Lao*, 'Milking-place of the calves', while Ballyclare, Co. Antrim is construed as *Bealach Cláir*, 'Pass of the plain'.

BAISLEAC: Derived from Greek βασιλικος, originally meaning 'kingly' and then giving 'basilica', 'church', appears very rarely (twice?) in Irish place-names: Baslick, Co. Monaghan and, in the diminutive, *baisleacán*, as Baslickane, Co. Kerry.

Bal(ly): See BAILE, BÉAL, BEALACH and BUAILE

BÁN: Means 'white' and appears frequently in place-names, very occasionally as a first element or prefix, as Banteer, Co. Cork, *Bántír*, 'White land'. Its normal adjectival position is after the noun qualified: as in Cregganbaun, Co. Mayo, *Creagán Bán*, 'White rocky place'; Gathabawn, Co. Kilkenny, *Geata Bán*, 'White gate'; Ferbane, Co. Offaly, *Féar Bán*, 'White grass', and even Strabane, Co. Tyrone, *Srath Bán*, 'White holm'.

Bane: See BÁN

Barnes: See BEARNA

BARR: Means 'top' and occurs quite frequently in place-names, usually in quite simple combinations such as Barnatra, Co. Mayo, *Barr na Trá*, 'Top of the strand', or in three different versions of *Barr na Coille*, 'Top of the wood' – Barnacullia, Co. Dublin, Barnakillew, Co. Mayo and Barnakilly, Co. Derry.

BEAG: Is an adjective meaning 'small' or 'little' which very commonly appears in place-names. It rarely appears as a first element except in compounds such as Beginish, Co. Kerry, *Beaginis*, 'Small island', or Beglieve, Co. Cavan, *Beagshliabh*, 'Small mountain'. Its normal position is after the noun it qualifies, often describing one member of a pair of correlatives, as in Rathmore and Rathbeg, in Co. Antrim, *Ráth Mór* and *Ráth Beag*, 'Large fort' and 'Small fort'. It occurs in reference to all sorts of feature, both natural and man-made: to rivers, as in Avanbeg, Co. Wicklow, *Abhainn Beag*, 'Small river'; to plains, as in Magherabeg, Co. Donegal, *Machaire Beag*, 'Small plain'; to churches, as in Killybegs, Co. Donegal, *Cealla Beaga*, 'Little churches'; to forts, as in Doonbeg, Co. Clare, *Dún Beag*, 'Small fort'.

BÉAL: Basically means simply 'mouth' but in place-names often has a more generalised sense of 'opening', 'approach' or 'access'. In this more general sense it would seem to appear in Bealadangan, Co. Galway, *Béal an Daingin*, 'Opening of the stronghold', while in others, such as Belclare, Co. Galway, *Béal Chláir*, 'Approach of/to the plain' appears the most appropriate translation. With Belturbet, Co. Cavan, *Béal Tairbirt*, 'Access of/to the isthmus' would seem sensible, and in Belgooly, Co. Cork, *Béal Guala*, 'Opening in/of the ridge'. With Beltra in Cos Mayo and Sligo, *Béal Trá*, 'Mouth of the beach' is as acceptable as anything. For Belvelly, Co. Cork, *Béal an Bhealaigh*, 'Mouth of the pass', and Belderg, Co. Mayo, *Béal Deirg*, 'Mouth of the (river) Derg' are appropriate. Very frequently *béal* is coupled with *átha*, 'ford', at its simplest in Bealaha, Co. Clare, *Béal Átha*, 'Mouth of the ford'; also in Bellanagh, Co. Cavan, *Béal Átha na nEach*, 'Mouth of the ford of the horses'; Bellanagare, Co. Roscommon, *Béal Átha na gCarr*, 'Mouth of the ford of the carts', and Bellacorick, Co. Mayo, *Béal Átha Chomraic*, 'Mouth of the ford of the confluence'.

BEALACH: Means both 'road' and 'pass', with the common concept of 'passage', the translation depending, presumably, on the geographical context. It occurs, without further qualification, and thus giving no indication of which translation should be preferred, as simply Ballagh, in Cos Fermanagh, Galway, Limerick and Tipperary. In Ballaghkeen, Co. Wexford, *Bealach Caoin*, 'Smooth passage', and Ballaghaderreen, Co. Roscommon, *Bealach an Doirín*, 'Passage of the little oak-grove', the description does not point any more clearly to the appropriate translation. In the case of Ballyfeard, Co. Cork, *Bealach Feadha Aird*, 'Pass of the high wood', it might be tempting to assume that here a mountain-pass was indicated. In the case of Baltinglass, Co.

Bearna(s)

Wicklow, Bealach Conglais, 'Pass of Conglas', Its
geographical situation in the Wicklow
Mountains again suggests a mountain-pass.

BEANN/BINN: Means 'peak' or 'mountain peak', not as a rule
with reference to the highest mountains, to
which sliabh is usually applied, but to good
mountains of the middle size. It appears in the
plural without qualification in Banna, Co. Kerry,
Beanna, 'Peaks'. The peak can be qualified as to
size: Benbeg, Co. Galway is of course Beann
Beag, 'Small peak', while Benmore, Co. Antrim
is Beann Mór, 'Large peak'. Benbane, Co. Antrim
is Beann Bán, 'White peak'; Bengorm, Co. Mayo
is Beann Gorm, 'Blue peak'; and Benbrack, Co.
Cavan is Beann Breac, 'Speckled peak'. The
description can refer to an animal, real or
imaginary, as Benbo, Co. Leitrim is Beann Bó,
'Peak of the cow(s)' and Bengore in Co. Antrim
Beann Gabhar, 'Peak of the goats'. There can be
applied the name of a person, real or
imaginary: Benbulbin, Co. Sligo, is Beann
Ghulbain, 'Gulban's peak', on which Gráinne's
Diarmaid is said to have met his end. In a
central position in a compound name it
appears in Ballyvangour in Co. Carlow, Baile
Bheanna Gabhar, 'Homestead of the peaks of the
goats'.

BEARNA(S): Means a 'gap' or 'pass' through mountainous
country. There are examples of the bare term
in Barna, Bearna, in Cos Galway, Limerick and
Offaly, and Barnes, in Co. Tyrone, while
simple qualified forms can be found in
Barnesmore, Co. Donegal, Bearnas Mór, 'Great
gap', which in the English form is often given
the pleonastic addition 'Gap'; and Barnaderg,
Co. Galway, Bearna Dhearg, 'Red gap'. Bearna
Gaoithe, 'Gap of the wind', or 'Windy gap', is a
common, and understandable, combination,
appearing as Barnageeha in Co. Limerick.

More complex combinations include Lisdoonvarna, Co. Clare, *Lios Dúin Bhearna*, 'Fort of the fort of the gap'.

Beg: See BEAG

BEITH/ BEITHEACH: Means a 'birch-tree/land' and is fairly common as an element in Irish place-names. It appears without qualification as Beagh, Co. Leitrim and Behy in Cos Donegal and Mayo; as Beaghmore, Co. Tyrone, *Beitheach Mór*, 'Large birchland'. It appears also as a qualifying element in names like Ballybay, Co. Monaghan, *Béal Átha Beithe*, 'Mouth of the ford of the birch', while Aghavea, Co. Fermanagh is *Achadh Beithe*, 'Field of the birch'. The pollen diagrams for the prehistoric site (stone circles and cairns) at Beaghmore, Co. Tyrone include one showing the more recent palaeoecological history of the site; this gives a maximum value for *betula*, i.e. *beith* or 'birch', at *c*. AD 360 (±75), suggesting that the naming of this area might well have taken place at or around this date, despite the fact that even then nearly twice as much pollen of *corylus*, in Irish *coll*, or 'hazel', was present. This may therefore be an interesting example of a place-name dated by radiocarbon-assisted pollen analysis. Unfortunately it is not often that pollen diagrams exist for a site named after its vegetation.

Bel: See BÉAL

Ben: See BEANN

BILE: Means a 'large, or sacred, tree' – a tree with ritual or historic attributes, and is quite common in place-names. It appears without qualification in Bellia, Co. Clare and Bellew, Co. Meath and even as 'The Bell' or 'The Bill' in Co. Kerry. Its importance can be inferred from the fact that in Moville, Co. Donegal and Movilla,

Co. Down the name of a plain is derived from such a tree, Má Bhile, 'Plain of the sacred tree'. It appears in association with forts, in Rathvilly, Co. Carlow and Rathvilla, Co. Offaly, Ráth Bhile, 'Fort of the sacred tree'. Such sacred trees were held in great esteem by their owners, clients or worshippers; wilful damage to one by an enemy was not taken lightly. For instance it is recorded in Annals of Ulster, under the year AD 1111 that Slogadh la hUlltu co Tealach nÓc co ro thescat a biledha, 'An expedition was made by the Ulaid to Telach Óc [Tullaghogue, Co. Tyrone] and they cut down its sacred trees'. Such profanity provoked immediate and dire consequences: Crech la Niall H. Lochlainn co tuc mile no tri mile do buaibh ina ndighail, 'A raid was made by Niall Ua Lochlainn, and carried off a thousand or three thousand cows in revenge for them.'

BINN: See BEANN

BIORRA: Means 'water' or 'stream'; its most notable appearance in place-names is in Birr, Co. Offaly; it also occurs in Birra, Co. Donegal.

BÓ: Simply means a 'cow' and is found with surprising frequency in place-names. Most appropriately it appears in Aghavoe and Aghaboe, Co. Laois, Achadh Bhó, 'Field of the cow(s)', and in Arboe, Co. Tyrone, Aird Bó, 'Cow promontory'. In more complex forms it appears in Drombofinny, Co. Cork, Droim Bó Finne, 'Ridge of the white cow', and of course in Inishbofin, in Cos Donegal and Galway, Inis Bó Finne, 'Island of the white cow'. Drumshanbo, Co. Leitrim is Droim Sean-bhó, 'Ridge of the old cow'. These last three are mythological references, as is Boyne, Bóinn, the river that wends its way through Co. Meath, with the full meaning of the 'White cow (goddess)'.

Boher: See BÓTHAR

Booley:	See BUAILE
Borris:	See BUIRÍOS
BOTH:	Means 'hut' and occurs fairly commonly in place-names throughout the country. It is seen, in the plural, without qualification, in Boho, Co. Fermanagh, *Botha*, 'Huts'. There is a diminutive form, *Bothán*, which appears in the form Bohaun in Cos Galway and Mayo, while another diminutive, *Bothóg*, appears as Bohoge, in Co. Mayo. In Boughadoon, Co. Mayo it represents *Both an Dúin*, 'Hut of the fort', while in Bolea, Co. Derry, we have *Both Liath*, 'Grey hut'. Understandably it is often qualified by a personal name: Bovevagh, Co. Derry is *Both Mhéibhe*, 'Maeve's hut', and Bohola, Co. Mayo is *Both Chomla*, Comla's hut. Its frequent religious affiliation is supported by Bodoney, Co. Tyrone, *Both Domhnaigh*, 'Hut of the church'. Sometimes *Both* itself is the qualifying element, as in Raphoe, Co. Donegal, *Ráth Bhoth*, 'Fort of the hut'.
BÓTHAR:	Means 'road' or 'avenue', originally for cattle, and is now very frequently observed in street-names in the Irish language. As an element in place-names it is not, understandably, quite as common. Its most common Anglicisation is 'boher', which appears without qualification in Boher, Cos Cork, Donegal and Limerick. Simple descriptive terms are often used to describe the road, as in Boherlahan, Co. Tipperary, *Bóthar Leathan*, 'Wide road', or in Boherboy, Co. Cork, *Bóthar Buí*, 'Yellow road'. Appropriately enough there is a Boherard, *Bóthar Ard*, 'High road', in Cos Cork and Waterford. In one instance it suggests a road not to be travelled by the faint-hearted after dark: Boheraphuca, Co. Offaly is *Bóthar an Phúca*, 'Road of the sprite'. A diminutive,

Bóithrín, 'Little road', appears as Bohereen, Co. Limerick. In this form, usually spelt as 'boreen', it has passed into the English language.

Boy: See BUÍ

BREAC: Simply means 'speckled' and appears frequently in place-names. The most obvious example is Ballybrack, Co. Dublin and Co. Kerry, which is *Baile Breac*, 'Speckled homestead'; Benbrack, Co. Cavan is *Beann Breac*, 'Speckled peak'. A derivative, *Breacnach*, 'Speckled place', occurs as Bracknagh, Co. Offaly, while in compounds, preceding the noun it qualifies, it appears as an initial element in place-names, as in Brackloon, Co. Mayo, *Breachluain*, 'Speckled field', or, with a rather different Anglicised form, in Bricklieve, Co. Sligo, *Bricshliabh*, 'Speckled mountain'.

BRÍ: Means a 'hill' or even a 'brae'. It occurs quite simply as Bray, Co. Wicklow; Bree, Cos Donegal, Monaghan and Wexford; Brigh, Co. Tyrone. Apart from these few examples it is not common.

BRIOTÁS: Is a direct borrowing of the Old French *Bretesche*, in modern English usually written as 'brattice', signifying 'boarding' or 'planking', and referring to wooden defences, usually associated with a castle: either a stone castle, where such wooden structures may have been used as ancillary defences, or, more appositely, a motte or castle-mound of the Anglo-Norman period, where wooden palisades and towers would have constituted the major defence-works. Evidence of such wooden structures has been observed on several excavated mottes, such as Ballyroney and Clough, Co. Down. The term occurs in several Irish place-names, usually in the forms 'Brittas', as in Brittas, Co. Dublin or Brittas Bay, Co. Wicklow. In slightly different form it appears as British, Co. Antrim, a location well outside the densest distribution of the term. The term, in place-names, would almost certainly refer to an earthen motte, and its use should serve as fairly clear evidence that the mound in question is, in fact, an Anglo-Norman motte, rather than a native Irish raised earthwork.

MAP **BRIOTÁS** as a sole or first element in the names of townlands; apart from the remote example of 'British' in Co. Antrim all are firmly located in the southern part of the country.

British:	See BRIOTÁS
Brittas:	See BRIOTÁS
BRUACH:	Means 'bank' or 'edge', of a river, for example. It occurs mainly in the North, as in Broughderg, Co. Tyrone, B*ruach Dearg*, 'Red bank', and Broughshane, Co. Antrim, B*ruach Sheáin*, 'Seán's bank'.
BRUGH:	Means a 'mansion', a 'palace', even a 'fairy mansion'. Apart from its many appearances in mythology, for example as B*rugh na Bóinne*, literally 'The fairy mansion of the white cow (goddess)', long identified with the complex of passage tombs in the Boyne Valley, it does appear in extant place-names: as Bruff, in Co. Limerick, without qualification, and as Bruree, Co. Limerick, B*rugh Rí*, 'Palace of the king', claimed to be the chief seat in Munster of Ailill Olom, who is said to have raped the love-goddess Áine, by whom his ear was cut off in retaliation.
BUAILE:	Is used to describe any area set aside for the tending of cattle and is usually translated simply as 'milking-place'. In a special sense it is associated with the summer, upland pastures to which cattle were transferred, sometimes accompanied by more or less the entire family. This practice, known as Seasonal Nomadism, or Transhumance, derived its name in Irish society, 'booleying', from the term *buaile*. Theoretically it would be possible to divide sites into the two classes: the established farm where the cattle would be kept in the winter and the location, possibly at some considerable distance, where they would be pastured in the summer. Since this is not feasible without extensive field-work, the term 'milking-place' is applied to all names containing the word. Some of the names containing the term (which can appear

misleadingly similar in English forms to *Baile*, 'Homestead') are delightfully straightforward, as in Ballinalea, Co. Wicklow, *Buaile na Lao*, 'Milking-place of the calves', or, in simple form, Boola, Co. Waterford. Some indicate the location of the milking, or booley, site, as in Ballynahown, Co. Westmeath, *Buaile na hAbhann*, 'Milking-place of the river'; others might, superficially, indicate a true transhumance site, as Ballyknockan, Co. Wicklow, *Buaile an Chnocáin*, 'Milking-place of the small hill'. Others call to mind the dangers previously experienced by dairy-farmers, as in Ballynabrackey, Co. Meath, *Buaile na Bréamhaí*, 'Milking-place of the wolf-plain'. As with other fields of human endeavour, very often the word is qualified by a personal or family name, as Boolakennedy, Co. Tipperary, *Buaile Uí Chinnéide*, 'Ó Cinnéide's milking-place'.

BUÍ/IDHE: Is an adjective, and a noun, meaning 'yellow'. It appears quite frequently in place-names: Boherboy, Co. Cork is *Bóthar Buí*, 'Yellow road'; Ballyboy, Co. Offaly is *Baile Átha Buí*, 'Homestead of the yellow ford'; Owenboy, Co. Cork and Owenwee, Co. Donegal are both *Abhann Bhuí*, 'Yellow river'. As a constituent of a compound it can precede the noun it qualifies, as Boyounagh, Co. Galway, *Buíbheanach*, 'Yellow marsh'.

BUIRÍOS: Seems to be a direct borrowing of the English medieval legal term 'burgage', meaning 'a tenure whereby lands or tenements in cities or towns were held of the king, or other lord, for a certain yearly rent'. It is not particularly common in Irish place-names, but where it does appear it is usually translated 'burgage', although the Anglicised form in place-names is mainly 'Borris', with 'Burris' and 'Burges' occurring as well. It is found only in the provinces of Munster, Leinster and Connaught.

In Borris, Co. Carlow it appears without qualification; Borrisnoe, Co. Tipperary is quite clearly Buiríos Nua, 'New borris', and Borrisbeg, Co. Kilkenny, Buiríos Beag, 'Small borris'. In most other instances it carries a qualification indicating either its location or the family who were involved: thus we have Borris-in-Ossory, Co. Laois, Buiríos Osraí, 'Burgage of Osraí' – an area and diocese in south-west Leinster; Borrisoleigh, Co. Tipperary, Buiríos Ó Luigheach, 'Burgage of Uí Luigheach'.

MAP   **BUIRÍOS** as a sole or first element in the names of townlands; the examples are all located in the southern part of the country. (1) represents the Anglicised form 'Borris', (2) 'Burges' and (3) 'Burgage'.

■ 1   ● 2   ★ 3

BUN: Simply means 'bottom', but in place-names has assumed the specialised meaning of 'river-mouth'. Sometimes it carries a descriptive qualifier, as in Bunbeg, Co. Donegal, *Bun Beag*, 'Small river-mouth'; elsewhere it is qualified by a term for a river or stream, as Bunnahowen, Co. Mayo, *Bun na hAbhna*, 'Mouth of the river', or Bunnanaddan, Co. Sligo, *Bun an Fheadáin*, 'Mouth of the stream'. In some cases the nature of the river is described, as in Bunduff, Co. Leitrim, *Bun Dubh*, 'Mouth of the black (river)'. Usually, however, the name of the river is used, as in Bunclody, Co. Wexford, *Bun Clóidí*, 'Mouth of the (river) Clóideach'; Bunmahon, Co. Waterford, *Bun Machan*, 'Mouth of the (river) Machain'; or even Bunratty, Co. Clare, *Bun Raite*, 'Mouth of the (river) Raite'.

Burgage: See BUIRÍOS

Bwee: See BUÍ

C

CÁBÁN: Means 'tent', 'cabin', and is Anglicised as 'cabin', as in Cabinteely, Co. Dublin, *Cábán tSíle*, 'Sheila's cabin'. It appears also in Rathcabban, Co. Tipperary, *Ráth Cabáin*, 'Fort of the cabin'.

CABHÁN: Means a 'hollow' or 'valley'; the most noteworthy example is the town and county, Cavan, Co. Cavan, *Cabhán*, 'Hollow'.

Caher: See CATHAIR

CAIPÍN: Means simply 'cap' or 'hood'; it seems uncommon but where it does occur, mainly in the extreme south, it appears as Cappeen, or Coppeen, without qualification, both in Co. Cork.

Cairn: See CARN

CAISEAL: Is derived from, or cognate with, the Latin *castellum*, is normally Anglicised 'cashel' and means 'stone wall, rampart, stone fort'. Normally the fort in question is seen to be a ring-fort, defended by stout stone walls instead of earthen banks and ditches. It is a term – like *cathair*, also meaning 'stone fort' – particularly common in the west of Ireland, where stone was the most abundant building material. *Caiseal* and *cathair* enjoy complementary, almost mutually exclusive, distributions, *caiseal* being the term preferred in the north-west. Some archaeologists employ the term 'cashel' to describe a stone fort regardless of its geographical location; 'cashel' is also used by some of them to describe the stone wall or rampart itself.

Most often in place-names it stands without qualification, especially on the fringes of the *caiseal*-areas. Of the fifty or so examples

recorded as townland names, representatives
– all, in Irish, *Caiseal*, Anglicised as 'Cashel',
and all meaning simply 'Stone fort' – are to be
found in counties as far apart in the north-
west as Galway and Donegal. Outside the
'home' area of the term is, of course, the most
famous example – Cashel, Co. Tipperary; this
enjoys no qualification in the place-name
itself, but is often described as *Caiseal
Mumhan*, 'Cashel of Munster', or as *Caiseal na
Ríogh*, 'Cashel of the kings', on the ground that
it was the royal seat of the kings of Munster.
The remaining fifty-odd examples of townland
names with *caiseal* as their first element
include Cashelgarran, Co. Sligo, *Caiseal an
Ghearráin*, 'Cashel of the horses', and
Cashelmore, Co. Donegal, *Caiseal Mór*, 'Large,
or great, cashel'. Some minor place-names
also contain the term as an initial element,
such as Cashelbane, Loughash, Co. Tyrone,
Caiseal Bán, 'White cashel'. Diminutive forms,
caislín and *caisleán*, also exist, the latter
generally as a translation of 'castle'. It
occasionally appears as a second or
qualifying element in place-names as in
Moygashel, Co. Tyrone, *Má gCaisil*, 'Plain of
the cashel', or Carracastle, Co. Roscommon,
Ceathrú an Chaisil, 'Quarterland of the cashel'.

CAISLEÁN: Means simply 'castle', but is probably a direct
derivation from the Latin *castellum* rather than a
borrowing of the English 'castle'. It is used
specifically of medieval and post-medieval
castles: Castlecomer, Co. Kilkenny, for example,
takes its name, *Caisleán an Chomair*, 'Castle of the
confluence', from a castle erected at the time of
the Anglo-Norman invasion, probably by
William the Marshall, while Castlelyons, Co.
Cork, *Caisleán Ó Liatháin*, is named after a
fortified house of the Tudor period. The

descriptors of other *caisleán*-names sometimes refer to their location, usually on rivers, such as Castlederg, Co. Tyrone, *Caisleán na Deirge*, 'Castle of the (river) Derg', or Castlemaine, Co. Kerry, *Caisleán na Mainge*, 'Castle of the (river) Maine', indicating their strategic position. Sometimes they simply describe the appearance, as in Castlegar, Co. Galway, *Caisleán Gearr*, 'Short castle', or Castlereagh, Cos Down and Roscommon, *Caisleán Riabhach*, 'Striped/grey castle'. More often than not they refer to the family who, at one stage or other in its history, occupied the castle, such as Castleconnell, Co. Limerick, *Caisleán Uí Chonaill*, 'Ó Conaill's castle'.

MAP **CAISEAL** as a sole or first element in the names of townlands; with a few notable exceptions it is essentially a term used in the north-western part of the country.

CALADH: Is a word with two compatible, but slightly different, meanings, both connected with water; it can mean low-lying land beside a river, liable to flooding, usually translated simply 'holm' in place-names, or, referring to the same sort of situation, it can mean a 'landing-place'. An example of the first can be seen in Callow, in Cos Mayo and Roscommon, in which instances, being inland, it probably means 'holm'; however, a minor name, *Caladh Buí*, on the island called Deenish in Co. Kerry, being coastal, is patently 'Yellow landing-place'. Ballinchalla, Co. Mayo, verging on Lough Mask, is *Baile an Chaladh*, 'Homestead of the landing-place'.

CAM: Means simply 'crooked', 'bent' or 'winding' and is applied in place-names to features such as lakes and rivers: Camowen, Co. Tyrone is *Camabhainn*, 'Crooked river', while Camlough, Co. Armagh, is *Camloch*, 'Crooked lake', and Camport, Co. Mayo is *Camport*, 'Crooked shore'. Less obviously, Camaross, Co. Wexford and Camross, Co. Laois are both *Camros*, 'Crooked grove or copse'.

CAOL: Is an adjective meaning 'narrow' or 'slender' and a noun meaning 'slender thing', with a particular reference in place-names to a 'marshy stream'. In either sense it can be Anglicised 'keal' or 'keel'. Keel, Co. Mayo is an instance of its use as a noun, while Kealkill, Co. Cork, *Caolchoill*, 'Narrow wood', exemplifies its use as an adjective. More often than not it follows the noun it qualifies, as in Kerrykeel, Co. Donegal, *Ceathrú Chaol*, 'Narrow quarter', or Ballykeel, Co. Down, *Baile Caol*, 'Narrow homestead'. In Kilkeel, Co. Down the noun possibly appears in *Cill an Chaoil*, 'Church of the narrow (i.e. strait)'. In Kealariddig, Co. Kerry the noun appears again, *Caol an Roidigh*,

'Marshy stream of the red mire'; a diminutive of the noun appears in Keeloges, Co. Leitrim, Caológa, 'Strips'.

CAONACH: Is another of the several words in Irish describing 'swamp' or 'moss'; it is not very common in place-names but occurs, without further elaboration, in a number of different forms. It appears as Keenagh and Kenagh, both in Co. Longford, and with simple qualification as Keenaghbeg, Caonach Beag, 'Small moss', in Co. Mayo.

CARN: Means a 'heap, pile of stones', and is common not only in Ireland but in Scotland and even Wales in this sense, often specifically of a stone-built burial mound. It is usually Anglicised as 'cairn', which is, in fact, the genitive case of the word. The types of burial-monument to which the term is applied range from the prominently sited round cairns of neolithic passage tombs and round cairns containing cisted burials of the earlier Bronze Age, through the long cairns covering neolithic court tombs, or the D-shaped cairns covering earlier Bronze Age wedge tombs, to ring cairns of late neolithic or earlier Bronze Age date. Carmavy, Co. Antrim, for example, is Carn Méibhe, 'Maeve's cairn', after a rather denuded passage tomb reused in the earlier Bronze Age; Carnkenny, Co. Tyrone, Carn Cainnech, 'Cainnech's cairn', appears to take its name from a rather unspectacular ring cairn. It should be noted that where a personal name appears as a qualifying element of carn it rarely, if ever, has any connection with the buried occupant of the monument (i.e. Maeve is certainly not the person interred in any of the cairns named after her), but is the result either of a romantic fiction to give prestige to a monument or of a simple declaration of current ownership at some stage in the subsequent history of the burial mound in question. The latter is likely to be the case with Carnoneen, Co. Galway, *Carn Eoghainín*, 'Burial cairn of Eoghainín'; similarly with Carndonagh, Co. Donegal, *Carn Domhnaigh*, 'Cairn of the church', where the pre-existing monument has been coupled with the church-name. Often in modern place-name usage the romantic qualifier has been suppressed, as with Carn, Co. Westmeath, which was at one time identified as *Carn Fiachach*, 'Fiacha's cairn', allegedly commemorating one Fiach, a son of Niall of the Nine Hostages. The term also appears in the form *carnán*, superficially a diminutive but occurring in the apparently self-contradictory Carnanmore, Co. Antrim, *Carnán Mór*, 'Big little cairn', after a quite impressive passage tomb. The term is also found in non-specific (i.e. not referring to an individual burial mound) contexts in place-names such as Carna, Cos Galway and Wexford, *Carna*, simply meaning 'Mounds' or 'Cairns'; similarly it appears as *Carnlach*, in Carnlough, Co. Antrim, 'Place of mounds or cairns'.

CARRAIG: Means 'rock', 'large prominent stone', and is usually Anglicised as 'carrick' or 'carrig'. Often it appears totally without qualification, as in Carrick, Cos Donegal and Wexford, or Carrig, Co. Tipperary, *Carraig*, simply meaning 'rock'. Sometimes the qualifying element is simply of size, such as Carrickbeg, Co. Waterford, *Carraig Bheag*, 'Small rock', or Carrickmore, Co. Tyrone, *Carraig Mhór*, 'Large rock'. Often the qualifying element describes the position of the rock in question, as in Carrickmacross, Co. Monaghan, *Carraig Mhachaire Rois*, 'Rock of the plain of the grove', or Carrigahorig, Co. Tipperary, *Carraig an Chomhraic*, 'Rock of the confluence'. Sometimes it reflects a use of the rock, as in Carrigaholt, Co.

Clare, *Carraig an Chabhaltaigh*, meaning 'Rock of the fleet', possibly as a result of its being employed as a leading mark or a moorage. Sometimes it is qualified by a personal name, as in Carrickfergus, Co. Antrim, *Carraig Fhearghasa*, 'Rock of Fergus', or Carrigaline, Co. Cork, *Carraig Uí Leighin*, 'Ó Leighin's rock'. It does occur as a second element in names like Ballynagarrick, Co. Armagh, *Baile na Carraige*, 'Town(land) of the rock'. Carrigart, Co. Donegal is to all appearance an obvious example, *Carraig Airt*, 'Art's rock'; it has been suggested, however, that these appearances are totally deceptive and that in fact it represents *Ceathrú Fhiodhghoirt*, 'Quarterland of the wood of the field'.

Carrick: See CARRAIG

Cashel: See CAISEAL

CATHAIR: Means 'stone enclosure, fortress, dwelling' and, by extension, 'monastic enclosure, monastery'. It is usually Anglicised 'caher' or 'cahir'. In contrast with *caiseal*, names with *cathair* concentrate in the southern part of the west coast. This term is well documented in Irish writing: Caherconree, Co. Kerry, *Cathair Con Raoi*, 'Stone fort of Cúrí', is classified in *The Irish Triads* as one of the three *dúine* (strongholds) of Ireland. In some instances *cathair* appears in a place-name totally without qualification, as in Caher, Cos Clare and Tipperary, meaning simply 'Stone fort'. Sometimes it is qualified simply by a reference to its size, as in Cahermore, Cos Cork and Galway, both in Irish *Cathair Mhór*, 'Large stone fort'; sometimes by a personal name as in Cahersiveen, Co. Kerry, *Cathair Saidhbhín*, 'Stone fort of Saidhbhín', or Caherloughlin, Co. Clare, *Cathair Lochlainn*, 'Lochlann's stone fort'.

Ceall

MAP **CATHAIR** as a sole or first element in the names of townlands; it is very strongly identified with the western and south-western parts of the country.

CEALL: See CILL

CEALTRACH: Is derived from *ceall* and simply means 'churchyard' or 'graveyard'. It is usually Anglicised as 'caltra(gh)' or 'caldragh', as in instances without further qualification at Caltra, Co. Galway and Caldragh, Co. Fermanagh. The latter is remarkable for containing a stone with twin cross-armed figures set back to back, which is almost certainly pre-Christian and may bestow on the graveyard antiquity greater than might be assumed from the palpably Christian graves around it. At times simple, and somehow appropriate, qualifiers are applied, as in Caltraghlea, Co. Galway, *Cealtrach Lia*, 'Grey graveyard'.

CEANN/CIONN: Means 'head', as of an animal, and is quite common in place-names, often, as might be expected, referring to coastal features – whether as a promontory or as the highest point reached by the tide in an inlet or river-mouth. In this latter sense are several notable examples, descriptive of precisely this feature: Kinsale, Co. Cork is *Cionn tSáile*, 'Head of the salt water', a smaller version of which exists at Kinsalebeg in Co. Waterford, *Cionn tSáile Beag*, 'Little head of the salt water'. A similar tidal situation is described by Kenmare, Co. Kerry, which is *Ceann Mara*, 'Head of the sea', and Kinvarra, Co. Galway. It can also be applied to the top of a sheet of fresh water, as in Kinlough, Co. Leitrim, *Cionn Locha*, 'Head of the lake'. In Kinnegad, Co. Westmeath it refers to the head, rather than the mouth, of a ford – *Cionn Átha Gad*, 'Head of the ford of the withies'.

In its more elevated sense, not always relating to a promontory, it can be qualified by a term describing its nature, as in Kingarrow, Co. Donegal, *Cionn Garbh*, 'Rough head', of an upland pass in rough moorland; a term describing its position, as in Kindrum, Co. Donegal, *Cionn Droma*, 'Head of the ridge'; or, as often is the case, a term describing the appearance of the head in question, in many instances comparing its shape to that of an animal: Kanturk, Co. Cork, for example, is *Ceann Toirc*, 'Head of the boar'; Kincun, Co. Mayo, is *Cionn Con*, 'Head of the dog'; Kineigh, in Co. Kerry and Kinnea in Cos Cavan and Donegal are all *Cionn Ech*, 'Head of the horse'.

CEAPACH/ÓG: Means a 'plot of land', 'green plot before a house', and in place-name contexts is usually translated simply as 'plot of land'. It is generally Anglicised as 'Cappa' or 'Cappagh'. It occurs commonly, without further qualification, in Cos Galway, Limerick, Kerry, Tyrone and Waterford, as Cappagh. Sometimes there is a very simple description, as in Cappamore, Co. Limerick, *Ceapach Mór*, 'Large plot of land', or Capparoe, Cos Kerry and Limerick, *Ceapach Rua*, 'Red/russet plot of land'. Sometimes the description is a little enigmatic, as in Cappanacush, Co. Kerry, *Ceapach na Coise*, 'Plot of land of the foot' – unless it indicates that the plot in question could be tilled only with the foot, i.e. with a spade. Sometimes, as in Cappaquin, Co. Waterford, the qualifying element is a personal name, *Ceapach Choinn*, 'Conn's plot of land'.

CEATHRÚ: Literally means 'quarter' and in the sense of 'quarterland' is regarded as a subdivision of a townland. Be that as it may, over 700 of the names of modern townlands begin with the usual Anglicised forms, 'carhoo' or – much more commonly – 'carrow'. The townlands may be large, as in Carrowmore, Co. Sligo, *Ceathrú Mhór*, 'Large quarterland', or small, as in Carrowbeg, Co. Mayo, *Ceathrú Bheag*, 'Small quarterland'; they may be striped, as Carrowreagh, Co. Roscommon, *Ceathrú Riabhach*, 'Striped quarterland', or they may be narrow, as in Carrowkeel, Co. Donegal, *Ceathrú Chaol*. They may be named after their position, as in Carrowmoreknock, Co. Galway, *Ceathrú Mhór an Chnoic*, 'Large quarterland of the hill', or their vegetation, as in Carrowtawy, Co. Sligo, *Ceathrú an tSamhaidh*, 'Quarterland of the sorrel'. Of course they can bear a personal name as an indication of the sometime owner, as in Carrowteige, Co. Mayo, *Ceathrú Thaidhg*, 'Taidg's quarterland'.

CÉIDE: Means a 'hill', especially one with a flat top. It is fairly common in place-names, especially in the North, where it appears as Keady, Co. Armagh; it occurs in diminutive form as the name of a mountain in Co. Wicklow, Keadeen, *Céidín*, and with a wholly different Anglicised form as Cadian, Co. Tyrone. It is regularly found in minor names throughout the country. An appropriate qualification for such a feature appears in Keadydrinagh, Co. Sligo, *Céide Droigneach*, 'Flat-topped hill of the blackthorns'.

CÉIM: Is a word meaning 'step' but in place-names describes a 'pass' or a 'gap'. Instances are not particularly common; the best-known example is Pass of Keimaneigh, Co. Cork, *Céim an Fhia*, 'Pass of the deer'. It is common in minor names, many of which have no Anglicised form.

CEIS/ACH: Basically means 'wickerwork' but in place-name contexts refers to a road of wicker across a bog; it is usually Anglicised as 'kesh' or 'kish', or, if the variant form is used, as 'cassagh'. It appears as Kesh, without qualification, in Co. Fermanagh; as Kish in Co. Arklow; Kisha in Co. Wexford; and Cassagh in Co. Waterford. In Co. Leitrim Keshcarrigan is *Ceis Charraigín*, 'Wicker causeway of the little rock'. Sometimes the term itself appears as a qualifying element, as in Ballinhassig, Co. Cork, *Béal Átha an Cheasaigh*, 'Mouth of the ford of the wicker causeway'. Traces of such wicker causeways are often discovered in bogs.

CELL: See CILL

CILL: Means 'church' and is the form which most frequently occurs in Irish place-names. It is the dative singular of the word *ceall*, derived from the Latin *cella*, which in Classical Latin referred to a 'room within a building', one of its special applications being to a 'shrine of a deity within the pagan *templum*. In place-names it has a range of associated meanings: 'church, monastic settlement or foundation, churchyard, graveyard'. Of these, in place-names, 'monastic settlement' is the commonest reference, particularly where the name can be shown to pre-date the ecclesiastical reforms of the twelfth century. It is the most prevalent ecclesiastical element in parish names, townland names and minor names.

It is usually Anglicised as 'kil(l)', which is unfortunate since it is rendered superficially indistinguishable from *coill*, 'wood', also Anglicised – since the seventeenth century at least – as 'kil(l)'. If the particular place-name is documented in Irish writing, as, fortunately, many are, the doubt is easily resolved; otherwise the only clue to which word is intended may consist in the associations, either documented or circumstantial, of the name. If it occurs in a parish name, for example, the chances of *cill*, rather than *coill*, as the relevant term, are vastly enhanced. In the case of Kilbride, Co. Down, for example, the qualifying element, 'bride', would suggest, even at first sight, that 'kil' in this instance is *cill* rather than *coill*, on the assumption that 'bride' represents Bríd, rather than being a corruption of something else. Oddly enough, while the place is referred to in the de Courcy Dower Charter of *c.* 1180, it is as 'Kelbide', in Lecale, which helps not a whit. It is only by good luck that in a document as late as 1609 it is recorded as 'Kilbriditche', and so is confirmed by documentation as representing *Cill Bhríde*, 'Brigid's church'.

Instances which are undocumented in Irish writing and therefore might be more doubtful were they not the names of parishes include Kilcoo, a parish in Co. Down, seen to be *Cill*

Chua, 'Cua's church'; Killyglen, Co. Antrim, a parish in Co. Antrim, seen to be *Cill Ghlinne*, 'Church of the glen'; Kilwaughter parish, Co. Antrim, seen to be *Cill Uachtair*, 'Upper church'. Other parish-names documented in Anglicised spelling include Killeeshil, Co. Tyrone, *Cill Íseal*, 'Low church'; Killagan, Co. Antrim, *Cill Lagáin*, 'Church of the low-lying place'; and Killashandra, Co. Cavan, *Cill na Seanrátha*, 'Church of the old fort'.

Names that are not parish-names present slightly greater difficulties, which early Anglicised spellings may occasionally resolve. In the case of Ballykilbeg, Co. Down, the existence of Anglicised forms such as 'Ballynegalbegge' or 'Ballynegalbeke' point to an Irish form *Baile na gCeall Beag*, 'Town(land) of the small churches'. Often, however, it is only the local tradition of an old church-site, or common local memory of the precise location of an old church-site, which may distinguish a *cill*-name from a *coill*-name. In the case of Kilvergan, Co. Armagh, for example, it was only the tradition of a church-site on Kilvergan Hill which suggested that the original name was *Cill Uí Mhuireagáin*, with the Ó Muireagán family seen as erenaghs, or hereditary stewards. Similarly, Kilfeaghan, Co. Down is not recorded any earlier than the seventeenth century: in this instance the clue was provided by local memory of a field known as Shankill, *Seanchill*, 'Old church', showing that the original name was likely to be *Cill Fhéichín*, 'Féichín's church'.

Archaeological evidence may cast light on the date of the site in question but does not necessarily demonstrate the date of the name. From the site of a *Seanchill*-name in Belfast (now an old graveyard) come two fragments of ninth-century crosiers and a circular mount with amber settings, showing that the site, at least, was in use before any surviving documentary records mention it; indeed the earliest indisputable reference to it is in the Papal Taxation of 1306, where it is described as 'Ecclesia Alba, the White church'. We do not know for certain, therefore, at precisely what period it first acquired the name of Shankill, *Seanchill*, 'Old church', now the name of the parish.

While *domhnach*-names are the ones that predominantly describe the churches of the Patrician mission, a total of twenty-six *cell*- or *cill*-names appear in the ninth-century 'Life of Patrick' (*Bethu Phátraic*). One is a church ascribed to Palladius, the precursor of Patrick, known as *Cell Fhine*, unfortunately not identified; another is *Cell Úsaill*, 'Church of Úsaile (= Auxilius)', identified with Killashee, Co. Kildare. Four are stated actually to have been founded by Patrick and thirteen to have direct Patrician associations. Apart from its occurrence in cited place-names, *cell* is one of the commonest terms used for an ecclesiastical foundation, often coupled with *congbháil*, which literally means 'holding' but in this context seems to refer to 'cloisters'. *Forothaigestar célla agus congbála and* ('There he founded churches and cloisters') is, with minor variations, almost a stock phrase in the text. Tírechán, Patrick's seventh-century biographer, normally uses the Latin *aeclesia* to describe a church-site; he also uses *cella*, both as a finite term with no apparent difference in meaning from *aeclesia*, and as an element in place-names – in Latin, however. Some of these have been identified and include *Cellola magna Muaide*, identified with Kilmoremoy, Co.

Mayo; *Cell Adrochtae*, identified with Killaraght, Co. Sligo; and *Cell Senchae*, identified with Shancoe, Co. Sligo.

With the development of the Irish monastic church from the sixth century onwards, *cell* or *cill* becomes the standard term for the monastic foundation. What credence or interpretation we ascribe to *cell* or *cill* in the context of the episcopal church founded by Patrick is a matter of opinion, bearing in mind the non-contemporary nature of the source-material. At the very least, it would appear that in our early ecclesiastical *seanchas* the use of *cell* was not regarded by the seventh- and ninth-century compilers as anachronistic. It is, after all, found in the earliest Columban material, both in Latin and in Irish. Adomnan, in his seventh-century *Vita Sancti Columbae*, 'Life of Saint Columba', uses it in two instances, once with a specifically monastic reference. In a eulogy of St Columba, *Amra Choluimb Chille*, ascribed to a secular poet, Dallán Forgaill, and thought to have been written shortly after the saint's death in 597, *cell* is the only significant ecclesiastical settlement term used. In this, and in two other seventh-century poems in praise of the saint, the sobriquet 'Collum Cille' appears. This would suggest that *cell* or *cill* had begun to enjoy a natural usage as an ecclesiastical settlement term by the seventh, if not as early as the sixth, century. Accordingly we might expect it to appear as a place-name element; and, with the *caveat* that early annalistic entries are not necessarily contemporary, by the sixth century it does start appearing as such, with examples such as *Cell Daro*, Kildare, Co. Kildare, 'Church of the oak-tree', and *Cell Cuilind*, Kilcullen, Co. Kildare, 'Church of the steep slope'. Many of the place-name compositions refer to a geographical or topographical feature of the site of the church, or more properly the monastery, such as Kilclief, Co. Down, *Cill Cléithe*, 'Church of the hurdle', and Kilroot, Co. Antrim, *Cill Ruaidh*, 'Church of the red' – referring to the red soil of the immediate area.

CLADACH: Is another word meaning 'shore' or 'beach'. Its best-known appearance is as The Claddagh, in Co. Galway, close to Galway city, whose fishing quarter it once was. It appears in the same form in Co. Kerry, and with a simple qualification as Claddaghduff, Co. Galway, *Cladach Dubh*, 'Black shore'.

CLAIS: Means any sort or depth of furrow from a 'drain' to a 'ravine', but in place-names is generally deemed to designate 'ravine'; it is usually Anglicised as 'clash', as which it appears in Clash, Cos Tipperary and Wicklow, and Clashmore, Co. Waterford, *Clais Mhór*, 'Big ravine'. It occurs as a qualifying element in Ballinaclash, Co. Wicklow and Ballinaclashet, Co. Cork, *Baile na Claise*, 'Homestead of the ravine'.

CLÁR: Basically means 'level surface', covering anything from a 'plank' to a 'plain'. Generally, but not invariably, in place-names it refers to a 'plain'. It is common throughout the country, and without further qualification appears as Clare in Cos Armagh, Clare (where it is the name of the county), Down and Tyrone; a diminutive, *Cláirín*, 'Little plain', occurs as Clareen, Co. Galway. It appears as a qualifying element in Kilclare, Co. Leitrim, *Coill an Chláir*, 'Wood of the plain', and in Ballyclare, Co. Antrim, *Bealach Cláir*, 'Pass of the plain'. In its narrower sense of 'plank' it is found in such names as Clarina, Co. Limerick, *Clár Aidhne*, 'Aidhne's plank (bridge)', and

Clarinbridge, Co. Galway, in a partially translated instance, Droichead an Chláirín, 'Bridge of the little plank'. A variant form, Clárach, appears as Clara, Co. Offaly.

CLOCH: Means 'stone', of any size or shape, and is even by extension applied to a stone building, usually a 'stone castle'. Where it appears by itself, as in Clough, Co. Down, it is likely that the reference is to a 'stone castle', which indeed in this case survives, located on an Anglo-Norman motte or castle-mound. Sometimes it applies to a large and conspicuous glacial erratic, as in Cloughmore, Co. Down, Cloch Mór, 'Large stone'. It is qualified by terms describing its shape or colour, as in Cloghbrack, Co. Mayo, Cloch Breac, 'Speckled stone', or Cloghroe, Co. Cork, Cloch Rua, 'Red stone', or even rather disguised, in Cloyfin, Co. Derry, Cloch Fionn, 'White stone'. Sometimes the second element describes the location of the stone in question, as in Clonakilty, Co. Cork, Cloch na Coillte, 'Stone of the woods'. It appears frequently in a secondary position, as in Ballynaclogh, Co. Tipperary, Baile na Cloiche, 'Homestead of the stone', Kilnacloghy, Co. Roscommon, Coill na Cloiche, 'Wood of the stone', or Aughnacloy, Co. Tyrone, Achadh na Cloiche, 'Field of the stone'. In some instances the qualifying element clearly indicates that the name refers to a stone castle, as Cloghjordan, Co. Tipperary, Cloch Shiurdáin, 'Jordan's castle'. There are diminutives: Cloichín, 'Little stone', which appears as Clogheen in Cos Tipperary and Waterford, and Clochóg, with the same meaning, which appears as Cloughoge, Co. Armagh. There are also derivatives, such as Clochán, meaning 'Stony place', which occurs as Cloghan, in Cos

Donegal, Offaly and Westmeath, and as
Cloghane in Co. Kerry. Clogher, in Cos Mayo
and Tyrone, Clochar, also means 'Stony place',
as does Clocharnach, represented by
Cloghernagh, Co. Waterford. Clochaigh, as in
Cloghy, Co. Down, simply means 'Stony'.

CLUAIN: Means 'meadow' or 'pasture-land' and is very
common in place-names; it is usually
Anglicised as 'clon' or 'cloon(e)'. In the form
'cloon' it appears without further qualification
in Cloon, Cos Clare and Mayo; as 'cloone' it
appears in Cloone, Co. Leitrim and even as
'cloyne' in Cloyne, Co. Cork. Often the
qualification is very simple, as in Cloonfad,
Co. Roscommon, Cluain Fada, 'Long pasture';
Clonard, Co. Wexford, Cluain Ard, 'High
pasture'; or Clonmore, in Cos Carlow and
Tipperary, Cluain Mór, 'Large pasture'. Often
the qualifying term prescribes the type of
livestock for which the pasture is used:
Clonygowan, Co. Offaly, Cluain na nGamhan,
'Pasture of the calves'; Clonmult, Co. Cork,
Cluain Molt, 'Pasture of wethers'; Clontarf, Co.
Dublin, Cluain Tarbh, 'Pasture of bulls'.
Sometimes a notable feature is recorded:
Clontibret, Co. Monaghan, Cluain Tiobrad,
'Pasture of the well'; Clondrohid, Co. Cork,
Cluain Droichid, 'Pasture of the bridge'; or
Cloondara, Co. Longford, Cluain dá Ráth,
'Pasture of two forts'. Clonmel, Co. Tipperary
is particularly attractive – Cluain Meala,
'Pasture of honey'. As so often with tracts of
land of any description, it is often a personal
or family name that is applied: Clonbern, Co.
Galway is Cluain Bheirn, 'Bearn's pasture';
Clondalkin, Co. Dublin is Cluain Dolcáin,
'Dolcan's pasture'; and Clongorey, Co. Kildare
is Cluain Guaire, 'Guaire's pasture'. Two
interesting examples are Clontuskert, Co.

Galway, Cluain Tuaiscirt, 'North pasture', implying there was a correlative south pasture, and Clonoulty, Co. Tipperary, Cluain Ultaigh, 'Pasture of the Ulstermen', which leaves us in no doubt what part of the north its namers had in mind.

CNOC: Means anything from a hill to a small mountain and is very common in place-names, not only in Ireland but in Scotland as well. Usually Anglicised as 'knock', it occasionally stands alone as a place-name, as in Knock, Co. Clare, and the well-known Knock, Co. Mayo, both of which are unadorned Cnoc, 'Hill'. Often it is qualified by a simple descriptive adjective, as in Knockmore, Co. Mayo, Cnoc Mór, 'Big hill'; Knockmoyle, Co. Galway, Cnoc Maol, 'Bald hill'; or Knockboy, of which there are examples in Cos Cork, Kerry and Waterford, Cnoc Buí, 'Yellow hill'. Sometimes it is found with a reference to some special feature: Knockaderry, Co. Limerick, Cnoc an Doire, 'Hill of the oakwood'; Knockadoon, Co. Cork, Cnoc an Dúin, 'Hill of the fort'; Knockloughrim, Co. Derry, Cnoc Clochdhroma, 'Hill of the stony ridge'; or even Knockcroghery, Co. Roscommon, Cnoc an Crochaire, 'Hill of the hangman'.

It often appears qualified by a personal name: Knockainy, Co. Limerick, is typical of several instances of Cnoc Áine, 'Áine's Hill', indicating a sort of primitive dedication to Áine, the goddess of love, of which there is another example in the north of the country, in south-west Donegal. Less obviously superhuman beings adding their names to hills are represented by Knockmealdown, and the mountains sharing the name, in Cos Tipperary and Waterford, Cnoc Maoldomhnaigh, 'Hill of

Maoldomhnach'. In the north-west of Ireland, particularly, the 'n' of *cnoc* is changed to 'r', so that near Killybegs, Co. Donegal, Crocknagapple appears representing C*noc na gCapall*, 'Hill of the horses'. A diminutive, *cnocán*, Anglicised 'knockan', is used as in Knockanevin, Co. Cork, C*nocán Aoibhinn*, 'Pleasant hillock'.

COILL: Is one of the standard Irish words for a 'wood'; unfortunately, since the seventeenth century at least, it has been Anglicised as 'kil(l)', thus causing confusion with 'kil(l)' as the usual Anglicisation of *cill*, meaning 'church, monastery'. The fact that many church-sites remain as parish-names, or are recorded as identifiable church-names in native, or even English, documentation, does not totally solve the confusion. With many 'kil(l)' names it is difficult, superficially, to distinguish between 'wood'-names and 'church'-names. If an Irish form can be found, the problem can be solved; if the associations of the name are helpful, a reasonable guess can at least be made. One particularly deceptive example is Kilnamanagh, Co. Tipperary, the obvious association of which is with monks, thus encouraging the interpretation 'Church of the monks'; fortunately the name is recorded in the Annals as C*oill na Manach*, making it clear that the name, contrary to expectation, means 'Wood of the monks'. Another disturbing example lies with the name Kildangan: Kildangan, Co. Kildare, is shown to be C*ill Daingin*, 'Church of the fortress', while Kildangan, Co. Offaly, is C*oill an Daingin*, 'Wood of the fortress'.

Generally a personal name, if it is known to be the name of a saint, is a reasonable indication that the reference is to a church. Of the simple descriptive adjectives used as qualifying elements, some colours are more pertinent to woods than they are to churches, thus Kilglass, Co. Galway is *Coill Ghlas*, 'Green wood' and Killylea, Co. Armagh is *Coillidh Liath*, 'Grey woodland', *coillidh* being a derivative of *coill* meaning 'woodland'. Where *coill* or *coillidh* is Anglicised 'cully', a useful indicator is provided that woodland is the subject, as in Cullybackey, Co. Antrim, *Coill na Baice*, 'Wood of the angle'. The plural of *coill* is *coillte*, which is Anglicised in several ways, including 'kilty' and 'quilty', as in Kiltyclogher, Co. Leitrim, *Coillte Clochar*, 'Woods of the stony place', and Quilty, Co. Clare, *Coillte*, 'Woods'.

COM/CÚM: Means 'hollow', especially with reference to the waist, or – like the similar-looking English word – 'coomb', and is quite common in place-names. It appears totally without qualification as Camp, Co. Kerry and also occurs in Co. Kerry as Coomatloukane, *Com an tSleabcáin*, 'Hollow of the edible seaweed' (i.e. 'sloke'), and in Co. Waterford as Coomnagoppul, *Com na gCapall*, 'Hollow of the horses'. In secondary position it appears, for example, in Baurtregaum, Co. Kerry, *Barr Trí gCom*, 'Top of the three hollows'. It is quite common in minor names.

COMAR: Simply means 'confluence', the place at which two rivers join; in a form totally without qualification it is, of course, found in Comber, Co. Down. It appears in two slightly different compositions, each with the same meaning: Ballycorick, Co. Clare and Ballycumber, Co. Offaly, the first of which is *Béal Átha Chomhraic*, the second *Béal Átha Chomair*, both meaning 'Mouth of the ford of the confluence'.

CONGBHÁIL: Literally simply means 'holding', but in ecclesiastical contexts can be interpreted as 'church', 'monastery' or, more specifically, 'cloister', since the expression *Forothaigestar célla agus congbála and*, 'There he founded churches and cloisters', is almost a stock expression in the ninth-century 'Life of Patrick', *Bethu Phátraic*. Despite the frequency with which this expression is used, the term itself appears only occasionally in place-names, without any qualification as Conwal, Co. Donegal, site of a monastery one of whose abbots, Fíachra, is said also to have been abbot of Clonard, Co. Meath, and again in Co. Leitrim. In Noughaval in Cos Laois and Clare it occurs as *Nuacongbháil*, 'New cloister/monastery'.

CORA: Means a 'weir' and is quite a common element in Irish place-names; it appears without qualification in Corry, Co. Leitrim but is usually present in more complex forms of name. One common combination is in Corrofin, Cos Clare and Galway, or Corofin, Co. Clare, *Cora Finne*, translated sometimes as 'Finn's weir', sometimes 'Weir of the white (river)'; a more sensible translation might well be 'Weir of the white (water)'. Possibly the most famous place-name containing the word is Kincora, Co. Clare, *Ciann Coradh*, 'Head of the weir', celebrated seat of the Dál gCais and of Thomond. Needless to say, it appears in the sense of 'Homestead of the weir', in Ballycarra, Co. Mayo and Ballycarry, Co. Antrim, *Baile Cora*, as well as in Ballinacarrow, Co. Sligo, and Ballinacurra, Cos Cork and Limerick, the same name but with the article, *Baile na Cora*. It also occurs as 'Ridge of the weir' in Drumcar, Co. Louth, *Droim Chora*.

CORCAIGH: Is the dative singular of the noun *corcach*, meaning 'swamp', and is the form generally found in place-name composition. The best-known example is, of course, the city and county of Cork, where the word appears without qualification, as it does at the other end of the country in Corkey, Co. Antrim. Inevitably it occurs as 'Homestead of the swamp', in Ballincurrig, Co. Cork, *Baile an Churraigh*. It appears in Kilcurry, Co. Louth, as *Cill an Churraigh*, 'Church of the swamp'.

CORR: Means a 'projection' of some kind or other, or a 'pointed hill'. It appears quite without qualification in Curr, Co. Tyrone and also with a range of descriptive predicates: some referring to its location, as in Cornamona, Co. Galway, *Corr na Móna*, 'Pointed hill of the bog', or Currandrum, Co. Galway, *Corr an Droma*, 'Pointed hill of the ridge'; some referring to the wildlife present, as in Cornafanog, Co. Fermanagh, *Corr na bhFeannóg*, 'Pointed hill of the crow'. Sometimes the description is not very helpful, as in Cornafulla, Co. Roscommon, *Corr na Fola*, 'Pointed hill of the blood', alluding, presumably, to some scantily remembered bloodshed. Sometimes it occurs simply in the plural, as in Currow, Co. Kerry, as does its diminutive, *Coiriní*, as Curreeny, Co. Tipperary. In the Curlew Mountains, in Cos Roscommon and Sligo, it appears as *Corrsliabh*, 'Pointed mountains (mountains)'.

CORRACH/ CURRACH: Is one of the many Irish words for a 'swamp' or 'morass'. It appears simply as Curragh, Co. Waterford and with various colour-descriptions, as in Curraghboy, Co. Roscommon, *Currach Buí*, 'Yellow marsh', or Curraghroe, Co. Roscommon, *Currach Rua*, 'Red marsh'. Size or shape descriptions exist too: Curraghmore, Co. Waterford, *Currach Mór*, 'Big marsh', and Curraghlawn, Co. Wexford, *Currach Leathan*, 'Broad marsh'. Sometimes there is a description of the vegetation, as in Currabeha, Co. Cork, *Currach Beithe*, 'Marsh of the birch'. It appears in a secondary position quite frequently, as in

Kilcurry, Co. Louth, *Cill an Churraigh*, 'Church of the marsh'. It also means simply 'low-lying plain', without any presumption of its being waterlogged, and in this sense appears as Curragh, in Co. Kildare, with the extended meaning of 'racecourse'.

CORRÁN: Means basically an 'angle', 'corner' or even 'sickle'. It appears simply as Curran, in Cos Antrim and Derry (in Antrim referring to the sickle-shaped promontory near Larne), and as Currane and Corraun in Co. Mayo.

Craig: See CREAG

CRANN: Is the standard word for a 'tree' and occurs in the simple forms Cran in Cos Cavan and Fermanagh, and Crann in Co. Armagh. It appears as the collective *Crannach*, 'Place abounding in trees', as in Crannagh, Cos Galway, Mayo, Laois, Roscommon and Tipperary; as Cranagh in Cos Tipperary and Wicklow; and as Cranny in Cos Derry, Donegal and Tyrone, and in the name of the Crana River in Co. Donegal. Some simple qualifications are observed, as in Crancam, Co. Roscommon, *Crann Cam*, 'Crooked tree', and Cranmore, Co. Mayo, *Crann Mór*, 'Large tree'. It is also, of course, the basis of the term *crannóg*, denoting an artificial island constructed from wooden beams and used as a habitation-site in lakes, which appears but rarely in place-names: unadorned as Crannogue, Co. Tyrone, and as Crannogue Boy, *Crannóg Buí*, in Co. Donegal.

CRAOBH: Means simply a 'tree' or 'branch' and is usually Anglicised as 'creeve' or 'crew'. It appears in this simple unqualified form as Creeve in Cos Antrim, Armagh, Donegal, Down, Longford, Monaghan, Roscommon, Tyrone and Westmeath; a collective form, *Craobhach*, 'Place of branches/trees', occurs as

Creevagh in Cos Clare, Donegal, Galway, Mayo, Meath, Monaghan, Offaly, Sligo, Tyrone and Westmeath. In Cos Antrim, Tyrone and Derry it appears as 'crew', a simply qualified version of which is Crewbane in Co. Meath, *Craobh Bán*, 'White tree'. Often it is associated with a hill, as in Crew Hill, Co. Tyrone, which, since it is a steeply rounded hill with an associated standing stone, is more likely to represent *craobh* + 'hill' than *Craobhchoill*, meaning 'Wood of branches/trees'. In many instances the *craobh* in question seems to have possessed almost totemic properties; *Craobh Ruadh*, Creeveroe, meaning 'Red branch/tree', occurs in Co. Armagh, in close proximity to Navan Fort. The term 'Red branch' was associated with a military band based there and in *Táin Bó Cúalnge* Cú Chulainn is referred to as the 'Smith's Hound from the Cráebrúad'. As with *bile*, the owners or devotees of a *craobh* guarded it jealously and their enemies regarded it as one of their sensitive points, hence in *Annals of Ulster*, under the year 1099, it is recorded that:

> *Slogadh la Domnall H. Lochlainn agus la Tuaiscert nErenn tar Tuaim i nUlltaibh; Ulaidh dano i Craibh Telcha i llongport. Comhraicit a ndi marcsloigh, maidhes for marcsluagh Uladh agus marbtair H. Amhrain ann. Facbaid Ulaidh iar sin a longport agus loiscit Cenel nEogain é agus tescait Craibh Tealcha.*

An expedition was made by Domnall Ua Lochlainn and the North of Ireland over Tuaim into Ulaid; the Ulaid, however, were in camp at Craeb Telcha. Their two forces of horsemen meet, the force of the Ulaid is defeated, and ua hAmráin is killed there. The Ulaid then leave their camp and Cenel Eogain burn it and cut down Craeb Telcha.

Needless to say, there was a sequel, which is recounted under B*ile*.

CREAG: Means 'rock' or 'crag' and is usually Anglicised as 'craig' or 'creg' in place-names. It is essentially a term of the North of Ireland, with a scatter in Co. Galway and around the mouth of the River Shannon. It sometimes occurs without qualification of any kind, as in Craigs, Co. Antrim and Cregg, Co. Sligo. Most of the names generated from it consist of *creag* followed by a fairly simple adjective, as in Craigmore, in Cos Derry and Antrim, C*reag Mór*, 'Large crag'; frequently the adjective concerns colour: Craigdoo, Co. Donegal and Cregduff, Co. Mayo are both examples of C*reag Dubh*, 'Black crag'; Craigban, Co. Antrim and Craigbane, Co. Derry of C*reag Bán*, 'White crag'; Craigboy, Co. Down and Cregboy, Co. Galway of C*reag Buí*, 'Yellow crag'. Speckled also occurs, as Craigbrack, Co. Derry, C*reag Breac*, 'Speckled crag', as does grey, in Craiglea, again in Co. Derry, C*reag Liath*, 'Grey crag'. Slightly more complex combinations are also seen, as in Craigavad, Co. Down, C*reag an Bháda*, 'Rock of the boat'. Sometimes the qualification refers to a beast or bird: Craignagat, Co. Antrim, is C*reag na gCat*, 'Crag of the cats', while in Craigatuke, Co. Tyrone, C*reag an tSeabhaic*, we find 'Crag of the hawk'. There is a diminutive form, C*reagán*, which appears without qualification as Creggan in Cos Armagh, Derry and Westmeath, and, in a more unusual form, as Doocregaun, Co. Mayo, D*ubh Creagán*, 'Little black crag'. There is also a collective form, C*reagach*, 'Abounding in rocks or crags', represented by Cregagh, Co. Down.

Croagh: See CRUACH

CROIS: Means simply 'cross', in the sense both of a Christian cross and of a crossroad. It appears

quite often in place-names, without any
qualification in Cross, in Cos Clare and Mayo.
There is no doubt which meaning it enjoys in
Crosspatrick, *Crois Phádraig*, which occurs as a
place-name in Cos Kilkenny and Wicklow,
'Pádraig's cross'. It also appears as Crossgar,
Co. Down, *Crois Gearr*, 'Short cross', and, in the
plural, as Crossabeg, Co. Wexford, *Crosa Beaga*,
'Small crosses'.

CRUACH: Originally described a rick, as of turf, but is also
applied to mountains or hills – sometimes an
isolated, symmetrical peak, sometimes a ridge,
or range, of mountains. It is usually Anglicised
in place-names as 'croagh'. The best-known
examples of both types of mountain to which it
is applied are Croaghpatrick, Co. Mayo, *Cruach
Phádraig*, 'Patrick's rick', and the Bluestack
Mountains, Co. Donegal, known in Irish as
Cruacha Gorma, 'Blue ricks'. The Irish name for
Macgillycuddy's Reeks, in Co. Kerry, is *Cruacha
Dubha*, 'Black ricks'. It appears in the names of
other mountains, such as a ridge in south-west
Donegal known as Croaghbeg, *Chruach Bheag*,
'Small rick', and – also in south-west Donegal –
in a slightly different Anglicised form, as
Crowbane, *Cruach Bán*, 'White rick'. The
diminutive form, *Cruachán*, Anglicised Croghan,
is even more common, with representatives in
Cos Offaly, Roscommon, Wexford and Wicklow,
all meaning 'Little rick'.

CUAN: Means 'curve', 'hollow', 'recess' and thence
'harbour', 'haven'. It appears totally without
qualification in Coon, Co. Kilkenny. *Loch Cuan*,
'Lough of the harbours', was an earlier name
for Strangford Lough.

CÚIL: Means a 'corner' or a 'nook'. It occurs without
qualification as Coole, Co. Westmeath, but
can easily be confused with *cúl*, 'hill'; for

example, Coolbaun, Co. Tipperary, *Cúil Bhán*, is 'White nook', and Coolbaun, Co. Kilkenny, *Cúl Bán*, is 'White hill'. Coolgreany, Co. Wexford is charmingly *Cúil Ghréine*, 'Nook of the sun'; Coolmeen, Co. Clare, *Cúil Mhín*, 'Smooth nook', and Culmore, Co. Derry, *Cúil Mór*, 'Big nook'. Coleraine, Co. Derry is *Cúil Rathain*, 'Nook of ferns', while Coolrain, Co. Laois is *Cúil Ruáin*, 'Nook of the red ground'. Killincooly, Co. Wexford is *Cillín Cúile*, 'Little church of the nook', and Collooney, Co. Sligo, *Cúil Mhuine*, 'Nook of the thicket'.

CUILLEANN: Is a word meaning 'steep unbroken slope' which appears as Cullen in Cos Cork and Tipperary, and Cullion in Cos Down and Tyrone. It is deceptively similar to the word *cuileann*, meaning 'holly', and as a result many names have been erroneously construed as referring to 'holly'. It appears as a qualifying element in Kilcullen, Co. Kildare, *Cill Chuillinn*, 'Church of the steep slope'.

CÚL: Means 'back', with special reference to the back of the head and thence to anything resembling the shape of the back of the head, i.e. a 'hill'. It is usually Anglicised as 'cool' or 'cul', which makes confusion with *cúil* almost inevitable. It appears with very simple qualification in Coolbaun, Co. Kilkenny, *Cúl Bán*, 'White hill'; Coolmore, Co. Donegal, *Cúl Mór*, 'Big hill'; and Coolboy, Cos Donegal and Westmeath, *Cúl Buí*, 'Yellow hill'. In Coolderry, in Cos Monaghan and Offaly, *Cúl Doire*, it is best rendered as 'Back of the oakwood', as is the case with Coolcullen, Co. Kilkenny, *Cúl an Chuillinn*, 'Back of the steep slope', or Culvin, Co. Westmeath, *Cúl Bhinn*, 'Back of the peak'.

Cully: See COILL

CURRACH: See CORRACH

D

DÁ: Means 'two', and is relatively common in place-name composition. The most notable example is Glendalough, Co. Wicklow, *Gleann dá Locha*, 'Valley of two lakes'; it also appears in a less obvious form in the name Duneane, in Co. Antrim, *Dún dá Éan*, 'Fort of two birds'.

DAINGEAN: Means 'fortress' or 'stronghold'. While not particularly common in Irish place-names there are a few notable examples, such as Daingean, Co. Offaly, *Daingean* (which takes its name from the medieval island fortress of O'Conor Faly). A less obvious example is Dingle, Co. Kerry, which in Irish is simply also *Daingean*. It sometimes appears as a descriptive element, as in Ballindine, Co. Mayo, *Baile an Daingin*, 'Homestead of the fortress'.

DAIR/DARACH: As a noun means 'oak' and as an adjective 'oaken' or 'abounding in oaks'. The first is best-known in Kildare, Co. Kildare, *Cill Dara*, 'Church of the oak-tree', and Adare, Co. Limerick, *Áth Dara*, 'Ford of the oak'. The second appears, without qualification, in Darragh, Co. Clare, meaning 'Place abounding in oaks'. Aghadarragh, Co. Tyrone, *Achadh Darach*, 'Field of the oak', and Clondarragh, Co. Wexford, *Cluain Darach*, 'Pasture of the oak', are two versions of virtually the same thing.

DAIRBHRE: Is a derivative of the above meaning 'Place abounding in oaks'. It is the ancient name of Valentia Island, Co. Kerry, and is also the retained name among Irish-speakers in Co. Kerry. It appears as Darrery in Cos Cork, Galway and Limerick and as Darraragh in

Co. Mayo. It also appears as the Irish name of Lough Derravaragh, Co. Westmeath, *Loch Dairbhreach*, 'Lake of the abundance of oaks'.

DEARG: In an adjective meaning 'red', usually Anglicised as 'derg', and most frequently found in river-names, as in the River Derg, Co. Tyrone, *Dearg*, 'Red + river'. Belderg, Co. Mayo has been expressed as *Béal Deirg* (Mouth of the (river) Derg); there is, however, a strongly held belief that 'derg' does not always mean 'red' in place-name contexts, especially with reference to rivers, but may simply be the name of the river in question, with no known translation. As a terminal element the Anglicised form 'derg' has been found suspect as representing *dearg* in the case of Lenaderg, Co. Armagh, for which a suggested Irish original is *Láithreach Dair-Thighe*, 'Site of the oratory'.

Derg: See DEARG

Derry: See DOIRE

Desert: See DÍSEART

DINNSEANCHAS: Means the 'lore of notable places'. A large body of such material exists in Irish literature, in both prose and verse; in the form in which it is preserved it goes back to the Middle Irish period, while the tradition of such place-name lore goes back further still. Notable topographical features, rather than centres of human activity, are the most common subjects. In general the purpose of the tale is to explain the origin of the name of the feature, occasionally to explain the meaning of the name. There could be several different tales about a feature, each giving a different version of how it acquired its name. (It is also the title of a journal published by *An Cumann Logainmneacha*.)

DÍSEART: Is derived from the Latin *desertum*, meaning 'deserted place', and is generally rendered as 'hermitage', and Anglicised in place-names as 'desert, disert, dysart'. Its strongest distribution is in Leinster and Munster, but it is reasonably common in Ulster, particularly in east Derry. Consideration of the Leinster and Munster examples suggests a connection between the spread of the element *díseart* and that of the ascetic *Céli Dé* movement of the eighth and ninth centuries. Some *díseart*-sites, however, have allegedly earlier associations, such as Desertegny, *Díseart Éignigh*, Co. Donegal, or Desertoghill, *Díseart Uí Thuathail*, Co. Derry, which are associated with Colm Cille and therefore have a claim to date to the sixth century.

MAP   **DÍSEART** as a sole or first element in the names of townlands; it is fairly evenly distributed throughout the country.

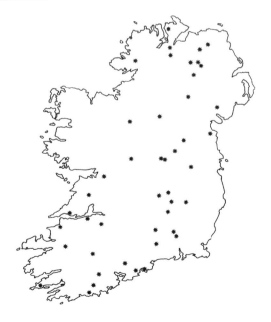

Frequently *díseart*-names appear without qualification, as in Dysart, Co. Westmeath; Desert, Co. Monaghan; Disert, Co. Donegal. If it is qualified, it is usually by a personal name as in the two instances cited above, though the surname *Uí Thuathail* is a later addition. A rarer example is Desertcreat, Co. Derry, *Díseart dá Chríoch*, 'Hermitage of two territories'.

Disert: See DÍSEART

DOIRE: Means simply an 'oak-grove' and is a common element in Irish place-names, though of course in the vast majority of examples the oak-grove itself has long since disappeared. It is usually Anglicised as 'derry': sometimes as the first element, as in Derrygolan, Co. Westmeath, *Doire an Ghabhláin*, 'Oak-grove of the fork'; sometimes as the second, qualifying, element, as in Dunderry, Co. Meath, *Dún Doire*, 'Fort of the oak-grove'. The best-known example, of course, is Derry, Co. Derry, originally known as *Doire Calgaich*, 'Calgach's oak-grove', and subsequently, since the establishment of a church there in 546 by Colm Cille, as *Doire Cholm Cille*, 'Colm Cille's oak-grove'.

DOMHNACH: Is derived from the Latin *dominicum*, which means 'church', and in the sense of 'church-building' is found in continental Latin manuscripts from the third to the fifth century. With this specialised meaning it has survived only in its Irish form in Irish place-names; it is usually Anglicised as 'Donagh' and in this sense almost invariably appears as the initial element in a place-name. It seems to be the earliest term used in Irish place-names to denote a 'church'. Such names are usually associated with the Patrician mission of the fifth century, as is attested by the number of *domhnach*-sites attributed to or associated with St Patrick in the Patrician biographical material, and particularly by a reference in the eighth-century *Liber Angeli* ('Book of the Angel'), contained in the *Book of Armagh*, which claims that 'any place anywhere that is called *domhnach* is . . . in special union with bishop Patrick and the heir of his see of Armagh'. The total validity, however, of this apparent exclusively Patrician association with *domhnach*-sites is open to question. The impression gained from the place-name evidence in its entirety is that some *domhnach*-names, particularly in the east and south of the country, may well have been independent of the Patrician mission, albeit probably contemporary with it; there is no positive evidence of *domhnach*-names earlier than the fifth century, while the evidence from the relevant documentation indicates that *domhnach*, as a term for 'church', had fallen out of natural use by the end of the seventh century. It is quite possible that *domhnach*-names were no longer being coined by the late sixth century; such names are not a feature of the Columban mission of the latter half of that century and there is no evidence that the term was exported from Ireland to Scotland, as other Irish terms for 'church' were. It is apparent, therefore, that *Donagh*-names recorded by the Ordnance Survey, with the exception of a few that are seen from earlier documentation to be misrepresentations of other elements, can be dated to the first few centuries of the Christian period in Ireland.

It has been argued that since the Irish Church in its earliest phase was episcopal and diocesan in its structure, *Domhnach* was the term used of the equivalent of a parish church, founded to serve a settled community. This interpretation is supported strongly by the frequency with which the element *domhnach* is qualified by the name of the district in which it was situated, as in *Domhnach Mór Mhá Iomchláir*, now Donaghmore Parish, Co. Tyrone, or *Domhnach Mór Mhá Cobha*, now Donaghmore Parish, Co. Down. It is possible that the change in the Christian Church in Ireland from an episcopal structure to a monastic structure was responsible for the decline of *domhnach* as a formative element in place-names.

The most common predicate of *domhnach* is *mór*, probably in the sense of 'great' rather than 'large', as in the two parish-names cited above. Other predicates do occur, usually personal names: e.g. *Domhnach Caoide*, 'Caoide's church', now Donaghedy, Co. Tyrone, or terms referring to the nature of the church's location, *Domhnach Riascadh*, 'Church of the marsh', now Donaghrisk, Co. Tyrone. In Leinster the usual Anglicisation of 'donagh' is sometimes replaced by 'donny-', as in Donnybrook, Co. Dublin, *Domhnach Broc*, 'Broc's church'. In a couple of superficially misleading examples, it is actually reduced to 'dun-', as in the case of Dunshaughlin, Co. Meath, where the Irish form is *Domhnach Seachnaill*, 'Seachnall's church', after a bishop who came to Ireland to assist St Patrick and established a church here, and Dunnamore, Co. Tyrone, which is an aberrant form of *Domhnach Mór*.

There are more than fifty place-names recorded by the Ordnance Survey that have *domhnach* as their initial element. The impressive spread is across the North from Cos Donegal and Leitrim to Down and Louth, with a marked cluster in Tyrone. There is a further significant cluster towards the middle of the

MAP **DOMHNACH** as a first element in the names of townlands; its strongest representation is in Ulster and along the eastern coastal strip, with a few examples in the south and west.

east coast, in the hinterland of Dublin, and a small pocket in the Kilkenny/Laois area. The northern spread corroborates the picture gained from the Patrician sources (particularly the late-ninth-century Irish biography, *Bethu Phátraic*) of a strong concentration of *domhnach*-names in the North: 'seven *domhnachs* to Patrick about the Faughan', 'seven *domhnachs* to Patrick among the Cianacht [mid-Derry]', 'seven *domhnachs* to Patrick among Uí Tuirtri [south-east Derry/north Tyrone]'. Some of the early *domhnach*-sites survived as monastic units in the post-Patrician period and as churches in the medieval period; many, however, disappear from the documentary records at a relatively early stage, suggesting, perhaps, that the church in question had fallen into disuse. Some *domhnach*-names, without earlier documentation, appear as church-names in post-twelfth-century records; in such instances the element *domhnach* is the sole indication of the antiquity of the site.

A commonly occurring place-name containing the element *domhnach* is Toberdoney, where it appears as the second, or qualifying, element. In these instances it seems that the term has no reference to a church building, but is employed in the common, later, sense of 'Sunday', *Tobar (an) Domhnaigh*, meaning (as it is often translated) 'Sunday's well', a well that is visited on Sundays, i.e. *'ar an Domhnach'*.

Don:	See DÚN
Donagh:	See DOMHNACH
Donny:	See DOMHNACH
Doon:	See DÚN
Dooneen:	See DÚN
Down:	See DÚN
DRAIGHEAN/ DRAIGHNEACH:	Is a noun meaning 'blackthorn' and an adjective meaning 'with abundant blackthorns'. It appears as Drinagh, in Cos Cork and Wexford, and as a qualifying element in Killadreenan, Co. Wicklow, *Cill Achaidh Draighnigh*, 'Church of the field of the blackthorns'.
DROICHEAD:	Means simply 'bridge'. The best-known example is Drogheda, Co. Louth, *Droichead Átha*, 'Bridge of the ford'. It also occurs, unqualified, in the names Drehid, Co. Kildare and Droghed, Co. Derry. Less obviously it occurs as Ballindrait, Co. Donegal (*Béal an Droichid*, 'The Mouth of the bridge').

DROIM· Means a 'ridge', Anglicised usually as 'drum' or 'drom', and as such is the origin of the term 'drumlin'. It is of frequent occurrence throughout Ireland (it is also found in Scotland) as a place-name element. It can appear either as the initial element, as in Drumraney, Co. Westmeath, *Droim Raithne*, 'Ridge of ferns', or Drumkeeran, Co. Leitrim, *Droim Caorthainn*, 'Ridge of the rowans', or as a second, qualifying, element, as in Dundrum, Co. Down, *Dún Droma*, 'Fort of the ridge'. Interestingly, where a *dún*-named site is located on a ridge called *droim*, often two names exist side by side in early documentation: one, *droim*, referring to the location, the other, *dún*, to the structure.

Drom: See DROIM

Drum: See DROIM

DUBH: Is an adjective meaning 'black', usually Anglicised as 'duff', as in Gulladuff, Co. Derry, *Guala Dhubh*, 'Black shoulder', or 'dub', as in Dublin, Co. Dublin, *Dubhlinn*, 'Black pool', the name preferred by the Vikings and, subsequently, the Anglo-Normans.

DÚN: Means 'fort' or 'fortress' and, in place-names, is used throughout Ireland. It is a prestige term in Irish writing and the one usually employed for the dwellings of kings and chieftains, as is reflected in heroic literature: when, for example, Cú Chulainn was being instructed in strategic topography on the day he took up arms, it was the name of every *Prímdún* ('Chief fort') that lay between Tara and Kells that his charioteer taught him. In the Irish Annals too *Dún* is the important dwelling-unit, the correlative of *cell*, the standard monastic unit. For instance, in 971 the *Annals of Ulster* record *co ro ort a n-ule cella agus dune* ('he spoiled all their churches and forts'); again, in 993, the *Annals of Inisfallen* record *fássugud cell Mide agus a dúne* ('the churches of Meath, and its forts, were devastated').

The types of fort or fortress to which the term *dún* is applied include several of the varieties of defended site recognised by archaeologists. Promontory forts, where a portion of an elevated promontory (not necessarily a coastal one) is heavily defended by means of ditches and raised earthworks, most usually are described by the term *dún*, as in Dún Bhinne, 'Fort of the cliff', and Dún Mór, 'Big fort', near Dunquin, Co. Kerry, or Dún Bhalair, 'Balar's fort' on Tory Island, Co. Donegal. The best-known is, perhaps, Dunseverick, Co. Antrim, Dún Sobhairce, 'Sobhairce's fort', which is attested as a royal stronghold in the early historic period and assigned an honourable antiquity by native historians (its destruction by Medb is mentioned in *Táin Bó Cúailnge*). Despite this, its storming by the Vikings in 870 is described as 'a thing that had never been effected before'. It is named as one of the three *dúine* of Ireland in the *Irish Triads*, along with Dún Cermna, on the Old Head of Kinsale, and – slightly confusingly – Caherconree, Co. Kerry, *Cathair Con Raoi*, 'Stone fort of Cúrí', an inland promontory fort.

Whether the term is applied to hill-forts, in the archaeological sense of the defended summit of a hill, is less easy to establish, since no excavated example of an accepted *dún*-named hill-fort exists. Dún Ailinne (also known as *Ráth Ailinne*) in Co. Kildare, although protected by a rampart and deep ditch, was shown by excavation to be a centre of assembly and ceremony, rather than a defended habitation-site. Among other *dún*-named sites accepted, pending excavation, as hill-forts is Dundrum, Co. Laois, Dún Droma, 'Fort of the ridge'.

Dún also occurs among the terms used for the most common type of fort or defended habitation-site in Ireland: the ring-fort. These are circular enclosures, normally some thirty metres in internal diameter, surrounded by one, two or even three banks of earth or stone, with or without ditches as appropriate. (There are, or were, 1,300 *recorded* examples in Co. Down alone!) Among examples of such forts to which the term *dún* is applied are Dunbeg, on Inishmaan, Co. Galway, Dún Beag, 'Small fort', and Dunfore, Co. Sligo, Dún Fuar, 'Cold fort'.

Another type of fort or fortress to which the term is applied is that consisting of a relatively high mound of truncated conical form; some of these are likely to be castle-mounds, or mottes, of the Anglo-Normans. Since, however, it has recently been demonstrated by excavations at Gransha, Co. Down that not all motte-like mounds are necessarily in fact mottes, and this form of structure was present in Ireland before the arrival of the Anglo-Normans, one problem attaching to the use of the term *dún* of such structures is solved. Many of these sites are qualified by personal names, often by patently Gaelic personal names. Examples of these include Dunmurry, Co. Antrim, Dún Muirí, 'Muireadhach's fort', and Dundonald, Co. Down, Dún Dónaill, 'Donall's fort'.

Examples such as Dungall, Co. Antrim, presumably representing the Irish Dún Gall, could possibly be interpreted as referring to 'the strangers', meaning the Anglo-Normans, while Donegal, Co. Donegal, Dún na nGall, 'Fort of the strangers', first documented in 1474, must with a fair degree of certainty be read as referring to the English rather than to Vikings.

A rather exceptional site to which the term is applied is Duneight, Co. Antrim; this, an oval enclosure, defended on three sides by a bank and a ditch five metres deep and wide in proportion, has been identified with a fort and town, Dún Echdach, 'Eochaid's fort', described by the Four Masters as having been destroyed in 1010. Outside the defences were found traces of occupation, much destroyed by ploughing, with a series of rather flimsy structures, of the same tenth- to eleventh-century date, suggesting that this was the site of the town. In the later twelfth century the oval enclosure was adapted as the bailey of a motte-and-bailey castle, complete with a triangular motte. Many ecclesiastical sites contain the term dún in their names, but presumably by association or inheritance, even in the case of Dunnamanagh, Co. Tyrone, Dún na Manach, 'Fort of the monks'.

In addition to the form 'dun', other Anglicised forms are 'Doon', as in Doonbeg, Co. Clare, Dún Beag, 'Small fort'; 'Down', as in Downpatrick, Co. Mayo, Dún Pádraig, 'Patrick's fort'; or the diminutive forms 'Dooneen', Dúinín, or even 'Downings', as in Downings, Co. Donegal (Na Dúnaibh in modern Irish, the dative case of Na Dúine; it is probably derived from Na Dúnáin, 'Forts', with an 's' added to pluralise it).

Dun: See DÚN, but also DOMHNACH

Dysart: See DÍSEART

DÚN as a sole or first element in the names of townlands; it enjoys a countrywide distribution.

E

E

ÉADAN: Means 'brow' or 'end-facing-out' and is reasonably common in place-names, especially in the northern part of the country. It is usually Anglicised straightforwardly as 'eden', and in this form, without further qualification, appears as Eden, Co. Antrim. A particularly common combination is Edenderry, *Éadan Doire*, 'Brow of the oakwood', which occurs in Cos Offaly and Antrim. Slightly more exotic combinations are found in Edendork, Co. Tyrone, *Éadan na dTorc*, 'Brow of the boars', and in Edentrillick, Co. Down, *Éadan Trilic*, 'Brow of the three stones', obviously referring to a megalith.

EAGLAIS: Is derived from the Latin *ecclesia* and, like it, means 'church'; it is usually Anglicised 'Eglish' or even 'Aglish' in place-names. Like *teampall* it is a term applied to parish churches of the post-Reform period, though less frequently. The distinction, if any, between the specific references of the two terms has not been established; it does not, however, appear to be dialectal. As preserved by the Ordnance Survey, *eaglais*-names are generally unqualified, suggesting that each was the only instance of an *eaglais*-named church in its own area. It is possible, if not probable, that many were qualified, not necessarily as place-names, by the name of the area they served. It appears both as a parish-name and a townland-name. Of the many examples extant it is sufficient to cite Eglish, Co. Tyrone and Aglish, Co. Waterford; there is a reasonable suggestion that 'aglish' is the form of Anglicisation preferred in the South, 'eglish' in the North.

MAP   **EAGLAIS** as a first element, usually unqualified, in the names of townlands; though not very common its distribution is fairly widespread except along the eastern coast.

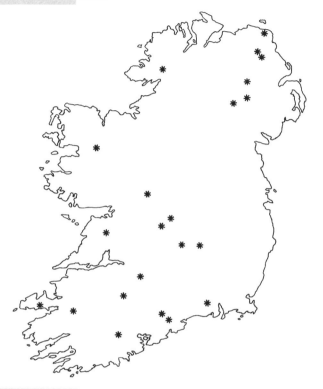

EANACH: Means 'watery place, fen, marsh or swamp'; since such areas are common in Ireland, the word, usually Anglicised as 'annagh, anna or anny', is common in Irish place-names throughout the country. Some examples are Annaduff, Co. Leitrim, *Eanach Dubh*, 'Black marsh'; Annabella, Co. Cork, *Eanach Bile*, 'Marsh of the sacred tree'; Annahilt, Co. Down, *Eanach Eilte*, 'Marsh of the doe'. It sometimes occurs, in the genitive, *eanaigh*, as a qualifying element, as in Raheny, Co. Dublin, *Ráth Eanaigh*, 'Fort of the marsh'.

EARAGAIL/ AIREAGAL:	Is usually construed in place-name contexts as meaning 'oratory', derived from the Latin *oraculum*, and indeed the number of times it appears as the name of a parish would seem to bear this out. It occurs as the name of a parish in Co. Tyrone, Errigal Keerogue, *Earagail Do Chiaróg*, 'Oratory of Do Chiaróg', a saint also known as Ciarán. Errigal Mountain in Co. Donegal probably took its name from an oratory that existed there at some time.
EAS(ACH):	Means 'waterfall' or 'cascade' and is quite common in place-names, especially minor names. Usually Anglicised as 'ass(a)' or 'ess', it seldom, if ever, appears totally without qualification. Assaroe, Co. Donegal, *Easa Rua*, is one straightforward example, meaning simply 'Red waterfall'; Ballysadare, Co. Sligo is *Baile Easa Dara*, 'Homestead of the waterfall of the oak'. Personal names are used as qualifying elements, as in Askeaton, Co. Limerick, *Eas Géitine*, 'Géitine's waterfall'.
EASC:	Is yet another word for a 'bog', though it seems sometimes rather to refer to a 'channel' in a bog. It is usually Anglicised as 'aska', as in Askamore, Co. Wexford, *Easca Mór*, 'Big bog', or Askanagap, Co. Wicklow, *Easca na gCeap*, 'Bog of the stumps', referring to the frequently observed phenomenon where a forest has been covered by the encroaching bog and, as the bog is cut over, the stumps of the trees appear.
Eglish:	See EAGLAIS
EIDHNEÁN/ EIDHNEACH:	Is a noun meaning 'ivy' and an adjective meaning 'ivy-covered'. The noun appears without qualification as Inan, Co. Meath and as Inane, Cos Cork and Tipperary. Clonenagh, Co. Laois is *Cluain Eidhneach*, 'Ivied pasture'.

EISCIR: Is a word meaning 'ridge', referring particularly to the long ridges of gravel deposited by glaciers; the word has been absorbed into standard geological terminology to describe such features. It is usually Anglicised as 'esker' and is common in place-names where such features occur. It appears in this simple unqualified form in Esker, Cos Dublin and Longford, and in Co. Tyrone – where many such features exist – a collective form, *Eiscreach*, meaning 'Abounding in ridges', appears as Eskra. In Co. Galway is Ahascragh, *Áth Eascrach*, 'Ford of the ridge'. There is even a place in Co. Tyrone known as Eskerridge, 'Ridge ridge'.

English Names Inevitably, after 800 years of settlement from England, and over 400 of organised plantation, many of the place-names of Ireland are of English origin. One of the largest groups consists of an English personal or family name with the suffix 'town'. These are common throughout the country: Edgeworthstown, Co. Longford takes its name from the Edgeworth family, of whom Richard, father of the celebrated Maria, built Edgeworthstown House in the later eighteenth century; Cookstown, Co. Tyrone is named from Alan Cook, the planter who laid it out in 1609; Thomastown, Co. Kilkenny takes the sequence back farther, taking its name from Thomas fitz Anthony, Anglo-Norman Seneschal of Leinster, the motte of whose castle still survives. Names which begin with the term 'Newtown' are Plantation, or post-Plantation, foundations: Newtownards, Co. Down, established between 1605 and 1616 by Hugh Montgomery, James Hamilton and Moyses Hill; Newtown Stewart, Co. Tyrone, after William Stewart, who acquired the site by marriage to a daughter of Robert Newcomen in about 1628; Newtown Forbes,

Co. Longford takes its name from Arthur Forbes, who acquired the land and began the building of the castle in 1619. 'Borough' is another element indicating an English creation, as in Maryborough, Co. Laois, the one-time name of Portlaoise. There are, in addition, some mildly eccentric English place-names, some deriving from the names of inns or hostelries, such as Fox and Geese, Cos Clare and Dublin, and Robinhood, Cos Dublin and Roscommon.

EO/EOCHAILL: The first means 'yew-tree', the second 'yew-wood'. The first appears in the name of the county of Mayo, Maigh Eo, 'Plain of the yew-tree', and in Killoe, Co. Longford, Cill Eo, 'Church of the yew-tree', while the second is to be seen unqualified in Youghal, Co. Cork and in Oghil on Inishmore in the Aran Islands, Co. Galway, as well as in Ahoghill, Co. Antrim, Áth Eochaille, 'Ford of the yew-wood'.

Exotic Names Scattered throughout the country are a few French, Italian and Spanish names, some deriving from the 'Grand Tour', some to commemorate Colonial experiences. French examples include Belle Vue, Belvoir and Ormeau, on the outskirts of Belfast, Belmont, Co. Galway and Beaulieu, Co. Louth, though this last acquired its name long before the 'Grand Tour' was introduced. Italian examples include Rialto and Marino, both in Co. Dublin, and Belvedere, Co. Westmeath. A rare Spanish example is Portobello, Co. Dublin, from Portobello in Panama, commemorating its destruction in 1739.

FADA: Means 'long', in both time and space, but in place-names, naturally, refers to space rather than time. It is applied to a wide range of features, both natural and artificial. Derrada, Co. Leitrim and Derryadd, Co. Armagh both represent *Doire Fhada*, 'Long oak-grove'; Dromada, Cos Limerick and Mayo, Drumfad, Cos Donegal, Down, Sligo and Tyrone, and Drumfadda, Cos Cork and Kerry, all represent *Droim Fhada*, 'Long ridge'.

FAICHE/ Means a 'lawn' or 'green', and was used of an
FAITHCHE: exercise green in front of a fort. In place-names it is normally translated simply as 'green' and Anglicised variously as Faha, with examples in Cos Kerry and Waterford, and as Fahy in Co. Offaly. Apart from these unqualified or unqualifying examples it appears in the simple guise of Fahamore, Co. Kerry, *Faiche Mór*, 'Large green'. It occurs as Fyfin in Co. Tyrone and Foyfin in Co. Donegal, both representing *Faiche Fionn*, 'Fair green'; excelling even this in appearance must have been Fahykeen, Co. Donegal, *Faiche Caoin*, 'Beautiful green'. It is found as a second element in Ballynafeigh, Co. Down, Ballynafey and Ballynafie in Co. Antrim, as well as Ballynafa, Co. Kildare, all representing *Baile na Faiche*, 'Homestead of the green'.

FAILL: Means, like AILL, 'cliff', but is the form most usually adopted in the south of the country (the coast of Co. Kerry is dotted with minor names such as *Faill Dhubh*, 'Black cliff', and *Faill Fhada*, 'Long cliff').
   It is often Anglicised as 'foil', as in Foilnaman, Co. Tipperary, *Faill na mBan*, 'Cliff of the women'.

FEARANN: Means 'land', especially 'ploughland', as a unit of land. It has been suggested that the *proper* Irish term for a 'townland' is *baile fearainn*, rather than simply *baile*. This is not accepted by the majority of scholars and is not attested by usage, the natural term for 'town' – even in the sense of 'townland' – being *baile* by itself. The term occurs in place-names all over the country, with a notably greater density in the south-west, especially in Cos Cork, Kerry and Tipperary. It appears totally without qualification in these counties, as Farran. It is seen with simple qualification in Farranfore, Co. Kerry, *Fearann Fuar*, 'Cold land'; Farranfadda, Co. Cork, *Fearann Fada*, 'Long land'; and in Co. Dublin, for example, as Farranboley, *Fearann Buaile*, 'Milking-place land'.

MAP   **FEARANN** as a sole or first element in the names of townlands; although it occurs throughout the country its densest concentration is in the south.

FEARN/FEARNÓG: Both mean 'alder', the second being a diminutive form of the first. Ferns, seductively posing as an English-looking word, in Co. Wexford, represents the plural of the first, *Fearna*, 'Alder-trees' or 'Place of alders', while Fern Lough in Co. Donegal is *Loch Fearna*, 'Lake of the alder'. Glenfarne, Co. Leitrim is simply *Gleann Fearna*, 'Valley of alders'. It appears in Ballyfarnan, Co. Roscommon, *Béal Átha Fearnáin*, 'Mouth of the ford of the alders'.

FERT/FEART: Means 'trench' or 'grave', and in the latter sense appears to relate particularly to a pagan grave. It occurs as a qualifying element in a number of names such as Clonfert, Co. Galway, *Cluain Fearta*, 'Pasture of the grave', and Ardfert, Co. Kerry, *Ard Fhearta*, 'Height of the grave', both important ecclesiastical sites associated with St Brendan, suggesting that there may have been a conscious effort to absorb, and thereby diminish, the pagan tradition. The plural, *Fearta*, appears as Farta, Co. Galway and Ferta, Co. Kerry, meaning 'Graves', while a derivative, *Feartach*, meaning 'Place of graves', gives its name to Fertagh, Cos Leitrim and Meath, as well as to Fartagh in Cos Cavan and Fermanagh.

FIODH: Is one of the words meaning 'wood' and is usually Anglicised as 'fee' or 'fi'. Often it carries a simple qualification, as in Feebane, Co. Monaghan, *Fiodh Bán*, 'White wood', Fethard, Cos Tipperary and Wexford, *Fiodh Ard*, 'High wood'. Sometimes its position or a notable feature is described, as in Finea, Co. Westmeath or Finnea, Cos Cavan and Westmeath, *Fiodh an Átha*, 'Wood of the ford', or Fiddown, Co. Kilkenny, *Fidh Dúin*, 'Wood of the fort'. The Figile River, in Co. Offaly, surprisingly contains it as an element, *Abhainn Fhiodh Gaibhle*, 'River of the wood of the fork'.

Sometimes the plural, *Feá*, 'Woods', appears, with an English plural 's' added, as in the districts known as The Fews in Cos Armagh and Waterford. A derivative, *Fiodhnach*, meaning 'Wooded place', appears, as in Feenagh, Co. Limerick and Fenagh, Co. Leitrim.

FIONN: Simply means 'white' and appears as a first element in a number of compounds used as place-names. Examples include Fennagh, Co. Carlow, *Fionnmhach*, 'White plain'; Finaghy, Co. Antrim, *Fionnachadh*, 'White field'; Finglas, Co. Dublin, *Fionnghlas*, 'White stream'; and Finvoy, Co. Antrim, *Fionnbhoth*, 'White hut'. It can also follow the noun it qualifies, as in Ballyfin, Co. Laois, *Baile Fionn*, 'White homestead'.

FUARÁN: See UARÁN

GABHLÁN/ GABHAL: Are both nouns meaning 'fork'; in place-names the reference is almost invariably to a river. Anglicised forms are varied. Gowlaun, Co. Galway, Gyleen and Guileen, Co. Cork, Gowlane, Co. Kerry and even Golden, Co. Tipperary are different versions of the two words and the diminutive, *Gabhailín*, 'Little fork', while Gola, Co. Donegal is the plural of *Gabhal*, meaning 'Forks'. It appears in compound names such as Derrygoolan, Co. Westmeath, *Doire an Ghabhláin*, 'Oakwood of the fork', and Galmoy, Co. Tipperary, *Gabhal Mhaí*, 'Fork of the plain'.

GALLÁN: Means a 'standing stone', whether it be a prehistoric one marking a grave or one erected as a mearing stone to mark a boundary. The term has given its name, without further qualification, to Gallan, Co. Tyrone and to Gallane, Co. Cork. It appears often as a secondary element identifying other features, as in Aghagallon, Cos Antrim and Tyrone, *Achadh an Ghalláin*, 'Field of the standing stone', or Maulagallane, Co. Kerry, *Meall an Ghalláin*, 'Knoll of the standing stone'.

GAORTHA: Is a term meaning 'wooded valley' which is virtually confined to Cos Cork and Kerry. It appears without qualification in Co. Kerry, as Gearha, and, again in Co. Kerry, as Gearhameen, *Gaortha Mín*, 'Smooth wooded valley', and with the type of wood specified in Gearhasallagh, *Gaortha Saileach*, 'Wooded valley of willows'.

GAOTH: Means 'wind' and features fairly often in place-names in reference to their exposure. Cahernageeha, Co. Kerry, *Cathair na Gaoithe*,

'Stone fort of the wind', must have been very exposed. Mountain-passes obviously frequently deserve this description, as in Barnageeha, Co. Limerick, *Bearna na Gaoithe*, 'Pass of the wind', often expressed in English as 'Windy gap'. It appears, almost as a warning, in Tanderagee, Co. Armagh, which is *Tóin re Gaoith*, 'Backside to the wind', as if to suggest that is the right stance in the area.

GAOTH: Is confusingly similar in the nominative singular to the previous word, but meaning 'inlet', particularly of the sea. It is most common in Ulster place-names such as Gweedore, Co. Donegal, *Gaoth Dobhair*, 'Inlet of the water'; it also occurs in Co. Mayo, in Gweesalia, *Gaoth Sáile*, 'Inlet of the sea'.

GARBH: Is an adjective meaning 'rough' which can appear in compounds before the noun it qualifies. It is quite common in Irish place-names, appearing in Garvagh, Co. Derry, Garvaghey, Co. Tyrone and Garvaghy, Co. Down, all of which represent *Garbhachadh*, 'Rough field'. It also appears, in slightly different form, in Garryhill, Co. Carlow, *Garbhchoill*, 'Rough wood', and in Glengarriff, Co. Cork, *Gleann Garbh*, 'Rough valley'.

GARRÁN: Means a 'clump' or 'grove' and is Anglicised both as Garrane, in Co. Tipperary, and Garraun, in Cos Clare and Galway. There are 'Broad groves', as in Garranlahan, Co. Roscommon, *Garrán Leathan*, and 'High groves' as in Garranard, Co. Mayo, *Garrán Ard*. There is a Garranamanagh, *Garrán na Manach*, 'Grove of the monks', in Co. Kilkenny and, perhaps to remind us of pre-Christian rituals, a Garnavilla, *Garrán an Bhile*, 'Grove of the sacred tree', in Co. Tipperary. Inevitably there is a Ballingarrane and a Ballingrane, in Co.

Limerick, both representing *Baile an Gharráin*, 'Homestead of the grove'.

GARRDHA: Means 'garden' and is usually Anglicised as 'garry'. The most famous name containing it is probably Garryowen, Co. Limerick, *Garraí Eoghain*, 'Eoghan's garden'. It appears, however, without qualification as Garry, Co. Antrim, *Garraí*, 'Garden', and with a simple qualification as Garryduff, Co. Cork, *Garraí Dubh*, 'Black garden'. Not surprisingly it is often qualified by a personal name, as Garryspillane, Co. Limerick, *Garraí Uí Spealáin*, 'Ó Spealáin's garden', or, less obviously, in Ballygomartin, Co. Antrim, *Baile Gharraí Mháirtín*, 'Homestead of Martin's garden'. A suitably homely version is Ballingarry, in Cos Limerick and Tipperary, *Baile an Gharraí*, 'Homestead of the garden'.

GLAS/GLAISE: Means 'small stream', 'rivulet'. It appears quite often in place-names: with very simple qualifiers, such as in Glashaboy, Co. Cork, *Glaise Buí*, 'Yellow stream'; with intriguing ascriptions, as in Glasnevin, Co. Dublin, *Glas Naíon*, 'Stream of the child'; with personal names, such as Glasthule, Co. Dublin, *Glas Tuathail*, 'Tuathal's stream'. A diminutive, *Glasán*, meaning 'Little stream', appears as Glassan, in Co. Westmeath.

GLAS: Is confusingly close to the preceding word but is an adjective meaning 'green', 'grey' or even 'blue-grey'. In place-name contexts it is usually translated as 'grey-green'. It can be placed either before the element it qualifies in compounds, or after it. Thus we have such formations as Glasdrumman, Co. Down, *Glasdromainn*, 'Grey-green little ridge', and Glaslough, Co. Monaghan, *Glasloch*, 'Grey-green lake'. Appearing after the term it describes, it occurs in simple combinations such as Ardglass, Co. Down, *Aird Ghlais*, 'Grey-green point', and Ardglass, Co. Cork, *Ard Glas*, 'Grey-green height'; similarly we have Kilglass, in Cos Roscommon and Sligo, representing *Cill Ghlas*, 'Grey-green church', and Kilglass, in Cos Galway and Sligo, representing *Coill Ghlas*, 'Grey-green wood'. There is also of course Ballyglass, Co. Mayo, *Baile Glas*, 'Grey-green homestead'.

GLEANN: Means 'valley', or 'glen', and is extremely common in Irish place-names. The most usual Anglicisations are 'glen' and 'glan' but 'glin' and 'glynn' also occur. The first and last two forms occur without qualification, in Glen, Cos Cavan, Kilkenny and Waterford; Glin, Co. Limerick; and Glynn, in Cos Antrim, Carlow and Wexford. Some qualifications are very simple: Glanmore, Co. Kerry and Glenmore, Co. Kilkenny are both simply *Gleann Mór*, 'Big valley', while Glenbeg, *Gleann Beag*, the opposite, appears in Co. Cork. Colours are represented in Glenduff, Co. Cork, *Gleann Dubh*, 'Black valley', and Glenboy, Co. Sligo, *Gleann Buí*, 'Yellow valley'; Glendowan, Co. Donegal, is *Gleann Domhain*, 'Deep valley', and Glenard, Co. Antrim, is *Gleann Ard*, 'High valley'. Glanmire, Co. Cork, is *Gleann Maghair*, 'Valley of the plain', and Glendalough, Co. Wicklow, is *Gleann dá Locha*, 'Valley of two lakes'. Glenbeigh, Co. Cork is *Gleann Beithe*, 'Valley of the birch', while Glenfarne, Cos Sligo and Leitrim, is *Gleann Fearna*, 'Valley of the alders', and Glenoe, Co. Antrim is 'Valley of the yews', *Gleann Eo*. Glenamaddy, Co. Roscommon, is 'Valley of the dogs', *Gleann na Madadh*. Indicating human interference with the natural scene, Glencairn, Co. Waterford is *Gleann an Chairn*, 'Valley of the cairn', and

Glentogher, Co. Donegal, *Gleann Tóchair*, 'Valley of the causeway'.

Inevitably some of the valleys have been allocated names of humans: Glencolumbkille, Co. Donegal is *Gleann Cholm Cille*, 'Valley of Colm Cille', whose three-mile-long *turas*, or pilgrimage, is celebrated there every year on 9 June, while Glenmalure, Co. Wicklow is *Gleann Maolúra*, 'Maolúra's valley'. Some have quite romantic or supernatural associations: Glennascaul, Co. Galway is *Gleann an Scáil*, 'Valley of the phantom', while Glanaruddery, Co. Kerry is *Gleann an Ridire*, 'Valley of the knight'. A diminutive form, *Gleanntán*, is exposed in Glantane, Co. Cork and Glentane, Co. Galway, while the plural appears as Glenties, Co. Donegal, *Gleannta*, 'Valleys'. As usual, however, care is needed: Glenavy, Co. Antrim has no valley, but is *Lann Abhaigh*, 'Church of the dwarf', and neither has Glenone, Co. Derry, which is *Cluain Eoghain*, 'Eoghan's pasture'.

Glen: See GLEANN, CLUAIN and LANN

GOB: Means 'mouth', 'bill' or 'beak' and occurs occasionally in place-names. It appears, for example, in Gubaveeny, Co. Louth, *Gob an Mhianaigh*, 'Mouth of the mine', and in Gubbacrock, Co. Fermanagh, *Gob dhá Chnoc*, 'Beak of two hills', the Anglicisation reflecting the northern pronunciation of *cnoc*.

GÓILÍN: Means an 'inlet' but appears to occur most frequently in minor names. It does occur, however, as Goleen, Co. Cork.

GORT: Is another word for 'field' but in the sense of an arable, or tilled, field, and especially a field producing cereals. It occurs totally without qualification in Gort, Co. Galway; a diminutive, *Goirtín*, 'Little tilled field', is

Anglicised in several forms: Gorteen, Co. Galway; Gortin, Co. Tyrone; Gurteen, Cos Galway and Sligo; while the plural, *Goirtíní*, 'Little tilled fields', appears as Gorteeny, in Co. Galway. Many of the qualifications give an indication of the location of the field in question: Gortatlea, Co. Kerry, *Gort an tSléibhe*, is 'Tilled field of the mountain'; Gortaclare, Co. Tyrone, *Gort an Chláir*, on the other hand, is 'Tilled field of the plain', as is Gortavoy, Co. Tyrone, *Gort an Mhaí*. A cave, possibly a souterrain in view of the late form of the name (i.e. noun followed by the genitive of the article and another noun), is quite common: Gortnahoo and Gurtnahoe, both in Co. Tipperary, represent *Gort na hUamha*, 'Tilled field of the cave', the cave possibly, as often nowadays, having been discovered in the course of the tillage. Sometimes a notable feature dictates the name: Gorticastle, Co. Tyrone, is *Gort an Chaisil*, 'Tilled field of the stone fort'; Gortahill, Co. Cavan, *Gort an Choill*, 'Tilled field of the wood'; Gortnahaha, Cos Clare and Tipperary, *Gort na hÁithe*, 'Tilled field of the kiln'; and Gortamullin, Co. Kerry, *Gort an Mhuilinn*, 'Tilled field of the mill'. Of course indications of ownership are common too, as in Gurtymadden, Co. Galway, *Gort Uí Mhadaín*, 'Ó Madaín's tilled field'.

GRÁIG: Is a term for a settlement, and in place-names is usually translated as 'hamlet'; it does not occur in Ulster. Usually deemed to have been introduced by the Anglo-Normans, it appears quite commonly without qualification, as Graig, in Cos Cork, Limerick, Galway and Tipperary, and as Graigue in Cos Cork, Galway, Sligo and Tipperary, and in its diminutive form, *Gráigín*, as Graigeen in Co. Limerick and Grageen in Co. Wexford. The best-known occurrence of the term is probably Graiguenamanagh, Co. Kilkenny, *Gráig na Manach*, 'Hamlet of the monks', referring to the great Cistercian abbey, on which building work began in 1204. In rather startling contrast is Graignagower, Co. Kerry, *Gráig na nGabhar*, 'Hamlet of the goats'.

MAP **GRÁIG** as a sole or first element in the names of townlands; it is confined to the southern part of the country.

GRÁINSEACH: Is derived from the Norman-French *grange* and means 'grange, monastic farm'. It occurs frequently in place-names, without further qualification, as Grange, sometimes in the Anglicised form Gransha. It refers to a land-unit, generally a townland, held as farmland (not necessarily solely for the production of cereals) by a monastic house of the twelfth century or later. Like the term, the concept was introduced from Europe with the arrival of the continental orders of monks. The grange need not adjoin the monastery by which it was held, or even be near it – it might, in fact, lie a considerable distance away. The cell of St Michael, at Duleek, Co. Meath, for example, was a grange of the Augustinian house of Llanthony II, near Gloucester. We know from the records that it was a very highly organised operation: it had bakeries and brew-houses; granaries, byres and sheep-pens; a water-mill (where the miller took half the flour from the cereals of strangers which were ground there). There were nearly 100 hectares of arable land, of which about one-fifth was to be ploughed. In the Lecale area of Co. Down, land-units such as Grangicam, *Gráinseach Cham*, 'Crooked grange', were granges held by one or other of the monastic foundations in the Downpatrick area. The term in some instances came to be used as the equivalent of a parish, where a block unit of adjoining land was held by a monastic house, as in the case of the Grange of Muckamore, Co. Antrim.

Grange: See GRÁINSEACH

Gransha: See GRÁINSEACH

GREANACH: Means a 'sandy or gravelly place', and is relatively common without qualification in several forms: Granagh, Co. Limerick; Graney, Co. Kildare; Grenagh, Co. Cork.

Greenan: See GRIANÁN

GRIANÁN: Is a term which occurs all over the country, normally without qualification. It is usually interpreted as meaning 'sunny place', though

MAP **GRÁINSEACH** as a sole or first element in the names of townlands; unlike other terms imported in medieval times it is reasonably widespread throughout the country because of its connections with continental religious orders.

there is a strong indication that it may refer to a place with a view and that in some of the earlier examples it was used metaphorically to mean 'important place'. The most common Anglicised form is Greenan, which appears throughout the country, with several instances in Co. Donegal, others in Cos Antrim, Fermanagh, Meath, Tipperary, etc. Greenane appears in Cos Kerry, Wicklow, etc., while Greenaun appears in Co. Leitrim and Co. Clare. The most famous example is on Greenan Hill, Co. Donegal, *Grianán Oileach*,

'Grianan of Ailech', which consists of an enormous stone-built hill-top fort, the central citadel of which is twenty-five metres in diameter. This gave its name to the early northern Uí Néill overkingdom of Ailech, which included modern Cos Donegal and Tyrone. 'Important place' would seem a most fitting title for this imposing structure.

GUALA: Means 'shoulder', in place-names referring usually to the 'shoulder' of a mountain. It appears in such names as Gulladoo, Co. Leitrim and Gulladuff, Co. Derry, both of which represent *Guala Dhubh*, 'Black shoulder', and Belgooly, Co. Cork, *Béal Guala*, 'Mouth of the ridge', to avoid the anatomical absurdity of talking of the 'Mouth of the shoulder'.

MAP **GRIANÁN** as a first element, usually unqualified, in names recorded by the Ordnance Survey; it is fairly widespread throughout the country.

Illan:	See OILEÁN
Illaun:	See OILEÁN
IMLEACH:	Means a 'boundary' or 'borderland' and is represented in a few surviving place-names. Emly, Co. Tipperary is the word without qualification, as is Emlagh, Co. Mayo. Emlaghmore, Co. Kerry is *Imleach Mór*, 'Large borderland'; Emlaghfad, Co. Sligo, *Imleach Fada*, 'Long borderland'.
INBHEAR:	Means 'river-mouth', 'estuary'; while it is common enough in Irish place-names it is even more common in Scotland. Inver, Co. Donegal is now simply *Inbhear*, but was originally *Inbhear Náile*, 'Náile's river-mouth'; Inveran, Co. Galway is a diminutive, *Inbhearán*, 'Little estuary'.
Inch:	See INIS
INIS/INSE:	Basically means 'island', but can also be used in the sense of 'water-meadow' – possibly in instances where one branch of a stream has silted or dried up, leaving what was once an island joined to the river-bank. Since without personal investigation or knowledge it is difficult to be certain which is meant in any specific occurrence, it is usual to translate the term simply as 'island'. Without qualification it appears frequently as Inch, *Inse*, which is to be found in Cos Cork, Down, Kerry and Wexford, and as Ennis, *Inis*, in Co. Clare. While general descriptive terms are applied, such as Inishkeen, Co. Monaghan, *Inis Caoin*, 'Beautiful island', which also appears as Inniskeen, Co. Louth, many of the terms used are locational. For example,

Inisheer, Co. Galway and Inishirrer, Co. Donegal are both Inis Oirthir, 'Eastern island'; Inishmaan, Co. Galway and Inishmeane, Co. Donegal are both Inis Meáin, 'Middle island'; while Inishtooskert, Co. Kerry is Inis Tuaisceart, 'Northern island'. In some cases the vegetation is described, as in Inishfree, Co. Donegal, Inis Fraoigh, 'Island of the heather'; in others the animal population, as in Inishkeeragh, Co. Donegal, Inis Chaorach, 'Island of sheep', or Inchnamuck, Co. Tipperary, Inse na Muc, 'Island of the pigs'. There is also, of course, Inishbofin, in Cos Donegal and Galway, Inis Bó Finne, 'Island of the white cow', though this is generally accepted to refer to a mythological white cow rather than an actual one. Personal names appear often as well, with Inishowen, Co. Donegal, Inis Eoghain, 'Eoghan's island' – which is clearly neither a water-meadow nor, indeed, an island, though *nearly* one. Other personally named examples are Inistioge, Co. Kilkenny, Inis Tíog, 'Tíog's island', and Inishmurray, Co. Sligo, Inis Muirí, 'Muireadhach's island'.

As a second element the term appears in a number of cases, where perhaps the reference is more likely to be to a river-meadow. It occurs in Ballynahinch, in Cos Down, Galway and Tipperary, Baile na hInse, 'Homestead of the island/river-meadow'; in Devenish, Co. Fermanagh, on the other hand, the reference, Daimh Inis, 'Island of oxen', is emphatically to an island in Lough Erne.

Inver: See INBHEAR

ÍOCHTAR: Means 'lower', and although it does occur as Eighter, Co. Cavan, without further ado, and in Co. Kerry as Eightercua, Íochtar Cua, 'Lower hollow', its normal function in place-names is to differentiate between two adjacent places with the same name – a divided townland, for example – often with the addition of *íochtar* to the one farther from the capital; *uachtar*, 'upper', to the other.

IOMAIRE: Means a 'ridge' of any kind and is generally Anglicised as 'ummera', as in Ummeracam, Co. Armagh, or 'umry' as in Umrycam, Cos Donegal and Derry, all of which are *Iomaire Cam*, 'Crooked ridge'. Killanummery, Co. Leitrim, is *Cill an Iomaire*, 'Church of the ridge'.

IORRAS: Is another word for a 'promontory'; its best-known example is Erris Head, Co. Mayo, which is simply *Iorras*, 'Promontory', with the pleonastic addition of 'head'. It also occurs in Errislannan, Co. Galway, *Iorras Fhlannáin*, 'Flannán's promontory'.

IUBHAR/IÚIR: Is another word for 'yew', the word still in use and the term more commonly used in place-names. It appears in a variety of combinations: inevitably as Ballynure, Co. Antrim (and many other places throughout the country), *Baile an Iúir*, 'Homestead of the yew'; and as in Terenure, Co. Dublin, *Tír an Iúir*, 'Territory of the yew'. There are fields distinguished by their yew-tree, as in Gortinure, Co. Derry, *Gort an Iúir*, 'Field of the yew'. It occurs, of course, in the name of Newry, Co. Down, where the definite article provides the initial 'n', *An tIúr*, 'The yew-tree'. This particular yew was allegedly planted by St Patrick himself, and is recorded as having been burned with the monastery beside which it stood in 1162.

K

Ken: See CEANN

Kil(l): See CILL and COILL

Knock: See CNOC

L

Labby:	See LEABA
Lack:	See LEAC
Lacken:	See LEACA

LADHAR: Is another word meaning 'fork' and as well as its anatomical application refers especially to the land between two converging rivers or hill-ridges. It is generally Anglicised as 'lear' in the northern part of the country, in Cos Cavan, Derry, Leitrim and Tyrone, the last of which has a Learmore, *Ladhar Mór*, 'Large fork'; Learmount, in the same county, possibly represents a situation where 'mount' has been added to the native *ladhar*. In southern parts it is generally Anglicised as 'lyre', which appears quite simply as Lyre, Co. Cork. Also in Co. Cork is Lyrenageeha, *Ladhar na Gaoithe*, 'Fork of the wind'. As if in compensation there is, in Co. Limerick, a place called Lyrenagrena, *Ladhar na Gréine*, 'Fork of the sun'.

LAG/LOG: Means a 'hollow' and is quite common in place-names, being Anglicised in a variety of ways. It is not much used in the extreme south, except in minor names. It appears as Lagnamuck, *Lag na Muc*, 'Hollow of the pigs', in Co. Mayo; Leggamaddy, *Lag an Mhadaidh*, 'Hollow of the dog', in Co. Down, and Luggacurren, *Log an Churraigh*, 'Hollow of the marsh', in Co. Laois. Lugnaquilla, in the Wicklow Mountains, is *Log na Coille*, 'Hollow of the wood'. There is a diminutive form, *Lagán*, meaning 'Little hollow' or even 'Little lake' – possibly a water-filled glacial hollow or 'cirque'; it gave its name to the district of Lagan in Co. Donegal and possibly also to the river of that name which rises in Co. Down.

LAITHEACH: Means 'mud' or 'mire' and is not very common in place-names; it does appear in Laghy, Co. Donegal without qualification and in Loughduff, Co. Cavan, rather surprisingly, as *Laitheach Dhubh*, 'Black mire'.

LÁITHREACH: Means 'site', even 'ruins (of a building)', and appears in this form under several different Anglicisations, as Laragh, in Cos Laois, Monaghan and Wicklow, and as Lauragh, in Co. Kerry. It appears as *Láithreach Cora*, 'Site of the weir', in Laracor, Co. Meath.

LANN: Has a primary meaning of 'land' or 'ground' and is attested in this sense as the secondary element in a range of early compound place-names, such as *Muclann* (pig-land) or *Eachlann* (horse-land). With the introduction of Christianity it acquired a new meaning as 'church'; in this sense it can be compared to its Welsh cognate *llan*, which became the standard term for 'church' or 'monastery' in Wales. *Lann*, in Ireland, did not, however, become a standard term, and the fact that instances of its use, where so far identified, lie in the eastern part of the country could be construed as indicating that its use in Ireland was suggested by the use of *llan* in Wales. All examples of place-names in Ireland with *lann* as the first element do have clear reference to ecclesiastical sites, some with attested early associations. Of these the earliest is Lynally, Co. Offaly, *Lann Eala*, founded by Colmán Eala, whose death is recorded as having taken place in AD 610. Lynn, Co. Westmeath, whose full name was formerly *Lann Mhic Luacháin*, was founded by Colmán Mac Luacháin, who died in AD 700 and with whom another *lann*-named church, Linns in Co. Louth, is associated. A well-known example is Lambeg, Co. Antrim, *Lann Bheag*, 'Little church', while

Glenavy, Co. Antrim, *Lann Abhaigh*, 'Church of the dwarf', after a dwarf associated with St Patrick, is a less obvious example.

MAP **LANN** as an element in place-names mentioned in the text; its distribution is markedly confined to the area east of the river Shannon.

Latin Names: Many of the medieval monastic houses founded by continental orders, especially by the Cistercians, bore Latin names – the Cistercian abbey at Kilbeggan, Co. Westmeath, for example, was known as *Benedictio Dei* ('Blessing of God'), while that at Baltinglass, Co. Wicklow was known as *Vallis Salutis* ('Valley of safety'). Only one of these names has survived as a place-name in current use: this, of course, is Mellifont, Co.

Louth, known as *Fons Mellis* ('Fountain of honey'). One other, now known as Abbeyleix, Co. Laois (*Mainistir Laoise*, 'Abbey of Laois'), was known in Latin as *Lex Dei* ('Law of God'), and it is very tempting to see in these two names a bilingual pun. In Holy Cross, Co. Tipperary, *Mainistir na Croiche Naoimhe*, known in Latin as *Sancta Crux*, it appears possible that the present English name is a translation directly from the Latin.

LEABA: Primarily means 'couch' or 'bed' but is consistently used in place-names to mean 'grave'; in fact *Leaba Dhiarmada agus Ghráinne*, 'Diarmaid and Gráinne's bed', is a term used, particularly in the west, from Co. Donegal to Co. Clare, to designate a neolithic or earlier Bronze Age megalithic tomb, often a court tomb, a portal tomb or a wedge tomb. It appears without qualification in Labby, Cos Derry, Donegal and Sligo; the common English term 'Giant's grave' is recalled in Labbyfirmore, Co. Monaghan, *Leaba an Fhir Mhóir*, 'Grave of the big man', actually an earlier Bronze Age wedge tomb.

LEAC: Means 'flagstone', 'tile', 'slate' and appears, without qualification, as Lack, Co. Fermanagh, 'Flagstone'; it occurs in more complex formations as Ballinalack, Co. Westmeath, *Béal Átha na Leac*, 'Mouth of the ford of the flagstones'; Bellanaleck, Co. Fermanagh, *Bealach na Leice*, 'Pass of the flagstone'; Belleek, Co. Fermanagh and Belleeks, Co. Armagh, both of which represent *Béal Leice*, 'Mouth of the flagstone'. There is a diminutive form, *Leaicín*, which appears in Lackeen, Co. Kerry. There is a derived word *Leacach*, 'Abounding in flagstones', which appears as Lackagh, Co. Kildare and in Athlacca, Co. Limerick, *Áth Leacach*, 'Ford abounding in flagstones'.

LEACA/LEACAN: Means any flat, sloping surface, like a cheek, and is generally construed as 'hillside'; it appears unqualified as Lackan, Co. Wicklow and Leckaun, Co. Sligo. With slight qualification it is found as Lackamore, Co. Tipperary, *Leaca Mhór*, 'Big hillside', and as Lackaroe, in Cos Cork and Offaly, *Leaca Rua*, 'Red hillside'.

LEACHT: Means 'grave' and is quite common in place-names, often referring to wedge tombs, though it can also refer to other sorts of megalith. It appears without qualification in Laght, Co. Cork, where there is a pillar-stone which may serve as a grave-marker. A diminutive form, *Leachtán*, 'Little grave', appears in Laghtane, Co. Limerick. Lachtcarn, Co. Tipperary, where there are remains of a burial cairn, is a curious term combining two words, *leacht* and *carn*, which are used for burial monuments. In Laghtneill, Co. Cork, *Leacht Néill*, are the remains of a wedge grave of the earlier Bronze Age which has been appropriated as the resting-place of a much later heroic figure, hence the name 'Niall's grave'; a similar fate seems to have befallen another wedge grave in Co. Derry, where *leacht* appears in its other Anglicised form of 'slaght' in Slaghtneill. Such appropriations are quite common: Slaughtmanus, Co. Derry, *Leacht Mhánasa*, is likely to pre-date its purported owner, Manas, by at least 2,000 years, in the same way as Laghtgeorge, Co. Galway, *Leacht Sheoirse*, 'Seoirse's grave', would long pre-date any known George in Ireland.

LEAMH/LEAMHÁN: Means 'elm-tree', the latter being the form more used. It occurs in various Anglicised forms, as Drumleevan, Co. Leitrim and Dromalivaun, Co. Kerry, both of which are *Droim Leamháin*, 'Elm-ridge', as is Droimlamph,

Co. Derry, *Droim Leamh*. It also appears in the name of the Laune River, in Co. Kerry. There are several derivative forms: *Leamhach*, meaning 'Abounding in elms', occurs in Lavagh, Cos Donegal and Sligo, as well as in Lavey, in Cos Derry and Cavan, and Lammy, in Cos Fermanagh and Tyrone. Other derivatives are *Leamhraidhe*, which appears as Lowery in Cos Donegal and Fermanagh, and *Leamhcán*, 'Place of elms', which appears as Lucan, Co. Dublin. The compound *Leamhchoill*, 'Elmwood', gives its name to Laughil, Cos Galway, Longford, Mayo, Offaly, Roscommon and Sligo; Laghil, Co. Donegal; Laghile, Cos Clare and Tipperary; Loghill, Co. Limerick; and Laughill, Cos Fermanagh and Laois.

LEARGA/
LEARGAIDH/
LEARGAN:

All mean 'slope'; Largy appears as a common Anglicised form, without qualification, or with a simple one, in Cos Antrim, Derry, Fermanagh, Leitrim, Meath and Monaghan, while Largan appears in Co. Mayo. It is a term most commonly found in northern counties. In Donegal it occurs as Largybrack, *Leargaidh Breac*, 'Speckled slope', and as Larganreagh, *Leargan Riabhach*, 'Striped slope', also seen as Largyreagh in Co. Derry. In Co. Sligo, it appears with a personal name, as Largydonnell, *Learga Uí Dhónaill*, 'Ó Dónaill's slope'.

LEATH:

Means a 'half' or a 'side', and in one guise or the other is found frequently in place-names. *Leath Mogha* and *Leath Cuinn* were terms used for the southern and northern parts of Ireland respectively, and it occurs, in the sense rather of 'portion', in Lecale, Co. Down, *Leath Cathail*, 'Cathal's portion'. It appears with *baile*, the usual name for the unit of land known as a townland, in the term *leth-baile*, signifying half of that unit, in *Annals of the Four Masters*, in an entry of 1239 referring to an endowment to the Canons of

Trinity Island, and this term, 'half townland', appears regularly in place names as Lavally, in Cos Clare, Cork, Galway, Roscommon, Sligo and Tipperary, and as Levally, in Cos Armagh, Down, Fermanagh, Galway, Laois and Mayo. It appears with other terms denoting land-measurement, in names like Lahesseragh, Co. Tipperary, *Leath Sheisreach*, meaning 'Half a *seisreach*', *seisreach* being a unit of land usually described as a 'ploughland'. It also appears as Laharan, in Cos Cork and Kerry, *Leath Fhearann*, 'Half of a *fearann*', another term used to indicate a land-division. *Leithghleann*, meaning 'Half a valley' or 'Side of a valley', is found in Leighlin, Co. Carlow, while Lahardaun, Co. Mayo, is *Leath Ardán*, 'Side of a plateau'. It also appears, slightly enigmatically, in the earlier names of Downpatrick, Co. Down, *Dún Lethglaise* and *Dún da Lethglas*, where the basic name-form is *Lethglas*, meaning either 'Green-sided place' or 'Land along one side of a stream or current'. It appears too in Lahinch, Co. Clare, *Leath Inse*, 'Half an island' or 'Peninsula'. Surprisingly, at Laragh, Co. Longford, *Leath Ráth*, 'Half a ring-fort', there actually is a semicircular earthwork (i.e. exactly half a ring-fort), locally believed to be the site of a church founded by St Patrick.

Leck: See LEAC

LÉIM: Means 'jump' or 'leap' and is, surprisingly, not uncommon in Irish place-names. It is found simply as Leap, Co. Cork, taking its name from a ravine at the head of Glandore Harbour, and as Loop, in Loop Head, Co. Clare. It also appears with animals to describe it: Leamlara, Co. Cork, *Léim Lára*, is the 'Leap of the mare', presumably a greater jump than that described in *Léim an Mhadaidh*, 'Leap of the dog', at Limavady, Co. Derry.

Leithghleann

LEITHGHLEANN: Is a word which literally means 'half valley' and is therefore construed as 'Side of a valley'. It appears in this form in Legland, Co. Tyrone and Leighlin, Co. Carlow.

LEITIR: Means 'hillside' and is found frequently in place-names: it appears simply as Letter, the usual Anglicised form, in Cos Fermanagh and Kerry, as Lettermore, *Leitir Móir*, in Co. Galway, and in its plural form, *Leitreacha*, in Latteragh, Co. Tipperary. Qualifying terms are usually descriptive, as in Letterfinnish, Co. Kerry, *Leitir Fionnuisce*, 'Hillside of bright water', or relate to the animal life, as in Letternadarriv, Co. Kerry, *Leitir na dTarbh*, 'Hillside of the bulls', or Letterbrick, Co. Mayo, *Leitir Bruic*, 'Badger hillside', or a personal name. In the case of Lettermullan, Co. Galway, *Leitir Mealláin*, this is somebody called Meallán, 'Meallán's hillside'.

LIA/LIATH: Means simply 'grey' and can go before the noun it qualifies in compounds as well as after it. It appears before its noun in Leitrim, Cos Down and Leitrim, *Liatroim = Liath Dhroim*, 'Grey ridge', and in Lemanaghan, Co. Offaly, *Liath Mancháin*, 'Grey place of Manchán'. *Liathmhuine*, 'Grey shrubbery', occurs in a number of different Anglicised guises: Leafonny, Co. Sligo; Leafin, Co. Meath; Liafin and Lefinn, Co. Donegal; Leighmoney in Co. Cork. After its noun it appears as Killylea, Co. Armagh, *Coillidh Liath*, 'Grey wood', and Caltraghlea, Co. Galway, *Cealtrach Lia*, 'Grey churchyard'.

LIAG: Is a word very similar to *leac* and with a very similar meaning of 'flagstone' or even 'monolith'. It is the form that appears unqualified as Leeg and Leek in Co. Monaghan and as Leeke in Cos Antrim and

Derry. Its best-known appearance, however, is in Slieve League, Co. Donegal, *Sliabh Liag*, 'Flagstone mountain', where the quartzite of which the mountain is composed does indeed split very obligingly into flagstones, which can be seen in the construction of the older houses, furnishing smooth flags for flooring and even tiles for roofing.

MAP **LIOS** as a first, sometimes a sole, element in the names of townlands; it is notably sparse in the south-east and in the extreme west and north-west.

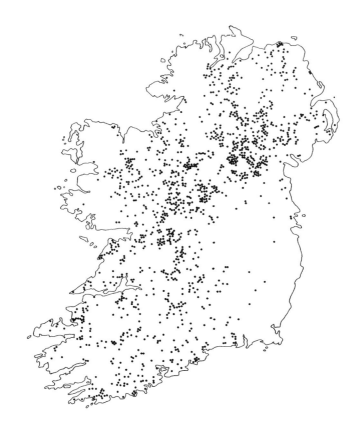

LIOS: While *lios, les* in Old Irish, literally means 'the space about a dwelling-house or houses enclosed by a bank or rampart', in place-names it refers to the dwelling-unit in its entirety, and is translated as 'fort'.

In Irish writing *lios*-names have nothing like the same currency or prestige as either *ráth*-names or *dún*-names. Both *dún* and *ráth* appear as place-name elements in heroic saga; *lios*, however, does not feature at all. *Lios*-names do not occur in *Lebor Gabála Érenn*, nor is any *lios* the subject of a *dindsenchas* poem. No *lios* is recorded as having been established by a well-known monarch; even in passing mention the incidence of *lios*-names is negligible. Such *lios*-names as appear in Irish writing are not heavily documented; the references tend to be late and rather incidental, except in the case of *lios*-named sites which had acquired additional status by dint of becoming ecclesiastical sites. Even *Ardd Senlis*, 'Height of the old fort', referred to in Tírechán's *Collections* in the *Book of Armagh*, a site which unfortunately has not yet been identified, is mentioned because of its claim to be the site of a church founded by St Patrick. Perhaps the lowlier status accorded to *lios*-sites is the very reason that *lios* does enjoy a higher incidence, as the first element in townland-names, than either *ráth* or *dún*; in the northern part of Ireland, indeed, it almost totally displaces *ráth* as the term for features for which *ráth* is the usual term, particularly in Leinster.

Unlike the term *dún*, both *ráth* and *lios* are often qualified by a word indicating colour. Lisbane, *Lios Bán*, 'White fort', is common, with examples in Cos Down and Limerick, as is Lisduff, *Lios Dubh*, 'Black fort', with examples in Cos Mayo and Cavan. *Lios Buí*, 'Yellow fort', appears in Lisboy, Cos Antrim,

Cork, Down, Fermanagh, Derry, Meath, Monaghan and Roscommon; *Lios Lfath*, 'Grey fort', appears in Lislea, Cos Armagh and Derry, while *Lios Ruadh*, 'Red fort', occurs in Lisroe, Cos Clare, Cork, Kerry and Waterford. Simple qualifications of size are common: Lismore, *Lios Mór*, 'Large fort', originally fully named as *Lios Mór Mo-Chuta*, Co. Waterford, is an instance of a *lios*-site which accrued fame because of its later ecclesiastical associations; *Lios Beag*, 'Little fort', appears regularly in the form Lisbeg, with an example near Aughrim in Co. Galway. A personal name as a qualifying element is not uncommon: Liscolman, Co. Antrim is *Lios Cholmáin*, 'Colman's fort', though whether the Colman in question gave the site ecclesiastical status is not documented. Lissue, Co. Antrim, *Lios Aedha*, 'Aedh's fort', is a rare example of a *lios*-site named after a notable king, Aedh, father of Ainbith, a powerful king of the Ulaid.

Qualifying elements consisting of the definite article and a noun – a form not significantly documented before the ninth century and not common until the eleventh and twelfth centuries – appear to be more common in *lios*-names than even in *ráth*-names. Examples are quite frequent, as in Lisnageer, Co. Cavan, *Lios na gCaor*, 'Fort of the berries'; Lisnamuck, Co. Derry, *Lios na Muc*, 'Fort of the pigs'; Lissatava, Co. Mayo, *Lios an tSamhaidh*, 'Fort of the sorrel'. Lisnagarvey, the former name of Lisburn, Co. Antrim, is *Lios na gCearrbhach*, 'Fort of the gamblers'. One particularly interesting example of this formation is to be seen in the common place-name Lissaniska, especially common in the southern part of Ireland, with instances in Cos Cork, Kerry, Limerick and Waterford; or in the form Lissanisky, with instances in Cos Cork, Roscommon and Tipperary. This is, in Irish, *Lios an Uisce*, 'Fort of the water', and it has long since been suggested that the name refers to the flooding of the ditch as an additional means of defence; the fact that the interior of the excavated ring-fort at Lissue, Co. Antrim was demonstrated to have been accessed by a wooden bridge over the ditch, rather than by the more common simple causeway, may lend support to this interpretation. Diminutive forms occur, such as Lissan, Co. Tyrone, *Leasán*, 'Little fort'. Sometimes the term is combined with one of the other terms with a somewhat similar meaning, the most notable example of which is Lisdoonvarna, Co. Clare, *Lios Dúin Bhearna*, 'Fort of the fort of the gap'.

While the archaeological entities to which the term *lios* is applied are for the most part rather unremarkable ring-forts, a few diverge from this rule, including the very impressive trivallate example in Co. Down, forming part, apparently, of the Dane's Cast complex, Lisnagade. This has been interpreted as *Lios na gCéad*, 'Fort of the hundreds', a name which remains rather enigmatic. Strategic importance could, however, be assumed of Lisbellaw, Co. Fermanagh, in view of its name *Lios Béal Átha*, 'Fort of the mouth of the ford'. Lisnalinchy, Co. Antrim, *Lios Uí Loingsigh*, 'Fort of Ó Loingsigh', another impressive ring-fort, is, unusually, named after, and associated with, one of the ruling families of Dál nAraidi. Sometimes *lios* is qualified by a patently Anglo-Norman personal name such as Robert (Lisrobert, Co. Mayo) or William (Liswilliam, Co. Roscommon), suggesting that *lios*-names were still being coined during the Anglo-Norman period.

In some instances the actual structure associated with the name appears to be a motte, or motte-like structure, as at Lismahon, Co. Down, where the qualification appears to be a native Irish personal name, *Móchán*; excavation of the site demonstrated that beneath the Anglo-Norman motte there lay a pre-Norman site to which the name probably originally applied. Since the excavation of the motte-like structure at Gransha, Co. Down, *Gráinseach*, 'Grange', we must bear in mind that the concept of motte-like structures was present in Ireland before the arrival here of the Anglo-Normans. The most impressive monument on a *lios*-named site is the third largest thirteenth-century castle in Ireland, at Liscarroll, Co. Cork; here the Irish form, *Lios Cearúill*, 'Cearúll's fort', strongly suggests that this splendid pile was erected on the site of an earlier native fortification.

MAP   **LIOS AN UISCE** as a townland name; it is virtually confined to the western part of the country.

LIS: See LIOS

LOCH: Is the standard Irish word for a 'lake', including an 'inlet of the sea'; since it is almost invariably Anglicised as 'lough' it is fairly straightforward – though other Irish words whose first syllables are Anglicised as 'lough' (e.g. *Luachair*, 'Rushy place', Anglicised as 'Lougher') may sometimes cause confusion, as may the collective suffix *-lach*, as in Carnlough, Co. Antrim, which has nothing to do with lakes but is actually *Carnlach*, 'Place of cairns'. Occasionally the lake's colour is described, as in Loughrea, Co. Galway, *Loch Ria*, 'Grey lake'; often some attribute of the lake is described, as in Lough Eske, Co. Donegal, *Loch Iasc*, 'Fish lake', or Loughanure, Co. Donegal, *Loch an Iúir*, 'Lake of the yew'. Frequently, however, the name of a person, real or mythical, is applied, as in Loughbrickland, Co. Down, *Loch Bricreann*, 'Bricriu's lake' – named after a character in *Táin Bó Cúailnge* who was trampled to death by the two fighting bulls; or Loughmacrory, Co. Tyrone, *Loch Mhic Ruairí*, 'Mac Ruairí's lake'. A diminutive *Lochán*, 'Little lake', exists, either simply as Loughan, Co. Meath, or as Loughanavally, Co. Westmeath, *Lochán an Bhealaigh*, 'Little lake of the valley'. With sea-loughs it should be noted that seldom, if ever, does the lough in question carry the name of the river that empties into it.

LONGPHORT: Is a term with two meanings, firstly a 'camp' or 'encampment', with an underlying assumption of its being of a temporary nature, appearing at first, in *Annals of Ulster*, in the ninth century with reference to the naval encampments or beach-heads of Viking raiders. Its second meaning as an 'established or permanent stronghold' does not begin to appear in the annalistic sources until the thirteenth century, while the primary sense of temporary encampment continued. One of the first to be documented in an onomastic sense is Longford, Co. Longford, with which the reference in *Annals of Ulster* of 1430, to *Senlongphort*, 'Old *longphort*', is identified, equated with *Longphort Uí Ferghail*, '*Longphort* of Ó Fergall'. In most of these early references the surname identifying the establishment is that of the local ruling family. The usual Anglicised form is Longford, of which sixteen instances occur as townland names. It also occurs as a qualifying term, in Ballylumford, Co. Antrim, *Baile Longphoirt*, 'Homestead of the stronghold'.

LORGA(N): Means literally 'shin' and is another anatomical term used in place-names to signify a 'ridge'; it appears unqualified in Lurga, Co. Mayo and Lurgan, Cos Armagh, Donegal and Westmeath. With simple qualification it appears in Lurganreagh, Co. Down, *Lorgan Riabhach*, 'Striped ridge'.

Lough: See LOCH

LUACHAIR: Means 'rushes' or 'sedges' and, in place-names, 'rushy place'; it appears without qualification in Lougher, Co. Kerry, and as Loughermore, *Luachair Mhór*, 'Big rushy place', in Co. Derry.

Lyn(n): See LANN

117

M

MACHAIRE: Is a common word in place-names meaning 'flat place' or 'plain'; it appears without qualification in Maghery, Co. Donegal and Maghera, Co. Down, but Maghera, Co. Derry is, deceptively, Machaire Rátha, 'Plain of the ring-fort'. Often quite simple qualifications are used: Magherabeg, Co. Donegal is Machaire Beag, 'Small plain'; Magheraboy, Co. Mayo is Machaire Buí, 'Yellow plain'. The plural form, Machairí, probably better translated as 'Flat places' rather than 'Plains', gives its name to islands in Co. Kerry. Magheralin, Co. Down is Machaire Lainne, 'Plain of the church', and Magheracloone, Co. Monaghan, Machaire Cluana, 'Plain of the pasture'. Magherafelt, Co. Derry, however, is Machaire Theach Fiolta, 'Plain of Fioghalta's house'.

MAGH/MÁ: Is the most common word for 'plain'; it appears without qualification as Moy, Co. Tyrone and Muff, Co. Donegal, and with very simple qualification as Moveen, Co. Clare, Má Mhín, 'Smooth plain'; Mowhan, Co. Armagh, Má Bhán, 'White plain'; Moyard, Co. Galway, Maigh Ard, 'High plain'; and Moymore, Co. Clare, Má Mhór, 'Big plain'. Sometimes the qualification is a natural feature pertinent to the plain, as in Muckamore, Co. Antrim, Má Chomair, 'Plain of the confluence'; Moyvally, Co. Kildare, Magh Bhealaigh, 'Plain of the pass'; Macroom, Co. Cork, Má Chromtha, 'Plain of the crooked ford'. Sometimes it is vegetation which decides the name: Moycullen, Co. Galway is Magh Cuilinn, 'Plain of holly'; Moville, Co. Donegal is Má Bhile, 'Plain of the sacred tree'; it can be planted vegetation, as in Moycarky, Co. Tipperary, Má Chairce, 'Plain ɔf oats'. Sometimes a human feature ɪnfluences the name: Moydow, Co. Longford ɪs Má Dumha, 'Plain of the mound', and ᴧoygashel, Co. Tyrone is Má gCaisil, 'Plain of the stone fort' Soɪnetimes there is a hint of mysteɪy: Moyvoughly, Co. Westmeath is Má Bhachla, 'Plain of the crosier'; sometimes of something that could make, or pay for, the crosier, as in Moyarget, Co. Antrim, Má Airgid, 'Silver plain'. In Damma, Co. Kilkenny we find Dá Mhagh, 'Two plains'.

MAINISTIR: Is, of course, derived from the Latin *monasterium*, meaning simply 'monastery'; the usual forms in English are 'Manister' and 'Monaster', both of which occur without further qualification as place-names in Co. Limerick. With a single great exception *mainistir*-names are not documented in pre-twelfth-century Irish writing. The exception is, of course, Monasterboice, Co. Louth, Mainistir Buite, founded by Buite, who died in 519 or 523, which is so uniquely named as to be frequently referred to simply as Mainistir. Often in modern English forms of the place-name in question *mainistir* is rendered as 'abbey', as in the case of Grey Abbey, Co. Down, which had previously been rendered, even in English documentation, as Monasterleigh, Mainistir Liath, 'Grey abbey'. In such instances as these it is difficult to tell whether the original name was coined in Irish or English. In the case of Abbeydorney, Co. Kerry, however, the fact that eclipsis after the genitive Ó, Mainistir Ó dTorna, 'Abbey of Uí Thorna', is retained even in the Anglicised form shows that the name was coined in Irish. Another well-known example is Monasterevin, Co. Kildare, Mainistir Eimhín, 'Eimhín's monastery'.

MÁS: With the meaning 'thigh' or 'buttock', is ⸜ of several anatomical terms which appear descriptively in place-names, referring, of course, to long, rather low hills. It is found without qualification in Maas, Co. Donegal and Mace in Cos Galway and Mayo. Most of the further descriptions seem compatible with the place or the feature after which it was named: Mausrevagh, Co. Galway, Más Riabhach, 'Striped thigh', as in a tabby cat; Mausrower in Co. Kerry, Más Ramhar, 'Fat thigh', is of fairly universal application.

MEALL: Means basically a 'lump' but is usually translated in place-names as 'knoll'. It is a term virtually confined to Munster, specifically to Cos Cork and Kerry, where it appears frequently and is generally Anglicised as 'maul'. In Co. Cork it appears as this, Maul, without qualification. Simple qualifications do appear: Maulmore and Maulbrack, in Co. Cork, Meall Mór, 'Large knoll', and Meall Breac, 'Speckled knoll'. More precise qualifying terms are usually to describe the vegetation, as in Maulnahorna, Co. Kerry, Meall na hEorna, 'Knoll of the barley'; the animal life, as in Maulnagower, Co. Kerry, Meall na nGabhar, 'Knoll of the goats'; or some outstanding feature, as in Maulagallane, Co. Kerry, Meall an Ghalláin, 'Knoll of the standing stone'. Inevitably, personal names appear as well, as in Maulyneill, Co. Kerry, Meall Uí Néill, 'Ó Néill's knoll'.

Meen: See MÍN

MÍN: Is an adjective meaning 'smooth', as in Moveen, Co. Clare, Má Mhín, 'Smooth plain', or Ballinameen, Co. Roscommon, Béal an Átha Mín, 'Mouth of the smooth ford'. It is also a noun meaning anything smooth, including a

MAP   **MEALL** as a first element in the names of townlands; it is confined not merely to Munster but to the counties of Cork and Kerry.

smooth green spot on a mountain or in rough land. In folklore it tends to mean a 'gentle' or 'kindly' spot, the sort of place where the 'hill-folk' have their dwellings. The form in English is usually 'Meen', which appears without qualification in Co. Kerry. Although it occurs all over the country it is rare in the east and south-east. Some of the qualifications are quite simple, such as Meenbane, Co. Donegal, *Mín Bán*, 'White gentle spot', or Meenmore, in Cos Donegal, Fermanagh and Sligo, *Mín Mór*, 'Large gentle spot'. In Co. Cork the plural appears in Meentyflugh, *Mínte Fliucha*, 'Wet gentle spots'. It is particularly common in Co. Donegal, as in Meenavean, *Mín na bhFiann*, 'Gentle place of the Fianna', where Fionn and his warriors were deemed to have set up their camp, though it occurs elsewhere as well, as in Tyrone's Meenagorp, *Mín na gCorp*, 'Smooth place of the dead bodies', so named possibly as a result of the discovery of human remains during cultivation.

MAP **MÍN** as a first element in the names of townlands; while it does occur in other parts of the country, its concentration in Co. Donegal and the fringes of adjoining counties is spectacular.

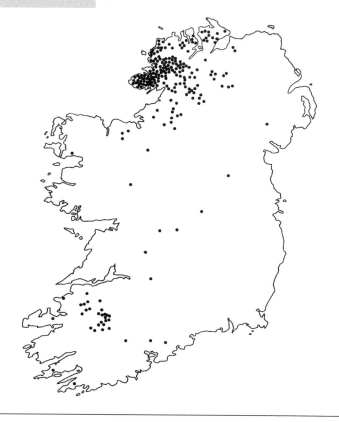

MÓIN/MÓNA: Is one of the many Irish words referring to a 'bog', in this case with particular reference to a 'peat-bog'. It is a common element in place-names, as peat-bogs are a common feature of the Irish countryside. Often it is qualified by a term referring to its position, as in Monard, Co. Tipperary, *Móin Ard*, 'High bog'; Monavullagh, Co. Waterford, *Móin an Mhullaigh*, 'Bog of the summit'; or Mountrath, Co. Laois, *Móin Rátha*, 'Bog of the fort'. Sometimes, as in Moneyreagh, Co. Down, it is simply a description of the bog, *Mónadh Riabhach*, 'Striped bog', or a statement of ownership, as in Mooncoin, Co. Kildare, *Móin Choinn*, 'Conn's bog'. It often occurs as a qualifying element, as in Ballinamona, Co. Cork, *Baile na Móna*, 'Homestead of the bog', seen in slightly different form in Ballymoney, Co. Antrim, *Baile Mónaidh*.

MUILEANN: Means 'mill'; it is sometimes found unqualified, as in Mullan, Co. Monaghan, but more often has an indication of ownership or location. In the case of Mullennakill, Co. Kilkenny, this could be either or both: *Muileann na Cille*, 'Mill of the church'; while in Mullinacuff, Co. Wicklow it is certainly the former, *Muileann Mhic Dhuibh*, 'Mac Duibh's mill'. Sometimes, however, the qualifying element is a little baffling: Mullinahone, Co. Tipperary is *Muileann na hUamhan*, 'Mill of the cave', while Mullingar, Co. Westmeath is *Muileann Cearr*, 'Crooked mill'. Frequently the term is itself the qualifying element: Ballymullen, Co. Kerry, is *Baile an Mhuilinn*, 'Homestead of the mill', while at Rathmullan, Co. Down, *Ráth an Mhuilinn*, 'Ring-fort of the mill', a motte-like mound, two hearths were found in deposits dating to about AD 1200, each of which was laid on a millstone.

MUINE: Means a 'thicket' and is common in place-names. Often the qualifying element refers to the size or nature of the thicket: Moneymore, Co. Derry is simply *Muine Mór*, 'Big thicket'; Moneyglass, Co. Antrim is *Muine Glas*, 'Grey/green thicket'; Moneygall, Co. Offaly is *Muine Gall*, 'Thicket of the stones'; Moneygashel, Co. Cavan, is *Muine na gCaiseal*, 'Thicket of the stone forts'; and Moneynick, Co. Antrim, is *Muine Chnoic*, 'Thicket of the hill'. Occasionally the description is more interesting: Monivea, Co. Galway, for example, is *Muine Mheá*, 'Thicket of the mead'; sometimes ownership, even of a thicket, is claimed, as in Monamolin, Co. Wexford, *Muine Moling*, 'Moling's thicket'.

MULLACH: Means 'summit' and appears in just this form, Mullagh, in Cos Cavan, Galway and Meath. Simple descriptions occur, as in Mullaghmore in Cos Derry and Sligo, *Mullach Mór*, 'Big summit', and Mullaghbawn, Co. Armagh, *Mullach Bán*, 'White summit'. Mullaghareirk, in Cos Cork and Limerick, *Mullach an Radhairc*, 'Summit of the vista', has a self-evident satisfaction about it, not shared, at first sight, by Mullaghcleevaun, Co. Wicklow, *Mullach Cliabháin*, 'Summit of the cradle', which presumably refers to a small cradle-like hollow at the summit. There is a diminutive form, *mullán*, which also appears in place-names, both without qualification in several counties and as a second element in examples such as Glassavullaun, Co. Dublin, *Glaise an Mhulláin*, 'Streamlet of the small summit'.

N

NEAD: Means 'nest', usually the nest of an eagle. It appears simply as Ned, in Cos Cavan, Fermanagh and Derry, and as 'Nad' in Co. Cork, in the name Nadanullar, *Nead an Iolair*, 'Eagle's nest'; a diminutive, *Neadín*, 'Little nest', appears as Nedeen, Co. Kerry. In Nedanone, Co. Kerry it appears as *Nead an Eoin*, 'Bird's nest', while in Nadnaveagh, Co. Roscommon, *Nead na bhFiach*, it represents 'Raven's nest'.

Norse Names: Despite the fact that the Norse or Vikings were in close (too close as far as their victims were concerned) contact with Ireland for some 200 years, both raiding and trading, there are surprisingly few totally Scandinavian names currently to be found in Ireland. This is despite the fact that the Anglo-Normans seem to have found Norse names more acceptable than Irish forms. Some Norse personal names did find their way into names that were otherwise totally Irish: Ballyfermot, Co. Dublin is one such, where the personal name, Thormund, is a Scandinavian one. Apart from these – and one inland name, Leixlip in Co. Dublin, which means 'Salmon leap' – all the major Scandinavian names refer to prominent coastal features: sea-loughs like Strangford, Co. Down, which means something like 'Bay with strong currents'; Carlingford, Cos Louth and Down, which means 'Bay of the hag'; Wexford, Co. Wexford, which appears to mean 'Sea-washed'; coastal settlements like Wicklow, Co. Wicklow, which means 'Viking meadow'; Arklow, Co. Wicklow which means 'Arnkell's meadow'; and Helvick, Co. Waterford, which means 'Rock-shelf bay'; or other prominent coastal features such as Howth, Co. Dublin, which simply means 'Head'. All in all they number no more than fifty.

NUA: Means 'new' or 'fresh' and is one of those adjectives which can precede the noun it qualifies in a compound or follow it. As a compound it makes Noughaval, Co. Cork, *Nuacongbháil*, 'New cloister', and, in connection with Anglo-Norman castles, it appears in Newcastle-Lyons, Co. Dublin, *Nuachaisleán Liamhna*, the location of an English royal castle. As an adjective following its noun it appears in the name of a parish in Co. Kerry, Templenoe, *Teampall Nua*, 'New church'; of a townland in Co. Down, Ballynoe, *Baile Nua*, 'New homestead', and one in Co. Tipperary, Borrisnoe, *Buiríos Nua*, 'New burgage'.

O

O

OILEÁN: Means an 'island' and is usually Anglicised as 'illan' or 'illaun' or even 'island'. As well as signifying 'island' in the sense of a piece of land surrounded by water, it also refers to an area of raised, and therefore, dry, land surrounded by what is, or was, bog. It is not, superficially, as common in place-names as *inis*, but does occur in Illanfad, Co. Donegal, *Oileán Fada*, 'Long island', which is also represented by Illaunfadda in Co. Galway. It appears as Illaunmore, *Oileán Mór*, 'Large island', an island in Lough Derg, Co Tipperary. Illauntannig, Co. Kerry, *Oileán tSeanaigh*, 'Seanach's island', takes its name from St Seanach, who founded a monastery here in the sixth or seventh century. The Anglicised form 'island' seems particularly to refer to dry areas in bogs: in this sense it occurs as 'Island' in Cos Cork and Mayo; Islandreagh, in Co. Antrim, is *Oileán Riabhach*, 'Grey/striped island', while Islandmoyle, Co. Down, is *Oileán Maol*, 'Bare island'.

Oran: See UARÁN

Oughter: See UACHTAR

Owen: See ABHA

PAILÍS: Is a word, derived from the Old French *palis* (from which is also derived the English word 'palisade'), introduced by the Anglo-Normans in the sense of a wooden defensive structure and translated by 'palisade' or 'stockade'. It is not very common and is restricted to the southern part of the country. It appears without qualification as Palace, in Cos Cork and Wexford, Pallas, in Cos Galway, Kerry and Longford, and Pallis in Cos Wexford and Kerry. Some simple qualifications do occur: there is a Pallasbeg, *Pailís Beag*, 'Small stockade' in Co. Limerick and a Pallasboy, *Pailís Buí*, 'Yellow stockade', in Co. Westmeath. At Pallis, Co. Wexford, to give substance to the name, is a motte constructed by a nephew of Raymond le Gros.

Pallas Green, Co. Limerick, is *Pailís Ghréine*, 'Stockade of Grian', Grian being another name for Áine, goddess of love, whose Otherworld abode was at nearby Cnoc Gréine, or Cnoc Áine, to which, as recently as 1879, flaming bunches of hay and straw were carried; earlier a great fair, known as *Aonach Áine*, was held at the beginning of harvest. There is also a fine motte, a relic of the Anglo-Norman manor established here by Geoffrey fitz Robert which in 1223 was granted to Maurice fitz Gerald. This motte, with its defences originally of wood, is obviously the structure which gave its name to the place, despite its usurpation by the goddess.

PÁIRC: Is a term introduced by the Anglo-Normans but readily and rapidly assimilated into the Irish language. While it can indicate a 'tilled field' it is more often used in the sense simply of a 'field' or 'pasture'. It is common throughout the country and is usually Anglicised as 'park'. Park, without qualification, appears frequently, with examples in Cos Derry and Mayo; Parkmore, *Páirc Mhór*, 'Big field', is also common, with examples in Cos Antrim, Galway and Tyrone. Slightly more interesting forms do occur, such as Rathfield, Co. Kerry, *Páirc na Rátha*, 'Field of the ring-fort'. It is, understandably, a very common element in minor names, with examples such as Parkgorm, *Páirc Gorm*, 'Blue field', and Parkreagh, *Páirc Riabhach*, 'Striped/grey field', in Co. Tyrone.

MAP   **PAILÍS** as a sole or first element in the names of townlands; like other Anglo-Norman secular terms it is confined to the southern part of the country.

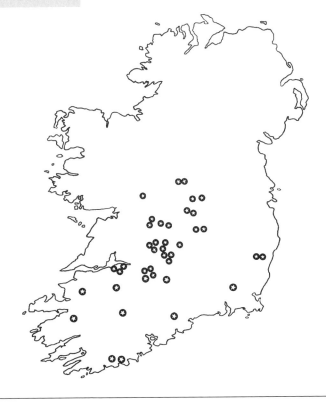

POLL: Means simply a 'hole' or even 'pool', and is quite common in place-names. It is usually Anglicised as 'pol(l)', 'pole', 'pool' or 'poul'. As Poolbeg, Co. Dublin, it represents *Poll Beag*, 'Little pool'; as Pollboy, Co. Galway, *Poll Buí*, 'Yellow pool'; as Poulargid, Co. Cork, *Poll an Airgid*, 'Silver pool'. Claims to own, or to have an association with, a *poll*, are indicated by Pollremon, Co. Galway, *Poll Réamainn*, 'Réamann's hole'. A little more interestingly, Poulaphuca, Co. Wicklow is *Poll an Phúca*, 'Pool of the sprite'. The plural, *Pollaí*, is represented in Poles, Co. Cavan, while *Pollach*, meaning 'Abounding in holes', appears in Pollagh, Co. Offaly. As a second element it occurs frequently: Ballinfull, Co. Sligo, is *Baile an Phoill*, 'Homestead of the pool', as is Ballyfoyle, Co. Kilkenny.

PORT: The fact that it basically means 'platform' or 'bank' explains why it should mean both 'port' and 'fort'. As 'port' it usually occurs on the coast, on lakes or on rivers. Portrush, Co. Antrim makes sense as *Port Rois*, 'Port of the promontory', as does Portballintrae in the same county as *Port Bhaile an Trá*, 'Port of the homestead of the beach'. Portnoo, Co. Donegal, as *Port Nua*, 'New port', also makes sense, and Portaferry, Co. Down as *Port an Pheire*, 'Port of the ferry'. In Portumna, Co. Galway, on the north bank of the river Shannon, it could be construed as either 'Bank of the tree-trunk' or 'Port of the tree-trunk', *Port Omna*. In Longford, Co. Longford, it is generally agreed to represent an element in a term which had come to mean 'Fort', or 'Fortified house', *Longphort*, as it does in Ballylongford, Co. Kerry, *Béal Átha Longphoirt*, 'Mouth of the ford of the fortress'.

Q

Quilty: See COILL

RAE/RÉ: Is a word meaning a 'level place', sometimes confused with *réidh*, which has a similar meaning. It appears occasionally in place-names, mainly in the south. It occurs as Rear Cross, Co. Tipperary, *Crois an Rae*, 'Cross of the level place', and again with slightly religious connotations in Reanascreena, Co. Cork, *Rae na Scríne*, 'Level place of the shrine'. It is a common enough term in minor names in Co. Kerry; possibly one reason for its not being so common in townland names is that the feature described is not sufficiently noteworthy, without a major qualifier, to merit broader recognition.

RAITH(EAN)/ RAITHNEACH: Severally mean 'fern', 'place of ferns' and, like the fern itself, are common elements in place-names throughout Ireland. Probably the most noteworthy place whose name contains this element is Coleraine, Co. Derry, *Cúil Rathain*, 'Nook of the ferns'. It appears in all sorts of combinations, but without qualification as *Raithean*, in Rahan, Co. Offaly. Since ferns grow almost everywhere, names such as Ardrahan, Co. Galway, *Ard Rathain*, 'Height of the ferns', and Drumraney, Co. Westmeath, *Droim Raithne*, 'Ridge of ferns', are only to be expected.

RÁTH: Is translated as an 'earthen rampart surrounding the residence of a chief, a fort; sometimes used of the enclosed dwelling also'. In place-names, however, *ráth* or *ráith*, denotes the settlement-unit *in toto*. While *dún* is the term commonly used in Irish writing of the residence of a king or chieftain, *ráth* also enjoys good associations. The earliest *ráth*-names mentioned in the pseudo-historical

Lebor Gabála Érenn are *rígrátha*, 'royal forts': *Ro class di rígráith la Nemed* ('Two royal forts were constructed by Nemed'), and when Éremón took the kingship of Ireland *ro classa da rígráith leis* ('two royal forts were constructed by him'). During the reign of Éremón important *dún*-sites, such as Dún *Sobhairce*, Dunseverick, Co. Antrim, 'Sobhairce's fort', were being constructed; it is evident that in the minds of the antiquarian compilers a *ráth*, or at least a *rígráth*, was of equal status with a *dún* and that the *ráth*-sites named in this context were regarded as enjoying acknowledged antiquity.

In heroic saga too, *ráth*-names appear to have the same status as *dún*-names: several *ráth*-names are mentioned in Táin Bó Cúailnge; four *ráth*-sites are the subject of Dindsenchas poems, and other *ráth*-names, some real, some fanciful, are scattered throughout the poems. In the Patrician literature *ráth*-names are quite common, as both civil and ecclesiastic sites, enjoying the same status as *dún*-sites to the extent that sometimes in the course of the narrative the term *dún* is applied to them. Unfortunately, few of the *ráth*-named sites recorded in early writing, particularly in saga and pseudo-history, can now be identified with any degree of certainty.

Place-names with the initial element *ráth* show a significantly different distribution pattern to those with *lios* as the initial element: *ráth*-names are sparse in the North, though not entirely absent, while *lios*, the prevalent term in the North, is sparse in the south-east. This variation cannot be totally explained in terms of regional usage, and at this stage it is difficult to find any convincing explanation for it. In most instances, where the actual eponymous monument can be identified it would appear that the great majority of the *ráth*-named sites are, like the great majority of *lios*-named sites, simple ring-forts. Some of the rare *ráth*-named sites in the North are seats of kings, such as Rathmore, Co. Antrim, *Ráth Mór*, 'Great fort', or Rademon, Co. Down, *Ráth Deamáin*, 'Deamán's fort'; others are attested ecclesiastical sites, such as Raholp, Co. Down, *Ráth Cholpa*, 'Fort of the bullock', or Raphoe, Co. Donegal, *Ráth Bhoth*, 'Fort of the huts'. In the parts of the country where *ráth* is the prevalent term, the very simplest, totally unqualified form can appear, such as Rath, Cos Offaly and Waterford, *Ráth*, 'Fort', or with simple descriptive or geographical qualifications such as Rathgar, Co. Dublin, *Ráth Garbh*, 'Rough fort'; Rathcool, Co. Cork, *Ráth Cúil*, 'Fort of the hill'; Rathlacken, Co. Mayo, *Ráth Leacan*, 'Fort of the hillside'; or Rathnure, Co. Wexford, *Ráth an Iúir*, 'Fort of the yew'.

Often the qualifying element is simply a personal name, as in Rathkeevin, Co. Tipperary, *Ráth Chaoimhín*, 'Kevin's fort'; Rathowen, Co. Westmeath, *Ráth Eoghain*, 'Eoghan's fort'; or Rathfran, Co. Mayo, *Ráth Bhrain*, 'Bran's fort'. In this part of the country too the site may have ecclesiastical associations, as in Rahugh, Co. Westmeath, whose full name was formerly *Ráth Aodha mic Bricc*, after its sixth-century founder, Aedh Mac Bricc. Diminutive forms are used, such as Raheen, which appears in Cos Cork, Westmeath and Wexford, *Ráithín*, 'Little fort'; sometimes too *ráth* is combined with one of the other words with a somewhat similar meaning, as in Rathdangan, Co. Wicklow, *Ráth Daingin*, 'Fort of the fortress'.

Like *lios*, *ráth* is sometimes qualified by a palpably Anglo-Norman name such as Walter (Rathwalter, Co. Tipperary), Gilbert

(Rathgilbert, Co. Laois) or Jordan (Rathjordan, Co. Limerick), indicating that the term was still incorporated in place-naming in the Anglo-Norman period. In one excavated example, Rathmullan, Co. Down, *Ráth an Mhuilinn*, 'Fort of the mill', the motte-like structure was shown to have been superimposed on an earlier, native Irish, site.

MAP **RÁTH** as a first element in the names of townlands; it is remarkably sparse in Ulster.

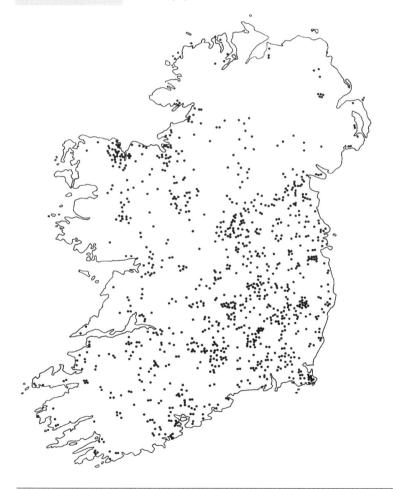

RÉIDH: Is a term meaning a 'level place' or 'clearing'. It appears in a number of place-names, possibly only in the south, and is sometimes confused with *rae*, which has a similar meaning. It appears in Reanaclogheen, Co. Waterford, *Réidh na gCloichín*, 'Clearing of the little stones', and Reacashlagh, Co. Kerry, *Réidchaisleach*, 'Clearing of the stone forts'.

RIA(BHACH): Is an adjective which means 'striped' or 'tabby', but is often translated as 'grey' in place-names. It can also mean 'fallow'. It normally follows the word which it qualifies and is quite common in place-names, where it is usually Anglicised as 'reagh'. Among the items it qualifies are natural features: a lake, as in Loughrea, Co. Galway, *Loch Ria*, 'Grey lake'; a hill, as in Correagh, Co. Westmeath, *Corr Riabhach*, 'Grey rounded hill'; a ridge, as in Mausrevagh, Co. Galway, *Más Riabhach*, 'Grey ridge'. It can be applied equally to man-made features, including those associated with agriculture, such as a field, as in Gortreagh, Co. Tyrone, *Gort Riabhach*, 'Grey or striped field'. With actual structures, of course, it is very common, as in Castlereagh in Cos Down and Roscommon, *Caisleán Riabhach*, 'Grey castle'.

RINN: Means 'point' or 'promontory' and is common in Irish place-names, particularly, of course, coastal ones. It appears without qualification in several different forms, as Reen in Co. Kerry and as Ring in Co. Waterford; the diminutive form, *Rinnín*, 'Little point', occurs without qualification in Rineen, Co. Clare and Rinneen, Cos Galway and Kerry. Simple qualifications such as Rinmore in Co. Donegal, *Rinn Mhór*, 'Big point', or *Rinn Fhada*, 'Long point', as in Ringfad, Co. Down, are common. Sometimes the shape of the point or promontory is described, as in Ringcurran, Co. Cork, *Rinn Chorráin*, 'Point of the sickle';

sometimes the location is described, as in Rindown, Co. Roscommon, *Rinn Dúin*, 'Point of the fort', or Rineanna, Co. Clare, *Rinn Eanaigh*, 'Point of the marsh'. The name can be dictated by reference to natural occupants of a promontory, as in Ringrone, Co. Cork, *Rinn Róin*, 'Seal point'. It is a term which occurs very frequently in minor names.

Rivers and Streams: The names of the major rivers are among the oldest and earliest of the place-names of Ireland. It has even been suggested that many of them are 'not Celtic at all and go back to a time long anterior to the Celtic invasion'. Be that as it may, it is, however, clear that many of the major river-names are associated with pagan beliefs. The river Boyne, for example, has been shown to mean 'Cow-white (goddess)', *Bóinn*; the rivers Bann, one in Ulster and one in Leinster, to mean 'Goddess', *Banna*; the river Bandon to be derived from the same word and also to mean 'Goddess'; and the greatest of them all, the river Shannon, *Sionainn*, to mean 'Ancient goddess'. In what appears to be descending order of size, the terms used for rivers and streams in Irish place-names are *Abha(inn)*, *Sruth(án)*, *Glaise/Glaisín* and *Feadán*.

ROS: Is an awkward word since it has two separate meanings. The first meaning is 'promontory', which can usually be identified by the simple question of whether or not a promontory exists. In The Rosses, *Na Rosa*, a series of promontories patently does, so there is little problem; in Rosbeg, Co. Donegal, which actually stands on a small headland, one can assume it to be *Ros Beag*, 'Little promontory'. Rosmuck, Co. Galway also stands on a promontory, so there should be little difficulty in deeming its meaning to be 'Pig promontory',

Ros Muc. With Roscrea, Co. Tipperary we would have misgivings were it not for the fact that we know that St Cronan founded a monastery on a promontory jutting into a lake then known as *Loch Cré*, after which the promontory was known as *Ros Cré*, and the name obviously refers to 'Promontory of (Lough) Cré'. Again with Ross Carbery, Co. Cork, we know that the place was originally known as *Ros Ailithir*, 'Pilgrim's promontory', after a pilgrim known as Colman; it should manifestly be *Ros Ó gCairbre*, 'Uí Chairbre's promontory'. With Rosslare, Co. Wexford again there is no problem; the name is obviously *Ros Láir*, 'Middle promontory'.

The other meaning of *ros* is 'grove', and unfortunately there is no easy way of determining whether a grove did previously exist; the palpable absence of a promontory would be a useful indicator. This seems satisfactorily to be the case with Roslea, Co. Fermanagh, so we can accept *Ros Liath* as meaning 'Grey grove'; Rossinan, Co. Kilkenny likewise appears to be lacking in a promontory, so we can accept that *Ros Fhíonáin* does mean 'Finian's grove'.

RUADH: Is an adjective meaning 'red', particularly a browny red or 'russet'; it is commonly Anglicised as 'roe'. It can be applied to natural features such as mountains, as in Slieveroe, Co. Kilkenny, *Sliabh Rua*, 'Red mountain', or promontories, as in Ardroe, Co. Galway, *Aird Rua*, 'Red point'. It can also be applied to man-made features, as in Balroe, Co. Westmeath, *Baile Rua*, 'Russet homestead', or Capparoe, Co. Kerry, *Ceapaigh Rua*, 'Russet plot'; or even to churches, as in Kilroot, Co. Antrim, *Cill Ruaidh*, 'Church of the red place'.

SCARBH: Means 'shallow ford' and appears without qualification as Scarriff, Cos Clare, Cork and Galway, as Scariff in Co. Kerry, and as Skerriff in Co. Armagh. A simply qualified form is to be found in Scarnageeragh in Co. Monaghan, *Scarbh na gCaorach*, 'Shallow ford of the sheep'. A sort of collective form, *Scarbhach*, 'Abounding in shallow fords', appears as Scarva, Co. Down.

SCEACH: Is the word for a hawthorn. Not surprisingly it features fairly frequently in Irish place-names, usually as Skeagh, in Cos Antrim, Cavan, Cork, Donegal, Down, Fermanagh, Kildare, Laois, Monaghan, Roscommon and Tipperary; Skea, in Cos Fermanagh and Tyrone; Skagh, in Cos Cork and Limerick; and Ska, in Skahard, Co. Limerick, *Sceach Ard*, 'High thorn'. Skeaghmore, Co. Westmeath is simply *Sceath Mhór*, 'Large hawthorn', while Skenarget in Co. Tyrone, *Sceath an Airgid*, 'Hawthorn of the silver', presents a lovely vignette of the blossom-laden tree coruscating in the sunlight. It occurs often as a second or qualifying element, as in the simple Ballinaskeagh, Co. Down, *Baile na Sceach*, 'Homestead of the hawthorn'.

SCEIR: Means a 'reef' and is best known in the form of Skerries, Cos Dublin and Antrim, *Sceirí*, 'Reef-islands'. The word is a borrowing from Norse.

SCRÍN: Is derived from the Latin *scrinium*, meaning 'shrine', and is usually Anglicised as 'skreen', as in Skreen, Co. Sligo, or 'screen', as in Screen, Co. Wexford. There is a strong tendency for *scrín*-names to show a connection with Colm Cille. The most illustrious example is Skreen, Co. Meath, which was fully titled *Scrín Choilm Chille*, to which in 878 the shrine of Colm Cille and his relics were transferred from Iona to preserve them from Viking marauders. If this documented instance may be taken as an exemplar of the origin of *scrín*-names in general, it suggests that such names are derived from the fact that the churches in question held important reliquaries and were, therefore, places of pilgrimage and devotional ritual. Ballynascreen, Co. Derry, 'Homestead of the *scrín*', was also known as *Scrín Cholm Chille*, which implies that some relic of the saint had been preserved there. Skreen in Co. Sligo, itself allegedly founded by Colm Cille himself, was known as *Scrín Adhamhnáin*; here had been deposited the reliquary of Adhamhnán, a seventh-century abbot of Iona and the biographer of Colm Cille. Of the seven other instances of *scrín* as a first element in place-names, without further qualification, all but one are in the northern part of the country. Unfortunately, early documentation for these names is lacking, but the probability is that most, at least, relate to pre-Reform sites, distinguished by their possession of a venerated shrine.

SEAN: Means 'old', 'ancient'. In compound formations it precedes the noun it qualifies and consequently appears quite commonly as the initial element in place-names, sometimes referring to natural features, as in Shanrahan, Co. Tipperary, *Seanraithean*, 'Old ferny place'; Shanagolden, Co. Limerick, *Seanghualainn*, 'Old shoulder'; Shanahoe, Co. Laois or Shanco, Co. Monaghan, in both of which it represents *Seanchua*, 'Old hollow'; Shanvaus, Co. Leitrim, where it represents *Seanmhás*, 'Old plain'. More often, however, it is used to qualify human artefacts, such as in Shanagarry, Co. Cork, *Seangharraí*, 'Old garden'; Shanbally, Co. Cork,

Seanbhaile, 'Old homestead'; Shankill, in Cos Antrim and Dublin, whcre it represents *Seanchill,* 'Old church'. Shanragh, Co. Laois is *Seanráth,* 'Old fort', while Santry, Co. Dublin, is *Seantreabh,* 'Old dwelling'. In these human contexts it may mean 'disused', 'abandoned', 'in ruins'.

MAP

SCRÍN as sole or first element in the names of parishes and townlands; (1) represents the name of a parish, (2) the name of a townland.

● 1 ★ 2

SEISCEANN: Is one of the many words in Irish for a swamp or marsh; it is Anglicised most commonly as 'seskin', 'seskan' or 'seskan'. It occurs throughout the country: sometimes without further qualification as in Seskin, Co. Tipperary; sometimes with very simple qualification as in

Seskinore, Co. Tyrone, *Seisceann Mhór*, 'Big swamp'; or dramatically qualified as in Sheskinshule, Co. Tyrone, *Seisceann Siúil*, 'Moving swamp'. Occasionally the qualification gives some information about the botanical make-up of the swamp, as in Sheskinatawy, Co. Donegal, *Seisceann an tSamhaidh*, 'Swamp of the sorrel'.

Seskan: See SEISCEANN

Seskin: See SEISCEANN

Shan: See SEAN

Sheskin: See SEISCEANN

SLIABH: Is the standard Irish term for a 'mountain', occasionally in the sense of 'mountain-land', and is usually Anglicised as 'slieve'. It does not appear without a qualifying element. The simplest of these are descriptive adjectives, as in Slievemore, Co. Tyrone, *Sliabh Mór*, 'Big mountain', or Slieveroe, Co. Kilkenny, *Sliabh Rua*, 'Red mountain'; sometimes nouns, as in Slieve League, Co. Donegal, *Sliabh Liag*, 'Mountain of flagstones', or Slieveardagh, in Cos Kilkenny and Tipperary, *Sliabh Ardachaidh*, 'Mountain of the high field'. Sometimes the weather conditions pertaining to the mountain dictate its name, as in Slieve Gamph, in Cos Mayo and Sligo, *Sliabh Gamh*, 'Mountain of storms', or, perhaps figuratively, in Slieve Snaght, Co. Donegal, *Sliabh Sneachta*, 'Mountain of snow'. Women seem to have influenced the naming of some mountains, as in Slievenamon, Co. Tipperary, *Sliabh na mBan*, 'Mountain of the women', and Slieve na Calliagh, Co. Meath, *Sliabh na Calliagh*, 'Mountain of the hag'. Some have quite intriguing names: the Glanaruddery Mountains in Cos Laois and Carlow are *Sléibhte Ghleann an Ridire*, 'Mountains of the valley of the knight', and the Derrynasaggart Mountains in Cork and

Kerry are *Sléibhte Dhoire na Sagart,* 'Mountains of the oak-grove of the priests'. Many of them, however, are identified by the names of people: Slieve Donard, Co. Down, *Sliabh Domhangairt,* 'Domhangart's mountain', takes its name from St Domhangart, who founded a monastery at nearby Maghera. Often *sliabh* is itself the qualifying element, as in Killeavy, Co. Armagh, *Cill Shléibhe,* 'Church of the mountain'.

SPIDÉAL: Simply means 'hospital' and occurs in several place-names throughout the country, appearing as Spiddal in Cos Galway and Meath. In the old name of Spittaltown, Co. Westmeath, it is found as *Baile an Ospidéil,* 'Town of the hospital'. In Co. Cork it appears in Ballinspittle, 'Mouth of the ford of the hospital', *Béal Átha an Spidéil.*

SRÁID: Means 'street', not merely in the sense of a 'passage between houses', but also in the sense (as it is still used in some districts in English) as 'the area in front of or round a house'. It is Anglicised usually as 'straid', as in unqualified examples of Straid in Cos Antrim, Donegal and Mayo; less often as 'street', as in Street, Co. Westmeath. In the compound Stradbally, *Sráidbhaile,* 'Street-town', it appears regularly as 'strad', with examples in Cos Kerry, Laois and Waterford.

SRATH: Basically means 'valley-bottom', or a 'flat place', e.g. beside a river or lake, a 'holm'. It is Anglicised 'srah', as in Srah, Co. Mayo, or Srahmore, *Srath Mór,* 'Large holm', also in Co. Mayo; or as 'stra', in Strabane, Co. Tyrone, *Srath Bán,* 'White holm', or in Stranorlar, Co. Donegal, *Srath an Urláir,* 'Holm of the (valley) floor'.

SRUTH: Is the basic word for 'stream' and occurs without qualification as Srue, Co. Galway, Sruh, Co. Waterford and Shrough, Co. Tipperary. Its diminutives and derivatives occur even more frequently: Shrule, Co. Mayo and Struell, Co. Down are unqualified examples of *Sruthail*, and Shroughan, Co. Wicklow and Stroan in Cos Antrim, Cavan and Kilkenny are similar examples of *Sruthán*. All these terms appear in more complex names: Ballystrew, Co. Down, is *Baile Sruth*, 'Homestead of the stream', as is Ballyshrule, Co. Galway, *Baile Sruthail*, while Stranmillis, Co. Antrim, is *Sruthán Milis*, 'Sweet stream', with reference to the point at which the stream became tidal and until which it remained sweet.

Stra:	See SRATH
Stra(i)d:	See SRÁID
Street:	See SRÁID
SUÍ(DHE):	Literally means a 'seat' and is usually qualified by a personal name. One example frequently encountered is Seefin, which occurs in, for example, Cos Cork, Down, Mayo and Waterford, and as Sheefinn in Co. Westmeath. It represents *Suí Finn*, 'Fionn's seat', the Fionn in question being the legendary Fionn Mac Cumhail, one of the most celebrated figures in Irish myth or legend. In Seadavog, Co. Donegal the 'seat' is ascribed to St Davog and there exists a palpable stone chair which is identified as the actual *suidhe*. In Shinrone, Co. Offaly, *Suí an Róin*, the zoological unlikelihood of a seal's requiring a seat so many miles from the sea – for the name means 'Seat of the seal' – is explained by the suggestion that in this instance *rón* refers not to an actual seal, but metaphorically to a hairy person. In Co. Antrim Sineirl appears, with the suggested interpretation of *Suí an Iarla*, 'Seat of the earl'.

T

TAMHLACHT: To all appearances this term denoted a burial-site of pagan, rather than Christian, association – often it is construed as 'plague-burial'; it is usually Anglicised as 'tamlaght', 'tamlat' or 'tawlaght'. It is an early word, attested mainly in place-names, with little significant documentation as a lexical item in Irish writing. It does occur in two versions of *Táin Bó Cúailnge*, as *Tamlachta Órláim*, 'Órlám's burial-place' – actually the place where he met his death at the hands of Cú Chulainn.

As a place-name element it appears surprisingly often in the names of early ecclesiastical sites. In this context its outstanding occurrence is as Tallaght, Co. Dublin, which was formerly known by the fuller name of *Tamhlacht Maolruáin*, an important monastery founded by Maolruain in 769. There was an important earlier Bronze Age cemetery in the vicinity. It has been argued that the siting of the monastery here was a conscious attempt to impose the Christian stamp on a site which had previously had strong pagan associations, an argument which might be extended to the term's occurrence in the names of other ecclesiastical foundations. Generally, as a modern place-name, it appears simply as Tamlaght, without qualification. It is of most frequent occurrence in the North of Ireland, with Co. Derry having the highest incidence. Of the six instances of *tamhlacht*-names in Co. Derry, four are documented early church-sites. Of these, Tamlaght O'Crilly bears the later qualification of the name of the erenaghs, or hereditary tenants and keepers of the church lands, while Tamlaght Finlagan bears the name of the founding saint, Fionnlugh, brother of St Fiontan and a disciple of Colm Cille. While there is not documented evidence that *all* names containing the term *tamhlacht* refer to ecclesiastical sites, it is possible that local tradition may show that they are likely to be such.

MAP **TAMHLACHT** as a sole or first element in the names of parishes and townlands; apart from one outlier in Co. Dublin it is confined to the northern part of the country. (1) represents a parish-name, (2) a townland-name.

● 1 ✱ 2

TAMHNACH: Is generally construed as a 'cultivated spot' or 'arable spot', often in otherwise unproductive land; 'kindly spot' is frequently used in areas where such spots occur. Its use increases towards the northern parts of Ireland. It is Anglicised in several different ways: 'tamney', as in Tamney, Co. Donegal, *Tamhnaigh*; 'tawnagh', as in Tawnalahan, Co. Donegal, *Tamhnach Lahan*, 'Broad field'; 'tawny', as in Tawnyeely, Co. Leitrim, *Tamhnaigh Aelaigh*, 'Field of the lime'; or 'tamnagh', as in Tamnaghbane, Co. Armagh, *Tamhnach Bán*, 'White field'. It appears that in some examples a personal name more recent than that of the original place-name has been added to signify ownership, as in Tamnyrankin, Co. Derry.

Tamn(e)y: See TAMHNACH

Tawna/y: See TAMHNACH

TEACH: Basically means 'house' but in place-names frequently is used of a saint's house, i.e. a 'church', especially in earlier compositions, where the *teach*-element is usually followed by a personal name. Examples of this use are common: Timahoe, Co. Laois, *Tigh Mochua*, 'Mochua's house', from the fact that a monastery was founded here by St Mochua, who died in 657; similarly Timoleague, Co. Cork, takes its name, *Tigh Molaige*, 'Molaga's house', from the fact that here St Molaga, a disciple of St David of Wales, founded a monastery. Timolin, Co. Kildare, takes its name, *Tigh Moling*, from St Moling; Tyrella, Co. Down, *Teach Riala*, from St Riail; and, of course, Tedavnet, Co. Monaghan, *Tigh Damhnata*, from St Davnet. In the Anglicisation process of the Anglo-Norman period the Anglicised form is often preceded by an 's', resulting in such names as Seagoe, Co. Armagh, in reality *Teach Daghobha*, 'Dagobha's house'; Stamullen, Co. Meath, in reality *Teach Maolin*, 'Maolin's house'; and Stillorgan, Co. Dublin, for *Teach Lorgan*, 'Lorcan's house'. The most droll example of this process is to be seen in St John's Point, Co. Down, where *Tigh Eoin*, 'John's house', became Anglicised early as 'Styoun', resulting, rightly, but in a roundabout way, as St John. In later name-formations such as Tinnakilla, Co. Wexford, *Tigh na Coille*, 'House of the wood', *teach* has reverted to its secular sense, while in Ticloy, Co. Antrim, where the *teach* in question is a neolithic portal tomb, the name *Tigh Cloiche*, 'House of stone', is not merely secular but tenderly antiquarianising.

TEAMPALL: Is derived from the Latin *templum* and means 'church'; in place-name formations it is Anglicised as 'temple' and is of frequent occurrence both as a townland-name and as a parish-name. For the most part it represents a church, frequently a parish church, of the post-Reform period. In annalistic records of post-twelfth-century date it is the term most commonly used of 'church', although *eaglais* is occasionally used. *Teampall* frequently appears with a dedication to one of the great saints of the Roman calendar, such as Michael, as in Templemichael, in Cos Cork and Wicklow, or Martin, in Templemartin, Co. Wexford. Dedications to Irish saints are not infrequent: Temple Brendan occurs in Co. Mayo and Templecronan in Co. Clare. Templepatrick is quite a common dedication, in Templepatrick, Caher Island, Co. Mayo and a parish in Co. Antrim. Simple descriptive qualifications occur as well, as in Templemoyle, Co. Mayo, *Teampall Maol*, 'Bald church', possibly indicating that the building was in ruinous condition; Templenakilla, Co. Kerry, *Teampall na Cille*, 'Church of the church', suggesting, possibly,

MAP   **TEAMPALL** as a first element in the names of parishes and
townlands; it is fairly widespread throughout the country.

that a post-Reform church was located on the
site of an earlier church; or Templefinn, Co.
Down, *Teampall Fionn*, 'White church'. While most
of the *teampall*-names, particularly those with
Anglicised forms, appear to relate to
foundations of the post-Reform period, there
are indications that *teampall* may have been in
use as a name-element in the pre-Reform era,
especially in the west of Ireland, with reference
to small, stone-built churches or oratories such
as *Teampall Mhic Dhuach*, dedicated to St Colmán
Mac Duach, on Inishmore, and *Teampall
Chaomháin*, close to which is St Caomhán's
grave, on Inisheer in the Aran Islands.

TEARMANN: Is derived from the Latin *terminus* and is applied to 'the lands of a church or monastery within which the rights of sanctuary prevailed', usually Anglicised as 'termon'. It has survived into modern Irish usage in the sense of 'sanctuary' or 'refuge'. Often it appears in place-names simply as Termon, with examples in Cos Cavan and Donegal. In Termonfeckin, Co. Louth, *Tearmann Feichín*, it is qualified by the name of its founder in the sixth century, St Feichín of Cong, Co. Mayo and Fore, Co. Westmeath. As a place-name, *tearmann* appears to cover not merely the monastic enclosure but the entire territorial extent of the adjoining monastic lands. As a result of this broadening of its scope it often appears as the initial element in names of parishes, such as Termonaguirk, Co. Tyrone, which was originally *Tearmann Cumaing*, after the patron saint, St Cumaing; here the original qualifying name has been replaced in the parish-name by the name of the associated erenagh family, that of the hereditary tenants and keepers of the parish land. Where *tearmann* survives in a place-name the reference seems to be to a pre-Reform foundation.

Temple: See TEAMPALL

Termon: See TEARMANN

THEAS: Means 'south' or 'southern' and appears in place-names most frequently in contrast to *thuaidh*.

THUAIDH: Means 'north' or 'northern' and appears in place-names most frequently to distinguish between two adjacent townlands bearing the same name, possibly as a result of a subdivision; its correlative is *Theas*. Thus Derrygarrane North, Co. Kerry is *Doire an Ghearráin Thuaidh*, while Derrygarrane South, Co. Kerry, is *Doire an Ghearráin Theas*. It is an alternative device to the use of *uachtar* and *íochtar*, 'upper' and 'lower'.

MAP   **TEARMANN** as an element, usually qualified, in the names of townlands; it is confined to the north-western part of the country.

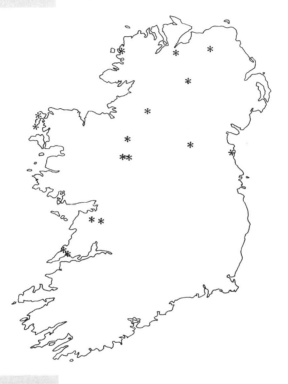

TIGH: See TEACH

TIOBRAID: Is another word for 'fountain', 'well' or 'spring'. It is Anglicised in several different fashions. The best-known instance of this element is, of course, Tipperary, town and county, *Tiobraid Árann*, 'Well of Ára', after the ancient territory in which the town is situated. It appears without qualification in Tubbrid, in Cos Kerry, Kilkenny and Tipperary; as 'tubbert' in Ballintubbert, Co. Laois, *Baile na Tiobrad*, 'Homestead of the well', and as 'tibret' in Clontibret, Co. Monaghan, *Cluain Tiobrad*, 'Pasture of the well'.

TÍR: Means broadly 'country', 'land', 'territory', and 'the people' of any of these concepts. It is a remarkable term in Irish place-names since it is applied to every size of land-division in the country, from provinces, through counties, baronies and parishes down to townlands, the smallest administrative unit recognised. (As *Tír Gaedheal* it is even used in the sense of 'Ireland'.) Of the names of the provinces it appears in three, where the eponymous population name – U*ladh* in the case of Ulster, M*umu* in the case of Munster, and L*aighin* in the case of Leinster – has been awarded a Norse possessive 's' followed by *tír*. Of the counties of Ireland only one, County Tyrone, *Tír Eoghain*, 'Eoghan's territory', retains *tír* as its initial element; *Tír Conaill*, named after Eoghan's brother Conall, has been supplanted as the county name by *Dún na nGall*, 'Fort of the foreigners', after the town of that name, which, ironically, is not even the administrative centre of the county. *Tír* also appears in the names of baronies, the largest unit into which counties were divided, as in the barony of Tirawley in Co. Mayo, *Tír Amhalghaidh*, 'Amhalghaidh's territory', or Tireragh in Co. Sligo, *Tír Fhiachrach*, 'Fiachra's territory'. As the name of a parish – a unit which has virtually become obsolete as a civil division, though it remains, of course, as an ecclesiastical one – the best-known, albeit obscured, instance of *tír* is in Terryglass, Co. Tipperary, which is *Tír dá Glas*, 'Territory of two streams' – conjuring up visions of an Irish Mesopotamia on a small scale. As an element in the names of townlands it is not quite so markedly northern: it appears in Tirboy, Co. Galway, *Tír Buí*, 'Yellow territory', and in Tirnamona, Co. Monaghan, *Tír na Móna*, 'Territory of the bog'.

MAP   **TÍR** as a first element in the names of counties, formerly to
Co. Donegal and still to Co. Tyrone; of baronies: (1)
Tirkeecon, Co. Derry; (2) Tirhugh, Co. Donegal; (3)
Tirkennedy, Co. Fermanagh; (4) Tirerill, Co. Sligo; (5)
Tireragh, Co. Sligo; (6) Tirawley, Co. Mayo; of parishes (the
larger symbols) and townlands (the simple stars).

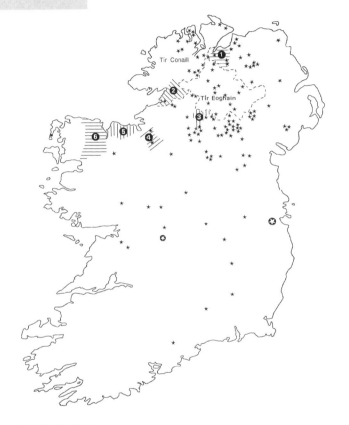

TOBAR: Means quite simply 'well', 'spring', 'source', and
is usually Anglicised in place-names as 'Tober'
or 'Tubber'. It is fairly widespread throughout
the country and often appears without
qualification: for example, as Tober, Co. Cavan
or Tubber, Co. Galway, each meaning simply
'well'. Sometimes it is graced with an indication
of its size or importance, as Tobermore, Co.

Derry, *Tobar Mór*, 'Big well'. Sometimes the description is more graphic, as in Tobercurry, Co. Sligo, *Tobar an Choire*, 'Well of the cauldron'; sometimes more evaluative, as in Toberbunny, Co. Dublin, *Tobar Bainne*, 'Well of milk', presumably as an indication of the sweetness of the water. The common name-form Toberavilla, as in an example from Co. Kerry, is *Tobar an Bhile*, 'Well of the sacred tree'. In this instance the well had also been known as *Tobar Crócháin*, 'St Cróchán's well', for sometimes a well with a reputation as a 'holy well' carries the name of the saint with which it is associated, as with Tobarmacdugh, at Keelhilla, Co. Galway, *Tobar Mhic Dhuach*, from Colman Mac Duach, whose hermitage was there; similarly Toberbreedy, in Co. Cork, is a well dedicated to St Bríd. The place-name Toberdoney, common throughout the country, is a well that is visited *ar an Domhnach*, 'on a Sunday', and, indeed, is often translated as 'Sunday's well'. Sometimes the term itself is the qualifier, as in Ballintober, Co. Roscommon, *Baile an Tobair*, 'Homestead of the well'.

TÓCHAR: Is another word meaning 'causeway' and is relatively common in place-names; it is usually Anglicised as 'Togher' and appears in just this form in Cos Cork, Louth and Offaly. It is not clear what the exact distinction between a *ceis* and a *tóchar* is, though the wickerwork associations of *ceis* suggest that *tóchar* might be the fitting term for the big wooden roadway, two kilometres long, built of great wooden planks laid edge to edge on supporting longitudinal runners to provide a broad, level roadway, found at Corlea, Co. Longford. This section of roadway has been dated precisely by dendrochronology to 148 BC. In contrast to this dating there is a reference in *Annals of Ulster*, in the year AD 1001, to the construction of a *tóchar*: *Tochur Atha Luain la Mael Sechnaill* – 'A causeway was constructed by Mael Sechnall at Athlone'. There are simply qualified forms of the name, as Togherbane, Co. Kerry, *Tóchar Bán*, 'White causeway', and Togherbeg, in Cos Galway and Wicklow, *Tóchar Beag*, 'Little causeway'. As might be expected, habitations are to be found adjacent to such means of communication, as is indicated by Ballintogher, Co. Sligo, *Baile an Tóchair*, 'Homestead of the causeway', while hills, which may have been used as fixed points during the construction of such roadways, are sometimes distinguished by the term, as in Knocktopher, Co. Kilkenny, *Cnoc an Tóchair*, 'Hill of the causeway'.

MAP **TÓCHAR** as a sole or first element in the names of townlands; apart from a few outliers it is virtually confined to the Midlands.

Toom(e):	See TUAIM
TRÁ(IGH):	Means 'strand', 'beach' or 'shore' and figures frequently in place-names throughout the country, usually Anglicised as 'tra', less often as 'traw'. It normally is qualified by some descriptor, even as simple as one indicating its size, as in Tramore, Co. Waterford or Trawmore, Co. Mayo, each representing *Trá Mhór*, 'Big strand'. Sometimes the qualifying word is descriptive of some feature of the strand in question, as in Trafrask, Co. Cork, *Trá Phraisce*, 'Strand of the kale', or its location, as in Tralee, Co. Kerry, *Tráigh Lí*, 'Strand of the (river) Lí', and Tranarossan, Co. Donegal, *Trá na Rosán*, 'Strand of the Rosses'. Often it, in its turn, acts as the qualifier, as in Portballintrae, Co. Antrim, *Port Bhaile an Trá*, 'Port of the homestead of the strand'.
Translated Names:	There are a number of instances throughout the country of names that are to all appearances English names, when, in fact, they are English translations of existing Irish names. The translations were executed with varying degrees of accuracy: Summerbank, Co. Meath is a reasonably close translation of *Droim Samhraidh*, and Silverwood, Co. Armagh of *Coill an Airgid*. Saintfield, Co. Down is a slightly less accurate rendering of *Tamhnach Naomh*; Saintcultivatedspot would be more exact as a translation, but as a place-name would not trip off the tongue so well. Freshford, Co. Kilkenny is a misplaced attempt at translating *Achadh Úr*, as a result of mistaking *achadh* for *átha*, 'field' for 'ford'. Sometimes the name is partially translated, as with Clarinbridge, *Droichead an Chláirín*, Co. Galway, 'Bridge of the little plank'.
TROM:	Is the word for an 'elder-bush' or 'elder-tree'. The best-known place to contain the word in

its name is Trim, Co. Meath, which in modern use retains only this word as a contraction of *Baile Átha Troim*, 'Homestead of the ford of the elder'. A derivative form, *Tromaire*, 'Place where elders grow', is represented by Trummery, Co. Antrim, while a diminutive, *Tromán*, 'Little elder' or 'Little place where elders grow', is to be found in Trumman, Co. Donegal, Tromman, Co. Meath and Tromaun, Co. Roscommon.

TUAIM: In place-names generally describes a 'mound', more often than not a 'burial mound', though rarely, if ever, can the eponymous mound be identified with sufficient certainty to establish what type or age of monument is involved. It is Anglicised in a variety of ways: as Toem in Co. Tipperary; as Toom, also in Co. Tipperary; as Toome in Co. Antrim; and, of course, as Tuam in Co. Galway. It sometimes has a simple descriptive qualifier, as in Toomard, Co. Galway, *Tuaim Ard*, 'High mound'. More often, however, it is qualified by a personal name, as in Tuamgraney, Co. Clare, *Tuaim Gréine*, 'Grian's mound' – but not necessarily the name of the actual or supposed occupant of the burial mound, as Toomyvara, Co. Tipperary demonstrates. *Tuaim Uí Mheára*, 'Ó Meára's mound', was bestowed on the site of a monastery founded by St Donnan in the seventh century only when the wardenship of the Augustinian priory there passed into the hands of the Ó Meára family in the fifteenth century; the change of name from *Teampall*, or *Tuaim Donnáin*, was effected because the Ó Meára family made the priory their place of sepulture. This does, however, indicate that the sense of 'burial' in the term was observed until quite recent times, even if the practice of building actual mounds was not.

TUAR: Is another word basically for 'field', particularly a dry or well-drained field, with a specialised sense of a 'bleach-green', which is the sense conventionally used in place-name translation. It appears without qualification as Tour, Co. Limerick; its diminutive, *Tuairín*, as Tooreen, Co. Mayo. Toormore, Co. Cork is *Tuar Mór*, 'Big bleach-green'. It occurs in other compounds, such as Tooraree, Co. Limerick, *Tuar an Fraoigh*, 'Bleach-green of the heather', and in Co. Kerry as Tooreennafersha, *Tuairín na Feirste*, 'Little bleach-green of the sandbank', and Tooreennahone, *Tuairín na hÓn*, 'Little bleach-green of the hole'. It appears as a qualifying element in names like Ballitore, Co. Kildare, *Béal Átha an Tuair*, 'Mouth of the ford of the bleach-green'. Inevitably some qualifying terms denote ownership, as in Tourmakeady, Co. Mayo, *Tuar Mhic Éadaigh*, 'Mac Éadaigh's bleach-green'.

TUATH: Meant originally a 'population-group' (defined as one capable of maintaining 3,000 soldiers in emergency) and, by extension, the land the group occupied; although it occurs infrequently in modern place-names, the best translation is probably 'district' or 'territory'. It does appear in Tuosist, Co. Kerry, *Tuath Ó Síosta*, 'Territory of the Uí Síosta'. It also occurs in Doe Castle, Co. Donegal, *Caisleán na dTuath*, 'Castle of the territories', because the Mac Sweeny family of that area were known as *na dTuath*, Anglicised as 'Doe'.

TULACH: Means 'hill' and is usually Anglicised as 'tulla', 'tullagh', 'tullow' or 'tully'. It is widespread throughout the country. Without qualification it appears as Tulla, Co. Clare, Tullagh, Co. Donegal, Tullow, Co. Carlow and Tully, Co. Galway. There is a diminutive, *Tulachán*, meaning 'Hillock', which appears as

Tullaghan, in Cos Leitrim and Sligo. There are the usual simple qualifiers, as in Tullamore, in Cos Kerry and Offaly, *Tulach Mhór*, 'Big hill', though Tullaghanmore, Co. Westmeath, *Tulachán Mór*, 'Big hillock', seems almost to offend the law of excluded middle. There is a Tullaherin, Co. Kilkenny, *Tulach Thirim*, 'Dry hill'; a Tullakeel, *Tulach Chaoil*, in Co. Kerry; and a Tullyallen, Co. Louth, *Tulach Álainn*, 'Lovely hill'. There are compounds in which relationship of the hill to another landmark is described: Tullycrine, Co. Limerick, *Tulach an Chrainn*, 'Hill of the tree', and Tulrahan, Co. Mayo, *Tulach Shrutháin*, 'Hill of the stream'.

Tully: See TULACH

TURLACH: Is a term applied to those areas of land, often beside rivers, which are liable to flood in winter but dry out, at least partially, in summer. Possibly 'fen' is the most appropriate translation; 'lake', or even 'winter lake', should be avoided, since the suffix -*lach* is deceptively similar to *loch*, with which it has no connection. It is not very common in place-names, but does occur in Co. Mayo as Turlough, and as Turloughmore in Co. Galway, *Turlach Mór*, 'Large fen'. It is also found in Co. Roscommon in the compound Ballinturly, *Baile an Turlaigh*, 'Homestead of the fen'.

U

UACHTAR: Means 'upper' and although it appears in its own right in place-names occasionally, as in Oughterard, Co. Kildare, *Uachtar Ard*, 'Upper height', or Kilwaughter, Co. Antrim, *Cill Uachtar*, 'Upper church', it is more frequently employed in place-names, often contrasting with *íochtar*, 'lower', to distinguish between two adjacent places with the same name, perhaps two portions of a townland that has been divided.

UAMA/UAIMH: Are two forms of a term meaning 'cave', 'cavern' or even 'souterrain', a kind of artificial cave. It appears with surprising frequency in place-names. Drumahoe, Co. Derry and Drumnahoe in Cos Antrim and Tyrone are all *Droim na hUamha*, 'Ridge of the cave'. Ballywee, Co. Antrim is *Baile Uaimh*, 'Homestead of the caves' – in this instance, however, the 'caves' are certainly souterrains, an amazing complex of which exists there. Rather surprisingly, Mullinahone, Co. Tipperary, is *Muileann na hUamhan*, 'Mill of the cave'.

UARÁN/FUARÁN: Both mean 'spring', 'cooling bath', the first form being more common in place-names. It appears unqualified in Oran, Co. Roscommon, and with the minimum qualification in Oranmore, Co. Galway, *Uarán Mór*, 'Big spring'. It appears also in more complex place-names such as Knockanoran in Cos Laois and Cork, *Cnoc an Uaráin*, 'Hill of the spring'; Carrickanoran in Cos Kilkenny and Monaghan, *Carraig an Uaráin*, 'Rock of the spring'; Mullinoran in Co. Westmeath, *Muileann Fhuaráin*, 'Mill of the spring'.

UBHALL: See ABHALL

UISCE: Is the general word for 'water' and, since water is usually in abundant supply in Ireland, it appears fairly often in Irish place-names, most frequently as a qualifying element. Ballyhisky, Co. Tipperary, for example, is *Bealach Uisce*, 'Pass of water'; Killisky, Co. Wicklow, is *Cill Uisce*, 'Church of water'; while Ballisk, Co. Dublin is *Baile Uisce*, 'Homestead of water'. Its appearance in names like Lissaniska, Cos Cork and Kerry, *Lios an Uisce*, 'Fort of the water', has been discussed under *Lios*.

LIST OF NAMES AND INDEX

In this section, names of counties have been abbreviated to save space; the system used is based on that for motor-vehicle registrations in the Republic of Ireland, but with modifications, not merely those necessary to cover the six counties of Northern Ireland. The abbreviations are as follows:

AH	ARMAGH
AM	ANTRIM
C	CORK
CE	CLARE
CN	CAVAN
CW	CARLOW
D	DUBLIN
DL	DONEGAL
DN	DOWN
DY	DERRY
FH	FERMANAGH
G	GALWAY
KE	KILDARE
KK	KILKENNY
KY	KERRY
L	LIMERICK
LD	LONGFORD
LH	LOUTH
LM	LEITRIM
LS	LAOIS
MH	MEATH
MN	MONAGHAN
MO	MAYO
OY	OFFALY
RN	ROSCOMMON
SO	SLIGO
TE	TYRONE
TY	TIPPERARY
WD	WATERFORD
WH	WESTMEATH
WX	WEXFORD
WW	WICKLOW

A

ABBEYDORNEY	KY (*Mainistir Ó dTorna*): Abbey of Uí Thorna, pp 119
ABBEYFEALE	L (*Mainistir na Féile*): Abbey of the (river) Feale
ABBEYLARA	LD (*Mainistir Leath Ráth*): Abbey of the half ring-fort
ABBEYLEIX	LS (*Mainistir Laoise*): Abbey of Laois, p. 106
ABBEYSHRULE	LD (*Mainistir Shruthla*): Abbey of the stream
ABINGTON	L (*Mainistir Uaithne*): Abbey of (the district of) Uaithne + town
ACHONRY	SO (*Achadh Conaire*): Field of Conaire, p. 12
ACLARE	SO (*Áth an Chláir*): Ford of the plain
ADARE	L (*Áth Dara*): Ford of the oak, p. 67
ADERAVOHER	SO (*Eadar dhá Bhóthair*): Place between two roads
ADRIGOLE	C (*Eadar Ghabhal*): Place between a fork
ADRIVALE	C (*Eadar Ghabhal*): Place between a fork
AGHA	CW (*Achadh*): Field, p. 12
AGHABOE	LS (*Achadh Bhó*): Field of the cow(s), pp 12, 31
AGHABOG	MN (*Achadh Bog*): Soft field, p. 12
AGHABRACK	WH (*Achadh Breac*): Speckled field
AGHABULLOGUE	C (*Achadh Bolg*): Field of the bulges, p. 12
AGHACASHEL	LM (*Achadh an Chaisil*): Field of the stone fort, p. 12
AGHACOMMON	AH (*Achadh Camán*): Hurling field
AGHADA	C (*Achadh Fada*): Long field, p. 12
AGHADARRAGH	TE (*Achadh Darach*): Field of the oak-tree, p. 67
AGHADAUGH	WH (*Achadh Damh*): Field of the oxen
AGHADOE	KY (*Achadh dá Eo*): Field of two yews
AGHADOWEY	DY (*Achadh Dubhthaigh*): Field of Dubhthach, p. 12
AGHADOWN	C (*Achadh Dúin*): Field of the fort
AGHAFATTEN	AM (*Achadh Pheatan*): Field of pets
AGHAGALLON	TE & AM (*Achadh Gallán*): Field of the standing stone, p. 89
AGHAGOWER	MO (*Achadh Fhobair*): Field of the spring
AGHALANE	FH (*Achadh Leathan*): Broad field, p. 12
AGHAMORE	MO (*Achadh Mór*): Big field, p. 12
AGHANACLIFF	LH (*Schadh na Cloiche*): Field of the stones
AGHANLOO	DY (*Áthán Lú*): Lú's small ford
AGHATUBRID	KY (*Achadh Tiobraid*): Field of the well
AGHAVANNAGH	WW (*Achadh Bheannach*): Hilly field
AGHAVEA	FH (*Achadh Beithe*): Birch field, p. 30
AGHAVOE	LS (*Achadh Bhó*): Ford of the cow(s), p. 31
AGHAWONEY	DL (*Achadh Mhóna*): Field of the bog

AGHER	MH (Achair): Space
AGHERN	C (Áth Chairn): Ford of the cairn
AGHERY LOUGH	DN (Loch Eachraí): Lake of the horses
AGHINVER	FH (Achadh Inbhir): Field of the river-mouth
AGHLEAM	MO (Eachléim): Horse-leap
AGHLISH	KY (Eaglais): Church, p. 80
AGHNABOHY	WH (Achadh na Boithe): Field of the huts
AGHNAHILY	LS (Achadh na hAille): Field of the cliff
AGHNASKEAGH	LH (Achadh na Scéithe): Field of the shields
AGHOWLA	L (Achadh Abhla): Field of the apple-tree, p. 11
AGHOWLE	L & WW (Achadh Abhla): Field of the apple-tree, pp 11, 12
AGHYARAN	TE (Achadh Uí Áráin): Field of the Uí Árán
AGHYOWLE	FH (Achadh Abhla): Field of the apple-tree, p. 12
AGIVEY	DY (Áth Geimhe): Ford of the roaring water
AGLISH	WD (Eaglais): Church, p. 80
AGOLA	AM (Áth Gobhlach): Ford of the fork
AHAFONA	KY (Áth an Phóna): Ford of the pound
AHAKISTA	KY (Áth an Chiste): Ford of the box or chest
AHALIA LOUGH	G (Loch an tSáile): Lake of the salt water
AHASCRAGH	G (Áth Eascrach): Ford of the gravel-ridge, p. 83
AHENNY	TY (Áth Thine): Ford of the fire
AHOGHILL	AM (Áth Eochaille): Ford of the yew-wood, p. 84
AILLE	CE & MO (Aille): Cliffs, p. 13
AILLENAVEAGH	G (Aill na Bhfiach): Ravens' cliff
ALLIHIES	C (Ailichí): Cliff-fields, p. 13
ALLOW RIVER	C (Abhainn Alla): River of (the district of) Ealla
ALTAGOWLAN	RN (Alt an Ghabhláin): Hillside of the fork, p. 15
ALTAMUSKIN	TE (Alt na Múscán): Hillside of the loose clay
ALTAN LOUGH	DL (Loch Ealtan): Lake of the flocks
ALTAN	DL (Altán): Little height, p. 15
ALTAVILLA	L (Alt a' Bhile): Hillside of the ritual tree, p. 15
ALTINURE	DY & CN (Alt an Iúir): Height of the yew-tree, p. 15
ALTISHAHANE	TE (Alt Inse Uí Chatháin): Hillside of the island of Uí Chatháin
ALTNAMACHIN	AH (Alt na Meacan): Hillside of the root-vegetables
ALTNAVEAGH	TY (Alt na Bhfiach): Hillside of the ravens
ALTORE	RN (Altóir): Altar
ANASCAUL	KY (Abhainn an Scáil): River of the phantom
ANKAIL	KY (Eing Caol): Narrow strip
ANNABELLA	C (Eanach Bile): Marsh of the sacred tree, p. 81
ANNACARTY	TY (Áth na Cairte): Ford of the cart
ANNACLONE	DN (Eanach Cluana): Marsh of the pasture

ANNACLOY	DN (*Áth na Cloiche*): Ford of the stone
ANNACOTTY	L (*Áth an Choite*): Ford of the boat
ANNACURRAGH	WW (*Eanach Churraigh*): Marsh of the bog
ANNADUFF	LM (*Eanach Dubh*): Black marsh, p. 81
ANNAGASSAN	LH (*Áth na gCasán*): Ford of the paths
ANNAGH	MO (*Eanach*): Marsh
ANNAGHDOWN	G (*Eanach Dúin*): Marsh of the fortress
ANNAGHMORE	AH, LS & OY (*Eanach Mór*): Big marsh
ANNAHILT	DN (*Eanach Eilte*): Marsh of the doe, p. 81
ANNAKISHA	C (*Áth na Cise*): Ford of the wicker causeway
ANNALEE RIVER	CN (*Abhainn Eanach Lao*): River of the marsh of the calf
ANNALONG	DN (*Áth na Long*): Ford of the ships
ANNALORE	MN (*Áth na Lobhar*): Ford of the leper
ANNAMOE	WW (*Áth na mBó*): Ford of the cows
ANNAVEAGH	MN (*Áth na Bhfiada*): Ford of the deer
ANTRIM	AM (*Aontraim*): One holding
ANYALLA	MN (*Eanaigh Gheala*): White marshes
Aonach Áine	p. 128
Aonach Tailtean	MH, p. 16
ARANMORE	DL (*Árainn Mhór*): Large ridge, p. 17
ARAN ISLANDS	G (*Árainn* + Islands): Ridge (islands), p. 17
ARBOE	TY (*Aird Bó*): Cow promontory, pp 14, 31
ARDAGH	L & LD (*Ardachadh*): High field, pp 13, 17
ARDAGHY	MN (*Ardachadh*): High field, pp 13, 17
ARDAKILLEN	RN (*Ard an Choillín*): Height of the little wood
ARDANLEAGH	L (*Ardán Liath*): Little grey height
ARDARA	DL (*Ard an Rátha*): Height of the fort, p. 17
ARDARAGH	DN (*Ard Darach*): Height abounding in oaks, p. 17
ARDATTIN	CW (*Ard Aitinn*): Height of the gorse, p. 17
ARDAVAGGA	OY (*Ard a' Mhagaidh*): Height of merriment
ARDBALLYMORE	WH (*Ardbhaile Mór*): Big high homestead
ARDCATH	MH (*Ard an Chatha*): Height of the battle
ARDCOLM	WX (*Ard Coilm*): Height of Colm
ARDCRONY	TY & WX (*Ard Cróine*): Cróine's height
Ardd Senlis	Height of the old fort, p. 112
ARDEE	LH (*Baile Átha Fhirdhia*): Ferdia's ford
ARDEEN	C & KY (*Ardín*): Small height
ARDERIN	LS & OY (*Ard Éireann*): Éire's height, p. 18
ARDFERT	KY (*Ard Fhearta*): Height of the grave, pp 18, 87
ARDFIELD	C (*Ard Ó bhFicheallaigh*): Height of Uí Fhicheallach
ARDFINNAN	TY (*Ard Fhíonáin*): Fíonán's height
ARDGARVAN	DY (*Ard Garbháin*): Garbhán's height, p. 18
ARDGIVNA	SO (*Ard Goibhne*): Height of the smith

ARDGLASS	C (Ard Glas): Grey/green height, pp 13, 92
ARDGLASS	DN (Aird Ghlais): Grey/green point, pp 13, 92
ARDGROOM	C (Dhá Dhrom): Two ridges
ARDINGARY	DL (Ard an Ghaire): Height of shouting
ARDIVAGHAN	WH (Ard Uí Mhocháin): Ó Mochán's height
ARDKEARAGH	KY (Ard Caorach): Height of sheep
ARDKEEN	DN (Ard Caoin): Pleasant height
ARDLEA	LS (Ard Liath): Grey height
ARDLOUGHER	CN (Ard Luachra): Height of the rushes, p. 17
ARDMILLAN	DN (Ard an Mhuilinn): Height of the mill, p. 18
ARDMORE	AH, DY, G, MO & WD (Aird Mhór): Big point, pp 13, 17
ARDMORE	KY & WH (Ard Mhór): Big height
ARDMORNEY	WH (Ard Murnaigh): Morna's height
ARDNACROHY	L (Ard na Croiche): Height of the gallows
ARDNACRUSHA	CE (Ard na Croise): Height of the cross
ARDNAGLUG	WH (Ard na gClog): Height of the bell
ARDNAGROGHERY	C (Ard na gCrochaire): Height of the hangman
ARDNAMOGHILL	DL (Ard na mBouchail): Height of the boys
ARDNAPREAGHAUN	L (Ard na bPréuchán): Height of the crows
ARDNAREE	MO (Ard na Ria): Height of the executions
ARDNURCHER	WH (Áth an Urchair): Ford of the cast
ARDPATRICK	L (Ard Pádraig): Patrick's height, p. 18
ARDRAHAN	G (Ard Rathain): Height of ferns, pp 17, 132
ARDROE	G (Aird Rua): Red point, pp 13, 138
ARDS	DN (Aird): Point/peninsula, p. 13
ARDSCULL	KE (Ard Scol): Height of schools
ARDSHEELANE	KY (Ard Síoláin): Height of Síolán
ARDSTRAW	TE (Ard Sratha): Height of the river-holm
ARDTOLE	DN (Ard Tuathail): Tuathal's height
ARDTREA	TE (Ard Tré): Tré's height
ARGIDEEN RIVER	C (Airgidín): Silver (river)
ARKLOW	WW: See NORSE NAMES, p. 125
ARLESS	LS (Ardlios): High fort, p. 19
ARMAGH	AH (Ard Macha): Macha's height/Height of the plain, p. 18
ARMOY	AM (Oirthear Maí): The east of the plain
ARRA MOUNTAIN	TY (Sliabh Ára): Mountain of the district of Ára
ARRYHEERNABIN	DL (Áirí Thír na Binne): Shieling of the country of the peak
ARTICLAVE	DY (Ard an Chléibh): Height of the wicker, p. 18
ARTIFERRALL	AM (Ard Tighe Fearghaill): Height of Fearghal's house
ARTIGARVAN	TE (Ard Tí Garbháin): Height of Garbhán's house
ARTNAGROSS	AM (Ard na gCros): Height of the cross

ARVAGH	CN (A*rmhach*): Battlefield
ASDEE	KY (|*Caisleán*| E*asa Duibhe*): (Stone fort of) the dark waterfall
ASKAMORE	WX (E*asca Mhór*): Big bog, p. 82
ASKANAGAP	WW (E*asca na g*C*eap*): Bog of the stumps, p. 82
ASKEATON	L (E*as Géitine*): Géitine's waterfall, p. 82
ASSAROE	DL (E*asa Rua*): Red waterfall, p. 82
ASSOLUS	C (Á*th Solais*): Ford of light
ASTEE	KY (|*Caisleán*| E*asa Duibhe*): (Stone fort of) the dark waterfall
ATHBOY	MH (|*Baile*| Á*tha Buí*): Yellow ford, p. 19
ATHCARNE	MH (Á*th Chairn*): Ford of the cairn
ATHEA	L (Á*th an t*S*léibhe*): Ford of the mountain
ATHENBOY	WH (A*iteann Buí*): Yellow gorse
ATHENRY	G (|*Baile*| Á*tha an Rí*): Ford of the kings, p. 19
ATHGARVAN	KE (Á*th Garbháin*): Garbhán's ford
ATHGREANY	WW (Á*th Gréine*): Gréine's ford
ATHLACCA	L (Á*th Leacach*): Ford abounding in flagstones, pp 19, 106
ATHLEAGUE	RN (Á*th Liag*): Ford of the boulders, p. 19
ATHLONE	WH (Á*th Luain*): Luan's ford, p. 18
ATHNID	TY (Á*th Nid*): Ford of the nest
ATHY	KE (Á*th Í*): Í's ford
ATTANAGH	LS (Á*th Tanaí*): Shallow ford
ATTATANTEE	DL (Á*it a' t*S*ean Tighe*): Place of the old house, p. 14
ATTICAL	DN (Á*it Tí Chathail*): Place of Cathal's house, p. 14
ATTICONOR	WH (Á*it Tí Chonuir*): Place of Conor's house
ATTYMACHUGH	MO (Á*it Tí Mhic Aodha*): Place of Mac Aodha's house, p. 14
ATTYMASS	MO (Á*th Tí Uí Mheasaigh*): Place of the house of Ó Measaigh
ATTYMON	G (Á*th Tiomáin*): Tiomán's ford
AUCLOGGEEN	G (Á*th Cloigín*): Ford of the little bell
AUGHAFATTEN	AM (A*chadh Pheatan*): Field of the pets
AUGHAGALLON	AM (A*chadh Gallánach*): Field of the standing stones
AUGHALL	TY (E*ochaill*): Yew-wood
AUGHAMORE	LM (A*chadh Mór*): Large field
AUGHAMULLEN	TE (A*chadh Uí Mhaoláin*): Ó Maolán's field
AUGHER	TE (E*ochair*): The brink
AUGHIL	DY (E*ochaill*): Yew-wood
AUGHINISH	G & L (E*achinis*): Horse island
AUGHNACLOY	TE (A*chadh na Cloiche*): Field of the stone, pp 12, 55
AUGHNAGOMAUN	TY (A*chadh na g*C*omán*): Hurling field

AUGHNAHOY	AM (Achadh na hÁithe): Field of the kiln
AUGHNAMULLEN	MN (Achadh na Muileann): Field of the mills, p. 12
AUGHNANURE	G (Achadh an Iúr): Field of the yew
AUGHNASHEELAN	LM (Achadh na Síleann): Field of the withies
AUGHRIM	G & WW (Eachdhroim): Horse-ridge
AUGHRIS	SO (Eachros): Horse promontory
AUGHVOLYSHANE	TY (Áth Bhuaile Sheáin): Ford of Seán's milking-place
AVAGHON LOUGH	MN (Loch an Mheatháin): Lake of the saplings
AVALBANE	MN (Abhall Bán): White orchard
AVANBEG	WW (Abhainn Bheag): Little river, pp 11, 27
AVONMORE	C, SO & WW (Abhainn Mhór): Big river, p. 11
AWBEG	C & L (Abha Bheag): Little river, p. 11
AYLE	MO (Aill): Cliff, p. 13

B

Baile Átha Cliath	Ford of the hurdles, pp 15, 19
Baile Uí Comgain	Homestead of the Ó Comgain family, p. 21
Baile Uí Uidrin	Homestead of the Ó Uidrin family, p. 21
BALBANE	DL (*Baile Bán*): White homestead
BALBORU	CE (*Béal Boromha*): Mouth of the (river) Borumha
BALBRIGGAN	D (*Baile Brigín*): Brigín's homestead
BALDOYLE	D (*Baile Dhúghall*): Homestead of Dúghall
BALFEDDOCK	LH (*Baile Feadóg*): Homestead of the plover
BALLA	MO (*Balla*): Spring
BALLACOLLA	LS (*Baile Cholla*): Colla's homestead
BALLADIAN	MN (*Bealach an dá Éan*): Pass of the two birds
BALLAGAN POINT	LH (*Gob Bhaile Uí Ágáin*): Point of the homestead of Ó Ágán
BALLAGH	FH, G, L & TY (*Bealach*): Pass, p. 28
BALLAGHADERREEN	RN (*Bealach an Doirín*): Pass of the little oak-grove, p. 28
BALLAGHANERY	DN (*Bealach an Aoire*): Pass of the shepherd
BALLAGHKEEN	WX (*Bealach Caoin*): Smooth pass, p. 28
BALLAGHMOON	CW (*Bealach Mughna*): Mughan's pass
BALLANAGARE	RN (*Béal Átha na gCarr*): Mouth of the ford of the carts
BALLANRUAN	CE (*Baile an Ruáin*): Homestead of the mystery
BALLARD	OY (*Baile Ard*): High homestead
BALLEEN	KY (*Bailín*): Little homestead
BALLICKMOYLER	LS (*Baile Mhic Mhaoilir*): Homestead of Mac Maolir
BALLINA	MO & TY (*Béal an Átha*): Mouth of the ford
BALLINABOY	G (*Béal Átha na Bá[ighe]*): Mouth of the ford of the bay
BALLINABRACKEY	MH (*Buaile na Bréamhaí*): Milking-place of the wolf-plain
BALLINABRANAGH	CW (*Baile na mBreatnach*): Homestead of Breatnaigh
BALLINACARRIGA	C (*Béal na Carraige*): Mouth of the rocks
BALLINACARROW	SO (*Baile na Cora*): Homestead of the weir, p. 60
BALLINACLASH	WW (*Baile na Claise*): Homestead of the ravine, p. 54
BALLINACLASHET	C (*Baile na Claise*): Homestead of the ravine, p. 54
BALLINACLOUGH	TY (*Baile na Cloiche*): Homestead of the stone
BALLINACOR	WW (*Baile na Cora*): Homestead of the weir
BALLINACURRA	C & L (*Baile na Cora*): Homestead of the weir, p. 60
BALLINADEE	C (*Baile na Daibhche*): Homestead of the well

BALLINAFAD	SO (*Béal an Átha Fada*): Mouth of the long ford, p. 26
BALLINAFID	WH (*Baile na Feide*): Homestead of the end
BALLINAGAR	OY (*Béal Átha na gCarr*): Mouth of the ford of the carts
BALLINAGH	CN (*Béal Átha na nEach*): Mouth of the ford of the horse
BALLINAGLERAGH	LM (*Baile na gCléireach*): Homestead of the clerics
BALLINAGORE	WH (*Béal Átha na nGabhar*): Mouth of the ford of the goat
BALLINAGREE	C (*Baile na Groighe*): Homestead of the stud
BALLINAHINCH	TY (*Baile na hInse*): Homestead of the water-meadow
BALLINAHOWEN	WH (*Buaile na hAbhann*): Milking-place of the river, p. 11
BALLINAKILL	LS (*Baile na Coille*): Homestead of the wood, p. 21
BALLINALACK	WH (*Béal Átha na Leac*): Mouth of the ford of the flagstones, p. 106
BALLINALEA	WW (*Buaile na Lao*): Milking-place of the calves, pp 26, 36
BALLINALEE	LD (*Béal Átha na Lao*): Mouth of the ford of the calves
BALLINAMALLARD	FH (*Béal Átha na Mallacht*): Mouth of the ford of the curses
BALLINAMARA	KK (*Baile na Marbh*): Homestead of the dead
BALLINAMEEN	RN (*Béal an Átha Mín*): Mouth of the smooth ford, p. 120
BALLINAMONA	C (*Baile na Móna*): Homestead of the bog, p. 123
BALLINAMORE	DL, G & LM (*Béal an Átha Móir*): Mouth of the big ford
BALLINAMUCK	LD (*Béal Átha na Muc*): Mouth of the ford of the pigs
BALLINAMULT	WD (*Béal na Molt*): Mouth of the wether
BALLINARD	TY (*Baile an Aird*): Homestead of the height
BALLINASCARTY	C (*Béal na Scairte*): Mouth of the thicket
BALLINASCORNY	D (*Baile na Scórnad*): Homestead of the gullet
BALLINASKEAGH	DN (*Baile na Sceach*): Homestead of the thorns, p. 139
BALLINASLOE	G (*Béal Átha na Sluaighe*): Mouth of the ford of the hostings
BALLINASPICK	WD (*Baile an Easpaig*): Homestead of the bishop, p. 21
BALLINATTIN	TY & WD (*Baile na Aiteann*): Homestead of the gorse, p. 14
BALLINCHALLA	MO (*Baile an Chaladh*): Homestead of the landing-place, p. 42
BALLINCLASHET	C (*Baile na Claise*): Homestead of the ravine, p. 54

BALLINCLOHER	KY (*Baile an Cloichir*): Homestead of the stony place
BALLINCOLLIG	C (*Baile an Chollaigh*): Homestead of the boar
BALLINCREA	KK (*Baile an Chraoibh*): Homestead of the sacred tree
BALLINCURRIG	C (*Baile an Churraigh*): Homestead of the marsh, p. 61
BALLINDAGGAN	WD (*Baile an Daingin*): Homestead of the fortress
BALLINDANGAN	C (*Baile an Daingin*): Homestead of the fortress
BALLINDARRAGH	FH (*Baile na Dara*): Homestead of the oak
BALLINDERREEN	G (*Baile an Doirín*): Homestead of the little oak-grove
BALLINDERRY	AM & TY (*Baile an Doire*): Homestead of the oakwood
BALLINDINE	MO (*Baile an Daingin*): Homestead of the fortress, p. 67
BALLINDRAIT	DL (*Béal an Droichid*): Mouth of the bridge, p. 74
BALLINEA	WH (*Béal an Átha*): Mouth of the ford
BALLINEDDAN	WW (*Baile an Fheadáin*): Homestead of the streamlet
BALLINEEN	C (*Béal Átha Fhinín*): Mouth of the ford of Finín
BALLINENAGH	L (*Baile an Aonaigh*): Homestead of the assembly
BALLINFULL	SO (*Baile an Phoill*): Homestead of the pool, p. 130
BALLINGADDY	L (*Baile an Ghadaí*): Homestead of the thief
BALLINGAR	OY (*Béal Átha na gCarr*): Mouth of the ford of the carts
BALLINGARRANE	L (*Baile an Gharráin*): Homestead of the grove, p. 90
BALLINGARRY	L & TY (*Baile an Gharraí*): Homestead of the garden, p. 91
BALLINGEARY	C (*Béal Átha Ghaorthaidh*): Mouth of the ford of the wooded valley
BALLINGLEN	WW (*Baile an Ghleanna*): Homestead of the valley
BALLINGRANE	L (*Baile an Gharráin*): Homestead of the shrubbery, p. 90
BALLINGURTEEN	C (*Baile an Ghoirtín*): Homestead of the little tilled field
BALLINHASSIG	C (*Béal Átha an Cheasaigh*): Mouth of the ford of the wicker causeway, p. 49
BALLINKILLEEN	CW (*Baile an Chillín*): Homestead of the little church
BALLINLEENY	L (*Baile an Laighnigh*): Homestead of Ó Leighin
BALLINLOUGH	MH & RN (*Baile an Locha*): Homestead of the lake
BALLINLUG	G (*Baile an Loig*): Homestead of the hollow
BALLINLUSKA	C (*Baile an Loiscthe*): Homestead of the burnt ground
BALLINODE	MN (*Béal Átha an Fhóid*): Mouth of the ford of the sod
BALLINRAN	DN (*Baile an Rathain*): Homestead of the rushes
BALLINRIDDERRA	WH (*Baile an Ridire*): Homestead of the knight
BALLINROBE	MO (*Baile an Róba*): Town of the (river) Róba
BALLINSKELLIGS	KY (*Baile an Sceillig*): Homestead of the rocks

BALLINSPITTLE	C (*Béal Átha an Spidéil*): Mouth of the ford of the hospital, p. 143
BALLINTAGGART	AH, DN & KY (*Baile an tSagairt*): Homestead of the priest
BALLINTANNIG	C (*Baile an tSeanaigh*): Homestead of the fox
BALLINTEEAN	MO (*Baile a' tSiodháin*): Homestead of the fairy hill
BALLINTEER	DY & D (*Baile an tSaoir*): Homestead of the craftsman
BALLINTEMPLE	C (*Baile an Teampaill*): Homestead of the church
BALLINTLIEVE	DN & MH (*Baile na tSléibhe*): Homestead of the mountain, p. 24
BALLINTOBER	MO & RN (*Baile an Tobair*): Homestead of the well, p. 154
BALLINTOGHER	SO (*Baile an Tóchair*): Homestead of the causeway, p. 155
BALLINTOY	AM (*Baile na Tuaighe*): Homestead of the *tuath*
BALLINTRA	DL (*Baile an tSratha*): Homestead of the holm
BALLINTRILLICK	SO (*Béal Átha an Trí Liag*): Mouth of the ford of the three flags
BALLINTUBBER	MO & RN (*Baile an Tobair*): Homestead of the well
BALLINTUBBERT	LS (*Baile na Tiobrad*): Homestead of the well, p. 151
BALLINTURLY	RN (*Baile an Turlaigh*): Homestead of the fen, p. 159
BALLINUNTY	TY (*Baile an Fhontaigh*): Font's homestead
BALLINURE	G & TY (*Baile an Iúir*): Homestead of the yew
BALLINVANA	L (*Baile an Bhána*): Homestead of the green field
BALLINVINNY	C (*Baile an Mhuine*): Homestead of the thicket
BALLINVONEAR	C (*Baile an Mhóinéir*): Homestead of the meadow
BALLINWULLY	RN (*Baile an Mhullaigh*): Homestead of the summit
BALLISK	D (*Baile Uisce*): Homestead of the water, p. 161
BALLISODARE	SO (*Baile Easa Dara*): Homestead of the waterfall of the oak
BALLITORE	KE (*Béal Átha an Tuair*): Mouth of the ford of the bleach-green, p. 158
BALLIVOR	MH (*Baile Íomhair*): Íomhar's homestead
BALLOUGHMORE	LS (*Bealach Mór*): Big pass
BALLOUGHTER	WX (*Baile Uachtair*): Upper homestead
BALLYAGRAN	L (*Béal Átha Grean*): Mouth of the ford of the gravel
BALLYALLAGHT	AM (*Baile Uí Allachta*): Homestead of Ó Allacht
BALLYALLINAN	L (*Baile Uí Áilleanáin*): Homestead of Ó hÁilleanáin
BALLYALTON	DN (*Baile Altúin*): Altoun's homestead
BALLYANDREEN	C (*Baile Aindrín*): Aindrín's homestead

BALLYANNE	WX (*Baile Anna*): Anna's homestead
BALLYARDLE	DN (*Baile Ardghall*): Homestead of the high standing stone
BALLYAUGHLIS	DN (*Baile na hEachlaisce*): Homestead of the whip
BALLYBAY	MN (*Béal Átha Beithe*): Mouth of the ford of the birch, p. 30
BALLYBEG	TY (*Baile Beag*): Small homestead, p. 25
BALLYBODEN	D (*Baile Baodáin*): Beodan's homestead
BALLYBOFEY	DL (*Bealach Féich*): Fiach's pass
BALLYBOGEY	AM (*Baile an Bhogaigh*): Homestead of the swamp
BALLYBOGHIL	D (*Baile Bachaille*): Homestead of the crosier
BALLYBOUGHT	AM (*Baile Bocht*): Poor homestead, p. 24
BALLYBOY	OY (*Baile Átha Buí*): Homestead of the yellow ford, p. 36
BALLYBOYLAND	AM (*Baile Uí Bhaolláin*): Homestead of Ó Baollán
BALLYBRACK	D, KY & TE (*Baile Breac*): Speckled homestead, pp 26, 33
BALLYBRITTAS	LS (*Baile Briotáis*): Homestead of the wooden palisade
BALLYBROOD	L (*Baile Bhrúid*): Homestead of the ashes
BALLYBROPHY	LS (*Baile Uí Bhróithe*): Homestead of Ó Bróithe
BALLYBUNION	KY (*Baile an Bhuinneánaigh*): Buinneán's homestead
BALLYCAHILL	TY (*Bealach Achaille*): Pass of Achall
BALLYCALLAN	KK (*Baile Uí Challáin*): Homestead of Ó Calláin
BALLYCANEW	WX (*Baile Uí Chonnmhaí*): Homestead of Ó Connmhaí
BALLYCARNAHAN	KY (*Baile Uí Chearnacháin*): Ó Cearnacháin's homestead
BALLYCARNY	WX (*Baile Uí Chearnaigh*): Homestead of Ó Cearnaigh
BALLYCARRA	MO (*Baile Cora*): Homestead of the weir, p. 60
BALLYCARRY	AM (*Baile Cora*): Homestead of the weir, p. 60
BALLYCASHIN	WD (*Baile Uí Chaisín*): Ó Caisín's homestead
BALLYCASSIDY	FH (*Baile Uí Chaiside*): Ó Caiside's homestead
BALLYCASTLE	AM (*Baile an Chaisleáin*): Town of the castle
BALLYCASTLE	MO (*Baile an Chaisil*): Homestead of the stone fort
BALLYCLARE	AM (*Bealach Cláir*): Pass of the plain, pp 26, 54
BALLYCLERAHAN	TY (*Baile Uí Chléireacháin*): Homestead of Ó Cléireacháin
BALLYCLERY	G (*Baile Uí Chléirigh*): Homestead of Ó Cléirigh
BALLYCLOGH	C (*Baile Cloch*): Homestead of the stones
BALLYCOMMON	OY & TY (*Baile Uí Chomáin*): Homestead of Ó Comán
BALLYCONNEELY	G (*Baile Conaola*): Homestead of Conaola

BALLYCONNELL	CN (*Béal Átha Conaill*): Mouth of the ford of Conall
BALLYCONREE	G (*Baile Con Raoi*): Homestead of Cúrí
BALLYCOOGE	WW (*Baile Chuag*): Homestead of the cuckoo
BALLYCORICK	CE (*Béal Átha Chomhraic*): Mouth of the ford of the confluence, p. 59
BALLYCOTTON	C (*Baile Choitín*): Coitín's homestead
BALLYCRADDOCK	WD (*Baile Chreadóig*): Homestead of the clay
BALLYCRISSANE	G (*Baile Crosáin*): Homestead of the cross
BALLYCROGHAN	DN (*Baile Cruacháin*): Homestead of the rick
BALLYCROSSAUN	G (*Baile Crosáin*): Homestead of the cross
BALLYCROY	MO (*Baile Chruaich*): Homestead of the rick
BALLYCULLANE	WX (*Baile Uí Choileáin*): Ó Coileáin's homestead
BALLYCULTER	DN (*Baile Uí Choltair*): Ó Coltar's homestead
BALLYCUMBER	OY (*Béal Átha Chomair*): Mouth of the ford of the confluence, p. 59
BALLYDAHEEN	C (*Baile Dáithín*): Dáthín's homestead
BALLYDANGAN	RN (*Baile Daingean*): Homestead of the stronghold
BALLYDAVID	G (*Baile Dháibhí*): Dóibhí's homestead
BALLYDAVID	KY (*Baile Dháith*): Dáith's homestead
BALLYDEHOB	C (*Béal Átha dá Chab*): Mouth of the ford of two openings
BALLYDESMOND	C (*Baile Deasmhumhna*): Town of south Munster
BALLYDONEGAN	C (*Baile Uí Dhonnagáin*): Ó Donnagáin's homestead
BALLYDONOHOE	KY (*Baile Uí Dhonnchadha*): Ó Donnchadha's homestead
BALLYDOOLEY	RN (*Baile Uí Dhúlaoich*): Homestead of Ó Dulach
BALLYDUFF	KY & WD (*Baile Dubh*): Black homestead
BALLYDUFF	WD (*Baile Uí Dhuibh*): Ó Duibh's homestead
BALLYDUGAN	DN (*Baile Uí Dhugáin*): Ó Dugán's homestead
BALLYEASTON	AM (*Baile Uistin*): Austin's homestead
BALLYEIGHTER	CE (*Baile Íochtair*): Lower homestead
BALLYENGLAND	L (*Baile an Aingleontaigh*): Aingleontach's homestead
BALLYFARNA	MO (*Baile Fearnach*): Homestead of the alder
BALLYFARNAN	RN (*Béal Átha Fearnáin*): Mouth of the ford of the alders, p. 87
BALLYFEARD	C (*Bealach Feadha Aird*): Pass of the high wood, p. 28
BALLYFERIS	DN = Perestoun, p. 24
BALLYFERMOT	D (*Baile Thormaid*): Homestead of Thormund, p. 125
BALLYFERRITER	KY (*Baile Feirtéaraigh*): Feirtéar's homestead
BALLYFIN	LS (*Baile Fionn*): White homestead, p. 88

BALLYFORAN	RN (*Béal Átha Feorainne*): Mouth of the ford of the brink
BALLYFORE	OY (*Baile Fuar*): Cold town
BALLYFOUNDER	DN = Punyerstoun, p. 24
BALLYFOYLE	KK (*Baile an Phoill*): Homestead of the pool, p. 130
BALLYGAR	G (*Béal Átha Ghártha*): Mouth of the ford of the garden
BALLYGARRETT	WX (*Baile Ghearóid*): Gearóid's homestead
BALLYGARVAN	C (*Baile Garbháin*): Garbhán's homestead
BALLYGAWLEY	SO & TE (*Baile Uí Dhálaigh*): Ó Dálaigh's homestead
BALLYGINNIFF	AM (*Baile Gainimh*): Sandy homestead, p. 24
BALLYGLASS	MO (*Baile Glas*): Grey/green homestead, p. 92
BALLYGLASS	WH (*Béal Átha Glas*): Mouth of the ford of the streams
BALLYGLUNIN	G (*Béal Átha Glúinín*): Mouth of the ford of the little bend
BALLYGOMARTIN	AM (*Baile Gharraí Mháirtín*): Homestead of Martin's garden, p. 91
BALLYGOREY	KK (*Baile Guaire*): Guaire's homestead
BALLYGORMAN	DL (*Baile Uí Ghormáin*): Ó Gormán's homestead
BALLYGOWAN	DN (*Baile Mhic Ghabhann*): Mac Gabhann's homestead
BALLYGRAINEY	DN (*Baile na Gréine*): Homestead of the sun
BALLYGUB	KK (*Baile Gob*): Homestead of the snout
BALLYHACK	WX (*Baile Chac*): Homestead of excrement
BALLYHACKAMORE	DN (*Baile Hacamar*): Homestead of the dung-stand
BALLYHAGHT	L (*Baile an Chéachta*): Homestead of the plough
BALLYHAHILL	L (*Béal Átha dhá Thuile*): Mouth of the ford of two floods
BALLYHAISE	CN (*Béal Átha hÉis*): Mouth of the ford of the track
BALLYHALBERT	DN (*Baile Thalbóid*): Talbot's homestead
BALLYHALE	KK (*Baile Héil*): Howel's homestead
BALLYHAR	KY (*Baile Uí Achir*): Ó hAichir's homestead
BALLYHEAN	MO (*Béal Átha hÉin*): Mouth of the ford of the bird
BALLYHEERIN	DL (*Baile Uí Shírín*): Ó Sírín's homestead
BALLYHEIGE	KY (*Baile Uí Thaidg*): Ó Taidhg's homestead
BALLYHISKY	TE (*Bealach Uisce*): Pass of water, p. 160
BALLYHOOLY	C (*Baile Átha Ubhla*): Mouth of the ford of the apple-trees, p. 11
BALLYHORNAN	DN (*Baile Uí Fhearnáin*): Ó Fearnáin's homestead
BALLYHOURA	C & L (*Bealach Abhradh*): Pass of Feabhra
BALLYHUGH	CN (*Bealach Aodha*): Aodh's pass
BALLYJAMESDUFF	CN (*Baile Shéamais Dhuibh*): Homestead of James Duff

BALLYKEAN	OY (*Baile Uí Chéin*): Ó Céin's homestead
BALLYKEEL	DN (*Baile Caol*): Narrow homestead, pp 24, 25, 42
BALLYKEERAN	WH (*Bealach Caorthainn*): Pass of the rowan-tree
BALLYKELLY	DY (*Baile Uí Cheallaigh*): Ó Ceallaigh's homestead
BALLYKILBEG	DN (*Baile na gCeall Beag*): Homestead of the small church, p. 51
BALLYKILLARE	DN (*Baile Cille Láir*): Homestead of the central church
BALLYKINLER	DN (*Baile Coinnleora*): Homestead of the candlesticks
BALLYKINSELLA	WD (*Baile an Chinsealaigh*): Ó Cinsealaigh's homestead
BALLYKNOCKAN	WW (*Buaile an Chnocáin*): Milking-place of the hillock, p. 36
BALLYLANDERS	L (*Baile an Londraigh*): de Londra's homestead
BALLYLANEEN	WD (*Baile Uí Laithnín*): Ó Laithnín's homestead
BALLYLAR	DL (*Baile Láir*): Homestead of the threshing floor
BALLYLESSON	DN (*Baile Leasáin*): Homestead of the fort, p. 24
BALLYLICKEY	C (*Béal Átha Lice*): Mouth of the ford of the flagstone
BALLYLIFFIN	DL (*Baile Lifín*): Homestead of the halfpenny
BALLYLINAN	LS (*Baile Uí Laigheanáin*): Ó Laigheanán's homestead
BALLYLONGFORD	KY (*Béal Átha Longphoirt*): Mouth of the ford of the fortress, pp 117, 130
BALLYLOOBY	TY (*Béal Átha Lúbaigh*): Mouth of the ford of the winding (river)
BALLYLOUGHBEG	AM (*Baile an Locha Beag*): Homestead of the small lake
BALLYLUMFORD	AM (*Baile Longphoirt*): Homestead of the fortress, p. 24
BALLYLYNAN	S (*Baile Uí Laigheanáin*): Ó Laigheanán's homestead
BALLYMACARBRY	WD (*Baile Mhac Cairbre*): Mac Carbre's homestead
BALLYMACARRET	DN (*Baile Mhic Ghearóid*): Mac Gearóid's homestead
BALLYMACART	WD (*Baile Mhac Airt*): Mac Art's homestead
BALLYMACAW	WD (*Baile Mhic Dháith*): Mac Dáith's homestead
BALLYMACELLIGOTT	KY (*Baile Mhic Eileagóid*): Mac Eileagód's homestead
BALLYMACKEY	TY (*Baile Uí Mhacaí*): Ó Macaí's homestead
BALLYMACODA	C (*Baile Mhac Óda*): Mac Códa's homestead
BALLYMACONNELLY	AM (*Baile Mhic Conaíle*): Mac Conaíle's homestead
BALLYMACURLY	RN (*Baile Mhic Thoirdhealaigh*): Mac Thoirdhealaigh's homestead
BALLYMACWARD	G (*Baile Mhic an Bhaird*): Homestead of Mac an Bhard
BALLYMADOG	C (*Baile Mhadóg*): Madóg's homestead
BALLYMAGAN	DL (*Baile Mhic Cionaoith*): Mac Cionaoith's homestead
BALLYMAGARRY	AM (*Baile mo Gharraí*): Homestead of my garden, p. 24
BALLYMAGORRY	TE (*Baile Mhic Gofraidh*): Mac Gofraidh's homestead

BALLYMAGUIGAN	DY (*Baile Mhic Ghuigín*): Mac Guigan's homestead
BALLYMAHON	LD (*Baile Uí Mhatháin*): Ó Matháin's homestead
BALLYMAKEERY	C (*Baile Mhic Íre*): Mac Íre's homestead
BALLYMANUS	WH (*Baile Mhánais*): Homestead of Mánas
BALLYMARTIN	DN (*Baile Mhic Ghiolla Mhártain*): Homestead of Mac Giolla Mhártain
BALLYMARTLE	C (*Baile Mhairtéal*): Mairtéal's homestead
BALLYMASCANLAN	LH (*Baile Mhic Scanláin*): Mac Scanlán's homestead
BALLYMENA	AM (*Baile Meánach*): Middle homestead, p. 26
BALLYMOE	G & RN (*Béal Átha Mó*): Mouth of the ford of Mogh
BALLYMONEY	AM (*Baile Monaidh*): Homestead of the bog, p. 123
BALLYMOON	CW (*Baile Móin*): Homestead of the bog
BALLYMORE	C, DL, KE & WH (*Baile Mór*): Big homestead
BALLYMORRIS	WD (*Baile Mhuiris*): Muiris's homestead
BALLYMOTE	SO (*Baile an Mhóta*): Homestead of the castle-mound, p. 25
BALLYMOYLE	WW (*Baile Maol*): Bald homestead
BALLYMULLEN	KY (*Baile an Mhuilinn*): Homestead of the mill, p. 123
BALLYMURN	WX (*Baile Uí Mhurúin*): Ó Murúin's homestead
BALLYMURPHY	CW (*Baile Uí Mhurchú*): Ó Murchú's homestead
BALLYMURRAGH	L (*Baile Mhurchadha*): Murchadh's homestead
BALLYMURRAY	RN (*Baile Uí Mhuirigh*): Ó Muireadhaigh's homestead
BALLYNABOLA	WX (*Baile na Buaile*): Homestead of the milking-place
BALLYNABRACKEY	MH (*Buaile na Bréamhaí*): Milking-place of the wolf-plain, p. 36
BALLYNACALLY	CE (*Baile na Caillí*): Homestead of the hag
BALLYNACARGY	WH (*Baile na Carraige*): Homestead of the rock
BALLYNACARRIGA	C (*Béal na Carraige*): Mouth of the rock
BALLYNACARRIGY	WH (*Baile na Carraige*): Homestead of the rock
BALLYNACLOGH	TY (*Baile na Cloiche*): Homestead of the stone, p. 55
BALLYNACOLE	C (*Baile Niocóil*): Niocól's homestead
BALLYNACORR	AH (*Baile na Cora*): Homestead of the weir
BALLYNACORRA	C (*Baile na Cora*): Homestead of the weir
BALLYNACOURTY	WD (*Baile na Cúirte*): Homestead of the mansion
BALLYNADRUMNY	KE (*Baile na Droimne*): Homestead of the ridge
BALLYNAFA	KD (*Baile na Faiche*): Homestead of the green, p. 85
BALLYNAFEIGH	DN (*Baile na Faiche*): Homestead of the green, pp 21, 85
BALLYNAFEY	AM (*Baile na Faiche*): Homestead of the green, p. 85
BALLYNAFID	WH (*Baile na Feide*): Homestead of the runnel

BALLYNAFIE	AM (*Baile na Faiche*): Homestead of the green, p. 85
BALLYNAGARRICK	DN (*Baile na Carraige*): Homestead of the rock, p. 45
BALLYNAGAUL	WD (*Baile na nGall*): Homestead of the stones
BALLYNAGEERAGH	DN (*Baile na gCaorach*): Homestead of the sheep, p. 24
BALLYNAGORE	WH (*Béal Átha na nGabhar*): Mouth of the ford of the goats
BALLYNAGREE	C (*Baile na Graí*): Homestead of the stud
BALLYNAGUILKEE	WD (*Baile na Giolcaí*): Homestead of the reeds
BALLYNAHATINNA	(*Baile na hAitinn*): Homestead of the gorse, p. 14
BALLYNAHATTEN	DN & LH (*Baile na hAitinn*): Homestead of the gorse, p. 14
BALLYNAHINCH	DN, G & TY (*Baile na hInse*): Homestead of the holm, p. 100
BALLYNAHOW	KY (*Baile na hAbha*): Homestead of the river, p. 12
BALLYNAHOWN	G & WH (*Buaile na hAbhann*): Milking-place of the river, pp 12, 36
BALLYNAHOWEN	WH (*Buaile na hAbhann*): Milking-place of the river, p. 12
BALLYNAKILL	CW (*Baile na Cille*): Homestead of the church
BALLYNAMEEN	DY (*Baile na Míne*): Homestead of the smooth place
BALLYNAMONA	C (*Baile na Móna*): Homestead of the bog
BALLYNAMULT	WD (*Baile na Muilt*): Homestead of the wether
BALLYNANTY	L (*Baile Uí Neachtain*): Ó Neachtan's homestead
BALLYNASCREEN	DY (*Baile na Scrín*): Homestead of the shrine, p. 140
BALLYNASHANNAGH	DL (*Baile na Seanach*): Homestead of the fox
BALLYNASKREENA	KY (*Baile na Scríne*): Homestead of the shrine
BALLYNEAL	TY (*Baile Uí Néill*): Ó Néill's homestead
BALLYNEANOR	TE (*Baile an Aonfhir*): Homestead of the lone man
BALLYNEASE	DY (*Baile Naois*): Naoise's homestead
BALLYNEETY	L (*Baile an Fhaoitigh*): de Faoite's homestead
BALLYNEILL	TY (*Baile Uí Néill*): Ó Néill's homestead
BALLYNESS	DY (*Baile an Easa*): Homestead of the waterfall
BALLYNICHOL	DN = Nicholtown, p. 24
BALLYNOE	C (*Baile Nua*): New homestead, p. 126
BALLYNONTY	TY (*Baile an Fhantaigh*): Homestead of the spectre
BALLYNURE	AM (*Baile an Iúir*): Homestead of the yew, pp 24, 25, 101
BALLYORGAN	L (*Baile Uí Árgáin*): Ó hÁrgáin's homestead
BALLYOTE	WH (*Baile Fhóid*): Homestead of the sod
BALLYPATRICK	TY (*Baile Phádraig*): Pádraig's homestead

BALLYPHEHANE	C (*Baile Féitheán*): Homestead of the osiers
BALLYPHILIP	DN = Phylippestown, p. 24
BALLYPHILIP	WD (*Baile Philib*): Philip's homestead
BALLYPOREEN	TY (*Béal Átha Póirín*): Mouth of the ford of the round stones
BALLYQUIN	WD (*Baile Uí Choinn*): Ó Coinn's homestead
BALLYQUIRK	TY (*Baile Uí Chuirc*): Ó Cuirc's homestead
BALLYRAGGET	KY (*Béal Átha Ragad*): Mouth of the ford of the churl
BALLYRAWER	DN (*Baile Ramhar*): Fat homestead
BALLYREE	DN (*Baile an Fhraoigh*): Homestead of the heather
BALLYROBERT	AM (*Baile Riobaird*): Robert's homestead
BALLYRONAN	DY (*Baile Uí Rónáin*): Ó Rónáin's homestead
BALLYRONEY	DN (*Baile Uí Ruanaí*): Ó Ruanaí's homestead
BALLYROOSKY	DL (*Baile Rusgaidh*): Homestead of the marsh
BALLYSADARE	SO (*Baile Easa Dara*): Homestead of the waterfall of the oak, p. 82
BALLYSAKEERY	MO (*Baile Easa Caoire*): Homestead of the waterfall of the berry
BALLYSALLAGH	DN (*Baile Salach*): Dirty homestead
BALLYSHANNON	DL (*Béal Átha Seanaidh*): Mouth of the ford of the slope
BALLYSHRULE	G (*Baile Sruthail*): Homestead of the stream, p. 143
BALLYSILLAN	AM (*Baile na Saileán*): Homestead of the willow-grove
BALLYSIMON	L (*Béal Átha Síomoin*): Mouth of Síomon's ford
BALLYSKEAGH	DN (*Baile na Sceiche*): Homestead of the thorn
BALLYSTEEN	L (*Baile Stiabhna*): Stiabhna's homestead
BALLYSTREW	DN (*Baile Sruth*): Homestead of the stream, p. 143
BALLYTARSNA	RN & TY (*Baile Trasna*): Homestead across
BALLYTORE	KE (*Béal Átha an Tuair*): Mouth of the ford of the bleach-green
BALLYVADE	WH (*Baile Bháid*): Homestead of the boat
BALLYVAGHAN	CE (*Baile Uí Bheacháin*): Ó Beacháin's homestead
BALLYVALDON	WX (*Baile Bhalduin*): Baldwin's homestead
BALLYVALTRON	WW (*Baile Bhaltairín*): Little Walter's homestead
BALLYVANGOUR	CW (*Baile Bheanna Gabhar*): Homestead of the peaks of the goats, p. 29
BALLYVARY	MO (*Béal Átha Bhearaigh*): Mouth of the ford of the heifer
BALLYVOGUE	C (*Baile Uí Bhuaigh*): Ó Buaigh's homestead
BALLYVOURNEY	C (*Baile Bhúirne*): Homestead of the stony place

BALLYVOY	AM (*Baile Bhóidh*): Homestead of the shaft
BALLYVOYLE	WD (*Baile Uí Bhaoill*): Ó Baoill's homestead
BALLYWALTER	DN (*Baile Bháltair*): Walter's homestead
BALLYWARD	DN (*Baile Mhic an Bhaird*): Macaward's homestead
BALLYWATER	WX (*Baile Uachtar*): Upper homestead
BALLYWEE	AM (*Baile Uaimh*): Homestead of the caves, p. 160
BALLYWILLIAM	WX (*Baile Uilliam*): William's homestead
BALNAMORE	AM (*Béal an Átha Móir*): Mouth of the big ford
BALRATH	MH (*Baile na Rátha*): Homestead of the fort
BALROE	WH (*Baile Rua*): Red townland, p. 138
BALROTHERY	D (*Baile an Ridire*): Homestead of the knight
BALTIMORE	C (*Baile Tigh Mór*): Homestead of the big house
BALTINGLASS	D (*Bealach Conglais*): Pass of Conglas, p. 29
BANADA	SO (*Muine na Fede*): Thicket of the stream
BANAGHER	OY (*Beannchar*): Peaked hill
BANDON	C: Goddess, p. 137
BANEMORE	KY (*Bán Mór*): Large pasture-land
BANGOR ERRIS	MO (*Beannchar Iorrais*): Peaked hill of Iorrais
BANGOR	DN (*Beannchar*): Peaked hill
BANNA	KY (*Beanna*): Peaks, p. 29
BANNOW	WX ([*Cuan an*] *Bhainbh*): (Bay of the) sucking pig
BANOGUE	L (*Bánog*): Courtyard
BANSHA	TY (*Báinseach*): Green
BANTEER	C (*Bántír*): White land, p. 26
BANTRY	C (*Beanntraí*): (District of) Beanntraí
BARNA	G, L & OY (*Bearna*): Gap, p. 29
BARNACULLIA	D (*Barr na Coille*): Top of the wood, p. 27
BARNADERG	G (*Bearna Dhearg*): Red gap, p. 29
BARNAGEEHA	L (*Bearna Gaoithe*): Windy gap, pp 29, 90
BARNAKILLEW	MO (*Barr na Coille*): Top of the wood, p. 27
BARNAKILLY	DY (*Barr na Coille*): Top of the wood, p. 27
BARNATRA	MO (*Barr na Trá*): Top of the strand, p. 27
BARNES	TE (*Bearnas*): Gap, p. 29
BARNESMORE	DL (*Bearnas Mór*): Great gap, p. 29
BARNMEEN	DN (*Bearn Mhín*): Smooth gap
BARNYCARROLL	MO (*Bearna Chearúill*): Cearúill's gap
BARRADUFF	KY (*Barra Dubh*): Black ridge
BARRYROE	C (*Barraigh Rua*): (District of) the Red Barraigh
BASLICK	MN (*Baisleac*): Basilica, p. 26
BASLICKANE	KY (*Baisleacán*): Small 'basilica', p. 26

BATTERSTOWN	MH (*Baile an Bhóthair*): Homestead of the road
BAURTREGAUM	KY (*Barr Trí gCom*): Top of three hollows, p. 59
BAUTEOGUE	LS (*Báiteog*): Morass
BAVAN	DL & DN (*Bádhún*): Cow-fortress, p. 20
BAWNBOY	CN (*Bábhún Buí*): Yellow cow-fortress, p. 20
BAYLIN	WH (*Béal Linne*): Mouth of the pool
BEAGH	LM (*Beitheach*): Birch-land, p. 30
BEAGHMORE	TE (*Beitheach Mór*): Large birch-land, p. 30
BEALADANGAN	G (*Béal an Daingin*): Opening of the stronghold, p. 28
BEALAHA	CE (*Béal Átha*): Mouth of the ford, p. 28
BEALNAMULLA	RN (*Béal na mBuillí*): Mouth of the blows
Beaulieu	LH, p. 84
BEGINISH	KY (*Beag Inis*): Small island, p. 27
BEGLIEVE	CN (*Beagshliabh*): Small mountain, p. 27
BEHAGHANE	KY (*Beitheachán*): Little place of birch
BEHY	DL (*Beitheach*): Birch-land, p. 30
BELCARRA	MO (*Baile na Cora*): Homestead of the weir
BELCLARE	G (*Béal Chláir*): Mouth of the plain, p. 28
BELCOO	FH (*Béal Cú*): Mouth of the narrow stretch of water between two larger stretches
BELDERG	MO (*Béal Deirg*): Mouth of the (river) Derg, pp 28, 68
BELFAST	AM (*Béal Feirste*): Mouth of the sandbank
BELGOOLY	C (*Béal Guala*): Mouth of the ridge, pp 28, 98
BELLACORICK	MO (*Béal Átha Chomraic*): Mouth of the ford of the confluence, p. 28
BELLAGHY	DY (*Baile Eachaidh*): Eochadh's homestead
BELLAHY	SO (*Béal Lathaí*): Mouth of the miry place
BELLANAGARE	RN (*Béal Átha na gCarr*): Mouth of the ford of the carts, p. 28
BELLANALECK	FH (*Bealach na Leice*): Pass of the flagstones, p. 106
BELLANAMORE	DL (*Béal an Átha Mhóir*): Mouth of the big ford
BELLANANAGH	CN (*Béal Átha na nEach*): Mouth of the ford of the horses, p. 28
BELLANEENY	RM (*Béal Átha an Aonaigh*): Mouth of the ford of the fair
BELLANODE	MN (*Béal Átha an Fhóid*): Mouth of the ford of the sod
BELLARENA	DY (*Baile an Mhargaidh*): Homestead of the market
BELLAVARY	MO (*Béal Átha Bhearaigh*): Mouth of the ford of Bearach
Belle Vue	AM, p. 84
BELLEEK	FH (*Béal Leice*): Mouth of the flagstones, p. 106

BELLEEKS	AH (*Béal Leice*): Mouth of the flagstones, p. 106
BELLEW	MH (*Bile*): Sacred tree, p. 30
BELLIA	CE (*Bile*): Sacred tree, p. 30
Belmont	G, p. 84
BELMULLET	MO (*Béal an Mhuirthead*): Sea-loop
BELTANY	DL (*Bealtaine*): Summer festival
BELTRA	MO & SO (*Béal Trá*): Mouth of the strand, p. 28
BELTURBET	CN (*Béal Tairbirt*): Mouth of the isthmus, p. 28
Belvedere	WH, p. 84
BELVELLY	C (*Béal an Bhealaigh*): Mouth of the pass, p. 28
Belvoir	DN, p. 84
BENAGH	DN (*Beitheanach*): Place of birch-trees
BENBANE	AM (*Beann Bán*): White peak, p. 29
BENBEG	G (*Beann Beag*): Little peak, p. 29
BENBO	LM (*Beann Bó*): Peak of the cow, p. 29
BENBRACK	CN (*Beann Breac*): Speckled peak, pp 29, 33
BENBULBIN	SO (*Beann Ghulbain*): Gulban's peak, p. 29
BENBURB	TE (*Beann Bhorb*): Bold peak
BENGORE	AM (*Beann Gabhar*): Peak of the goats, p. 29
BENGORM	MO (*Beann Gorm*): Blue peak, p. 29
BENMORE	AM (*Beann Mór*): Large peak, p. 29
BENWEE	MO (*Beann Bhuí*): Yellow peak
BINEVENAGH	DY (*Binn Fhoibhne*): Foibhne's peak
BIRR	OY (*Biorra*): Stream, p. 31
BIRRA	DL (*Biorra*): Stream, p. 31
BLACKWATER	AH, C & TE (*Abhainn Mór*): Big river, p. 11
BLANEY	FH (*Bléinigh*): Creek
BLARIS	DN (*Bláráis*): Exposed field
BLUESTACK MOUNTAINS	DL (*Cruacha Gorma*): Blue ricks, p. 65
BODERG	LM & RN (*Both Derg*): Red hut
BODONEY	TE (*Both Domhnaigh*): Hut of the church, p. 32
BOFEENAUN	MO (*Both Faonáin*): Faonán's hut
BOGARE	KY (*Both Chearr*): Crooked hut
BOGAY	DL (*Both Ghaoith*): Windy hut
BOHACOGRAM	KY (*Both an Chograim*): Hut of the whispering
BOHACULLIA	KY (*Botha Coille*): Huts of the wood
BOHAUN	MO (*Bothán*): Little hut, p. 32
BOHEESHIL	KY (*Both Íseal*): Low hut
BOHER	L (*Bóthar*): Road, p. 32

BOHERAPHUCA	OY (*Bóthar an Phúca*): Road of the sprite, p. 33
BOHERARD	C & WD (*Bóthar Ard*): High road, p. 32
BOHERBOY	C (*Bóthar Buí*): Yellow road, pp 32, 36
BOHERBUE	C (*Bóthar Buí*): Yellow road
BOHEREEN	L (*Bóithrín*): Little road, p. 33
BOHERLAHAN	TY (*Bóthar Leathan*): Broad road, p. 32
BOHERMEEN	MH (*Bóthar Mín*): Smooth road
BOHERMORE	G (*Bóthar Mór*): Large road
BOHO	FH (*Botha*): Huts, p. 32
BOHOGE	MO (*Bothóg*): Little hut, p. 32
BOHOLA	MO (*Both Chomhla*): Comla's hut, p. 32
BOLEA	DY (*Both Liath*): Grey hut, p. 32
BONMAHON	WD (*Bun Machan*): Foot of the (river) Machan
BONNICONLAN	MO (*Muine Chonalláin*): Conallán's thicket
BOOLA	WD (*Buaile*): Milking-place, p. 36
BOOLAKENNEDY	TY (*Buaile Uí Chinnéide*): Ó Cinnéide's milking-place, p. 36
BOOLANANAVE	KY (*Buaile na nDamh*): Milking-place of the oxen
BOOLAVOGUE	WX (*Baile Mhaodhóg*): Maodóg's homestead
BORNACOOLA	LM (*Barr na Cúile*): Top of the hollow
BORRIS	CW (*Buiríos*): Burgage, p. 36
BORRIS-IN-OSSORY	LS (*Buiríos Osraí*): Burgage of Osraí, p. 37
BORRISBEG	KK (*Buiríos Beag*): Small burgage, p. 37
BORRISNOE	TY (*Buiríos Nua*): New burgage, pp 37, 126
BORRISOKANE	TY (*Buiríos Uí Chéin*): Burgage of Ó Céin
BORRISOLEIGH	TY (*Buiríos Ó Luigheach*): Burgage of Uí Luigheach, p. 37
BOUGHADOON	MO (*Both an Dúin*): Hut of the fort, p. 32
BOULADUFF	TY (*Buaile Dhubh*): Black milking-place
BOVEVAGH	DY (*Both Mhéibhe*): Maeve's hut, p. 32
BOYLE	RN ([*Mainistir na*] *Búille*): (Monastery of the river) Búill
BOYOUNAGH	G (*Buibheanach*): Yellow marsh, p. 36
BRACKAHARAGH	KY (*Brá Chathrach*): Neck of the stone fort
BRACKLOON	KY & MO (*Breac Chluain*): Speckled pasture, p. 33
BRACKLYN	WH (*Breaclainn*): Speckled place
BRACKNAGH	OY (*Breacnach*): Speckled place, p. 33
BRACKNAHEVLA	WH (*Breacach na hAibhle*): Speckled land of the orchard
BRADOGE	DL (*Bráideog*): Little throat
BRADOX	MN (*Bráideoga*): Little throats
BRAID	AM (*Braghad*): Throat

DRANDON	KY ([Cé] Dhréanain). (Quay, etc. of) Dréanainn
BRAY	WW (Bré): Brae, p. 33
BREADY	TE (Brédach): Broken ground
BREAGHWY	MO & SO (Bréachmhaigh): Wolf-plain
BREDAGH	WH (Brédach): Broken ground
BREE	WX (Brí): Brae, p. 33
BREEDOGE	RN (Bráideog): Little throat
BRICKLIEVE	SO (Bricshliabh): Speckled mountain, p. 33
BRIGH	TE (Brí): Brae, p. 33
BRINLACK	DL (Bun na Leaca): Foot of the flagstones
BRISKA	WD (Brioscach): Brittle land
BRITISH	AM (Briotás): Wooden palisade, p. 34
BRITTAS	D & WW (Briotás): Wooden palisade, p. 33
BRITWAY	C (Breachmhaí): Wolf-plain
BROCKAGH	WH (Brocach): Badger-field
BROUGHDERG	TE (Bruach Dearg): Red bank, p. 35
BROUGHNAMADDY	DN (Bruach na Madadh): Bank of the dogs
BROUGHSHANE	AM (Bruach Sheáin): Seán's bank, p. 35
BRUFF	L (Brú): Palace, p. 35
Brugh na Bóinne:	Fairy palace of the white cow (goddess), p. 35
BRUREE	L (Brú Rí): Palace of the king, p. 35
BUCKODE	LM (Bocóid): Spot
BUGGAN	FH (Bogán): Soft place
BULLAUN	G (Ballán): Round hillock
BUN	OY (Bun): Bottom
BUNAW	KY (Bun Abha): River-mouth
BUNBEG	DL (Bun Beag): Small river-mouth, p. 38
BUNBRUSNA	WH (Bun Brosnaí): Mouth of the (river) Brosna
BUNCLODY	CW & WX (Bun Clóidí): Mouth of the (river) Clóideach, p. 38
BUNCRANA	DL (Bun Cranncha): Mouth of the (river) Crannach
BUNDORAN	DL (Bun Dobhráin): Mouth of the little water
BUNDORRAGHA	MO (Bun Dorcha): Mouth of the dark river
BUNDUFF	LM (Bun Dubh): Mouth of the black (river), p. 38
BUNMAHON	WD (Bun Machan): Mouth of the (river) Machain, p. 38
BUNNACURRY	MO (Bun an Churraigh): Foot of the swamp
BUNNAHOWEN	MO (Bun na hAbhna): Mouth of the river, pp 11, 38
BUNNANADDAN	SO (Bun an Fheadáin): Mouth of the stream, p. 38
BUNNYCONNELLAN	MO (Muine Chonalláin): Conallán's thicket
BUNOWEN	MO (Bun Abhann): Mouth of the river, p. 11

Bunratty

BUNRATTY	CE (*Bun Raite*): Mouth of the (river) Raite, p. 38
BUNREE	MO (*Bun Rí*): Mouth of the (river) Rí
BURREN	CE & DN (*Boireann*): Stony district
BURRENBANE	DN (*Boireann Bán*): White stony district
BURRENREAGH	DN (*Boireann Riabhach*): Grey stony district
BWEENG	C (*Boinn*): Swelling

C

CABINTEELY	D (*Cábán tSíle*): Síle's cabin, p. 39
CABRA	DN (*Cabrach*): Bad land
CABRAGH	D & TE (*Cabrach*): Bad land, p. 16
CADAMSTOWN	KE & OY (*Baile Mhic Ádaim*): Homestead of Mac Ádaim
CADDY	AM (*Cadaigh*): Moss
CADIAN	TE (*Céidín*): Little hill, p. 49
CAHER	CE & TY (*Cathair*): Stone fort, p. 45
CAHERAGH	C (*Cathrach*): Abounding in stone forts
CAHERBARNAGH	C (*Cathair Bearnach*): Gapped stone fort
CAHERCONLISH	L (*Cathair Chinn Lis*): Stone fort of the head of the ford
CAHERCONREE	KY (*Cathair Con Raoi*): Stone fort of Cúrí, pp 45, 76
CAHERDANIEL	KY (*Cathair Dónaill*): Dónall's stone fort
CAHERELLY	L (*Cathair Ailí*): Stone fort of the boulder
CAHERGAL	KY (*Cathair Geal*): White stone fort
CAHERLOUGHLIN	CE (*Cathair Lochlainn*): Stone fort of Lochlann, p. 45
CAHERMORE	C & G (*Cathair Mhór*): Big stone fort, p. 45
CAHERNAGEEHA MOUNTAIN	KY (*Cathair na Gaoithe* + Mountain): Stone fort of the wind + mountain, p. 89
CAHERSIVEEN	KY (*Cathair Saidhbhín*): Stone fort of Saidhbhín, p. 45
CAHIR	TY (*Cathair*): Stone fort, p. 16
CAIME	WX (*Céim*): Gap
Caladh Buí	KY: Yellow landing-place, p. 42
CALDRAGH	FH (*Cealtragh*): Graveyard, p. 46
CALLOW	MO & RN (*Caladh*): Holm, p. 42
CALTRA	G (*Cealtrach*): Graveyard, p. 46
CALTRAGHLEA	G (*Cealtrach Lia*): Grey graveyard, pp 47, 110
CAMAROSS	WX (*Camros*): Crooked grove, p. 42
CAMLOUGH	AH (*Camloch*): Crooked lake, p. 42
CAMOWEN	TE (*Camabhainn*): Crooked river, p. 42
CAMP	KY (*Com*): Hollow, p. 59
CAMPILE	WX (*Ceann Poill*): Head of the creek
CAMPORT	MO (*Camport*): Crooked shore, p. 42
CAMPSIE	DY (*Camsain*): Meanders
CAMROSS	LS (*Camros*): Crooked copse, p. 42
CAPPAGH	G, L, TE & WD (*Ceapach*): Plot of land, p. 48

CAPPAMORE	L (*Ceapach Mhór*): Big plot of land, p. 48
CAPPANACUSH	KY (*Ceapach na Coise*): Plot of land of the foot, p. 48
CAPPAQUIN	WD (*Ceapach Choinn*): Conn's plot of land, p. 48
CAPPAROE	TY (*Ceapach Rua*): Red plot of land, pp 48, 138
CAPPATAGGLE	G (*Ceapach an tSeagail*): Plot of rye
CAPPEEN	C (*Caipín*): Cap, p. 39
CARK	DL (*Cearc*): Hen
CARLINGFORD	LH: See NORSE NAMES, p. 125
CARLOW	CW (*Ceatharloch*): Quadruple lake
CARMAVY	AM (*Carn Méibhe*): Maeve's cairn, p. 43
CARN	WH (*Carn*): Cairn, p. 44
CARNA	G & WX (*Carna*): Cairns, p. 44
CARNAGH	AH (*Carnach*): Place of cairns
CARNALBANAGH	AM (*Carn Albanach*): Cairn of the Scotsman
CARNANMORE	AM (*Carnán Mór*): Big little cairn, p. 44
CARNDONAGH	DL (*Carn Domhnaigh*): Cairn of the church, p. 44
CARNEW	WW (*Carn an Bhua*): Cairn of the victory
CARNEY	SO ([*Fearann Uí*] *Chearnaigh*): (Territory of Ó) Ciarnaigh
CARNEY	TY (*Carnaigh*): Abounding in lumps
CARNKENNY	TE (*Carn Cainnech*): Cainnech's cairn, p. 43
CARNLOUGH	AM (*Carnlach*): Place of cairns, pp 44, 116
CARNMONEY	AM (*Carn Monaidh*): Cairn of the bog
CARNONEEN	G (*Carn Eoghainín*): Eoghainín's cairn, p. 44
CARNTEEL	TE (*Carn tSiail*): Sial's cairn
CARNTIERNA	C (*Carn Tighernaigh*): Tighernach's cairn
CARNTOGHER	DY (*Carn Tóchair*): Cairn of the causeway
CARRA	MO (*Cairthe*): Standing stone
CARRACASTLE	RN (*Ceathrú an Chaisil*): Quarter of the stone fort, p. 40
CARRAROE	G (*Ceathrú Rua*): Red quarter
CARRAUNTOOHIL	KY (*Corrán Tuathail*): Inverted crescent
CARRICHUE	DY (*Carraig Aodha*): Aodh's rock
CARRICK	DL & WX (*Carraig*): Rock, pp 16, 44
CARRICK-ON-SUIR	TY (*Carraig na Siúre*): Rock on the (river) Suir
CARRICKABOY	CN (*Carraigeach Buí*): Yellow rocky place
CARRICKAHORIG	TY (*Carraig an Chomraic*): Rock of the confluence, p. 44
CARRICKANORAN	KK & MN (*Carraig an Uaráin*): Rock of the spring, p. 160
CARRICKBEG	WD (*Carraig Bheag*): Small rock, p. 44
CARRICKFERGUS	AM (*Carraig Fhearghasa*): Rock of Fergus, p. 45

CARRICKMACROSS	MN (*Carraig Mhachaire Rois*): Rock of the plain of the grove, p. 44
CARRICKMORE	TE (*Carraig Mhór*): Big rock, p. 44
CARRICKROE	MN (*Carraig Rua*): Red rock
CARRIG	TY (*Carraig*): Rock, p. 44
CARRIGAFOYLE	TY (*Carraig an Phoill*): Rock of the pool
CARRIGAHOLT	CE (*Carraig an Chabhaltaigh*): Rock of the fleet, p. 45
CARRIGAHORIG	TY (*Carraig an Chomhraic*): Rock of the confluence, p. 44
CARRIGALINE	C (*Carraig Uí Leighin*): Ó Leighin's rock, p. 45
CARRIGALLEN	LM (*Carraig Álainn*): Lovely rock
CARRIGAN	CN (*Carraigín*): Little rock
CARRIGANIMMY	C (*Carraig an Ime*): Rock of the butter
CARRIGANS	DL (*Carraigín*): Little rock
CARRIGANURRA	KK (*Carraig an Fhoraidh*): Rock of the mound
CARRIGART	DL (*Ceathrú Fhiodhghoirt*): Quarterland of the wood of the field, p. 45
CARRIGATOGHER	TY (*Carraig an Tóchair*): Rock of the causeway
CARRIGCANNON	KY (*Carraig Cheannann*): White-headed rock
CARRIGFADA	C (*Carraig Fhada*): Long rock
CARRIGKERRY	L (*Carraig Chiarraí*): Rock of Ciarraí
CARRIGNAVAR	C (*Carraig na bhFear*): Rock of the men
CARRIGROHANE	C (*Carraig Crócháin*): Cróchán's rock
CARRIGTOHILL	C (*Carraig Thuathail*): Tuathal's rock
CARRON	CE (*Carn*): Cairn
CARROWBEG	MO (*Ceathrú Bheag*): Small quarter, p. 48
CARROWBEHY	RN (*Ceathrú Bheithí*): Quarterland of the birches
CARROWDOAN	DL (*Ceathrú Domhain*): Deep quarter
CARROWDORE	DN (*Ceathrú Dobhair*): Quarter of the water
CARROWHOLLY	MO (*Ceathrú Chalaidh*): Quarter of the landing-place
CARROWKEEL	DL (*Ceathrú Chaol*): Narrow quarter, p. 48
CARROWMENA	DL (*Ceathrú Meánach*): Middle quarter
CARROWMORE	G, MO & SO (*Ceathrú Mhór*): Big quarter, p. 48
CARROWMOREKNOCK	G (*Ceathrú Mhór an Chnoic*): Large quarterland of the hill, p. 48
CARROWNACON	MO (*Ceathrú na Con*): Quarter of the hound
CARROWNEADAN	SO (*Ceathrú an Éadain*): Quarter of the brow
CARROWNISKY	MO (*Ceathrú an Uisce*): Quarter of the water
CARROWREAGH	RN (*Ceathrú Riabhach*): Striped quarter, p. 48

CARROWTAWY	SO (*Ceathrú an tSamhaidh*): Quarter of the sorrel, p. 48
CARROWTEIGE	MO (*Ceathrú Thaidhg*): Taidg's quarter, p. 48
CARRYDUFF	DN (*Ceathrú Aodha Duibh*): Black Aodh's quarter
CARTRONLAHAN	G (*Cartúr Leathan*): Broad quarter
CASHEL	G & TY (*Caiseal*): Stone fort, p. 40
CASHELBANE	TE (*Caiseal Bán*): White stone fort, p. 40
CASHELGARRAN	SO (*Caiseal an Ghearráin*): Stone fort of the horse, p. 40
CASHELMORE	DL (*Caiseal Mór*): Large stone fort, p. 40
CASHLA	G (*Caisle*): Stream
CASSAGH	WX (*Ceasach*): Wicker causeway, p. 49
CASTLEBAR	MO (*Caisleán an Bharraigh*): de Barra's castle
CASTLECOMER	KK (*Caisleán an Chomair*): Castle of the confluence, p. 40
CASTLECONNELL	L (*Caisleán Uí Chonaill*): Ó Conaing's castle, p. 41
CASTLECONNOR	SO (*Caisleán Mhic Chonchobhair*): Mac Conchuír's castle
CASTLECOR	C (*Caisleán na Cora*): Castle of the weir
CASTLEDERG	TE (*Caisleán na Deirge*): Castle of the (river) Derg, p. 41
CASTLEDERMOT	KE (*Caisleán [Díseart] Diarmada*): Castle of (the hermitage of) Diarmaid
CASTLEFINN	DL (*Caisleán na Finne*): Castle of the (river) Finn
CASTLEGAL	SO (*Caisle Geala*): White inlet
CASTLEGAR	G (*Caisleán Gearr*): Short castle, p. 41
CASTLEGARREN	SO (*Caiseal an Ghearráin*): Stone fort of the horse
CASTLEKNOCK	D (*Caisleán Chnucha*): Castle of the hill
CASTLELYONS	C (*Caisleán Ó Liatháin*): Uí Liatháin's castle, p. 40
CASTLEMAINE	KY (*Caisleán na Mainge*): Castle of the (river) Maine, p. 41
CASTLEMARTYR	C (*Caisleán na Martra*): Castle of the relics
CASTLERAGHAN	CN (*Caisleán Rathain*): Castle of ferns
CASTLEREAGH	DN & RN (*Caisleán Riabhach*): Striped castle, pp 41, 136
CASTLESHANE	MN (*Caisleán an tSiáin*): Castle of the fairy hill
CASTLETOWN KINNEIGH	C (*Baile Chaisleáin Chinn Eich*): Town of the castle of the horse's head
CASTLETOWNROCHE	C (*Baile Chaisleáin an Róistigh*): Town of the castle of the Roches
CASTLEWELLAN	DN (*Caisleán Uidhilin*): Castle of Hugolin
Cathair na Mart	MO: Stone fort of the market, p. 15

CAVAN	CN (*Cabhán*): Hollow, p. 39
CAVANAGARDEN	DL (*Cabhán an Gharraí*): Hollow of the garden
Cell Fhine	p. 52
CHAFFPOOL	SO (*Lochán na Catha*): Little lake of the battle
CHANONROCK	LH (*Carraig na gCanónach*): Rock of the canons
CHAPELIZOD	D (*Séipéal Iosóid*): Iseult's chapel
CHEEKPOINT	WD (*Pointe na Síge*): Streak point
CLADDAGH	G & KY (*Cladach*): Shore, p. 54
CLADDAGHDUFF	G (*Cladach Dubh*): Black shore, p. 54
CLADY	DL & TE (*Cladach*): Shore
CLAGGAN	DL (*Cloigeann*): Head
CLANABOGAN	TE (*Cluain Uí Bhogáin*): Ó Bogáin's pasture
CLANDEBOYE	DN (*Clanna Aodha Buí*): Clan of yellow Aodha
CLANE	KE (*Claonadh*): Slanted ford
CLARA	OY (*Clárach*): Level place, p. 55
CLARE	AH, DN & TE (*Clár*): Plain, p. 54
CLARE ISLAND	MO (*Cléir* + Island): Clergy + Island
CLAREEN	OY (*Cláirín*): Little plain, p. 54
CLAREGALWAY	G (*Baile an Chláir*): Plain of Galway
CLAREMORRIS	MO (*Clár Clainne Muiris*): Plain of the children of Muiris
CLARINA	L (*Clár Aidhne*): Plank-bridge of Aidhne, p. 54
CLARINBRIDGE	G (*Droichead an Chláirín*): Bridge of the little plank, pp 54, 156
CLASH	TY & WW (*Clais*): Ravine, p. 54
CLASHMORE	WD (*Clais Mhór*): Big ravine, p. 54
CLEGGAN	G (*Cloigeann*): Head
CLIFFONY	SO (*Cliafuine*): Hurdle thicket
Clochán	G: Stony place, p. 15
CLOGH MILLS	AM (*Muileann na Cloiche*): Mill of the stone
CLOGH	AM & KK (*Cloch*): Stone castle
CLOGHAN	DL, OY & WH (*Clochán*): Stony place, p. 55
CLOGHANE	KY (*Clochán*): Stony place, p. 55
CLOGHANEALY	DL (*Cloch Chionnfhaolaidh*): Cionnfhaoladh's stone
CLOGHBOLEY	SO (*Clochbuaile*): Stone of the milking-place
CLOGHBRACK	MO (*Cloch Breac*): Speckled stone, p. 55
CLOGHEEN	TY & WD (*Cloichín*): Little stone, p. 55
CLOGHER	MO & TE (*Clochar*): Stony place, p. 55
CLOGHERNACH	WD (*Clocharnach*): Stony place, p. 55
CLOGHJORDAN	TY (*Cloch Shiurdáin*): Jordan's stone castle, p. 55

CLOGHMORE	MO & MN (*Cloich Mór*): Big stone
CLOGHORE	DL (*Cloich Óir*): Gold stone
CLOGHRAN	D (*Clochrán*): Stepping-stones
CLOGHROE	C (*Cloch Rua*): Red stone, p. 55
CLOGHY	DN (*Clochaigh*): Stony, p. 55
CLOHAMON	WX (*Cloch Ámainn*): Hamon's stone castle
CLOMANTAGH	KK (*Cloch Mhantach*): Gapped stone
CLONADACASEY	LS (*Cluain Fhada Uí Chathasaigh*): Ó Cathasaigh's long pasture
CLONAKENNY	TY (*Cluain Uí Chionaoith*): Ó Cionaoith's pasture
CLONAKILTY	C (*Cloch na Coillte*): Stone of the woods, p. 55
CLONALVY	MH (*Cluain Ailbhe*): Ailbhe's pasture
CLONARD	MH (*Cluain Ioraird*): Iorard's pasture
CLONARD	WX (*Cluain Ard*): High pasture, p. 56
CLONASLEE	LS (*Cluain na Slí*): Pasture of the path
CLONBANIN	C (*Cluain Báinín*): Pasture of the white tweed
CLONBERN	G (*Cluain Bheirn*): Bearn's pasture, p. 56
CLONBULLOGE	OY (*Cluain Bolg*): Pasture of the bulges
CLONCAGH	L (*Cluain Chath*): Pasture of the battle
CLONCREEN	OY (*Cluain Crainn*): Pasture of the tree
CLONCURRY	KE (*Cluain Curraigh*): Pasture of the marsh
CLONDALKIN	D (*Cluain Dolcáin*): Dolcán's pasture, p. 56
CLONDARRAGH	WX (*Cluain Darach*): Pasture of the oak-tree, p. 67
CLONDAW	WX (*Cluain Dáith*): Dáith's pasture
CLONDROHID	C (*Cluain Droichead*): Pasture of the bridges, p. 56
CLONDULANE	C (*Cluain Dalláin*): Dallán's pasture
CLONEA	WD (*Cluain Fhia*): Pasture of the deer
CLONEE	MH (*Cluain Aodha*): Aodh's pasture
CLONEEN	TY (*Cluainín*): Little pasture
CLONEGALL	CW (*Cluain na nGall*): Pasture of the stones
CLONENAGH	LS (*Cluain Eidhneach*): Ivied pasture, p. 82
CLONES	MN (*Cluain Eois*): Pasture of Eos
CLONEY	KE (*Cluainaidh*): Pasture
CLONEYGOWAN	OY (*Cluain na nGamhan*): Pasture of the calves
CLONFERT	G (*Cluain Fearta*): Pasture of the grave, p. 87
CLONFINLOUGH	OY (*Cluain Fionnlocha*): Pasture of the white lake
CLONGOREY	KE (*Cluain Guaire*): Guaire's pasture, p. 56
CLONKEEN	KY (*Cluain Chaoin*): Pleasant pasture
CLONLEIGH	DL (*Cluain Lao*): Pasture of the calf
CLONLOST	WH (*Cluain Loiste*): Burnt meadow

CLONMACNOISE	OY (*Cluain Mic Nois*): Pasture of the descendants of Noas
CLONMANY	DL (*Cluain Maine*): Maine's meadow
CLONMEL	TY (*Cluain Meala*): Pasture of honey, p. 56
CLONMELLON	WH (*Cluain Miláin*): Milán's meadow
CLONMORE	CW & TY (*Cluain Mhór*): Large pasture, p. 56
CLONMULT	C (*Cluain Molt*): Pasture of wethers, p. 56
CLONOE	TE (*Cluain Eo*): Meadow of the yew
CLONOULTY	TY (*Cluain Ultaigh*): Pasture of the Ulstermen, p. 57
CLONROCHE	WX (*Cluain an Róistigh*): Roches' pasture
CLONROOSK	OY (*Cluain Rúisc*): Pasture of the bark
CLONSILLA	D (*Cluain Saileach*): Pasture of the willow
CLONTALLAGH	DL (*Cluain tSalach*): Dirty pasture
CLONTARF	D (*Cluain Tarbh*): Pasture of bulls, p. 56
CLONTIBRET	MN (*Cluain Tiobrad*): Pasture of the well, pp 56, 152
CLONTOE	TE (*Cluain Tó*): Tó's pasture
CLONTUSKERT	G (*Cluain Tuaiscirt*): North pasture, p. 57
CLONTYGORA	AH (*Cluainte Gabhra*): Pastures of the goats
CLONYGOWAN	OY (*Cluain na nGamhan*): Pasture of the calves, p. 56
CLOON	CE & MO (*Cluain*): Pasture, p. 56
CLOONACOOL	SO (*Cluain na Cúile*): Pasture of the nook
CLOONAGH	WH (*Cluanach*): Meadowland
CLOONAGHMORE	MO (*Cluaineach Mór*): Large horse-meadow
CLOONDAFF	MO (*Cluain Damh*): Ox-meadow
CLOONDARA	LD (*Cluain dá Ráth*): Pasture of two forts, p. 56
CLOONE	LM (*Cluain*): Pasture, p. 56
CLOONEE	KY (*Cluainaigh*): Pasture
CLOONEY	DL (*Cluanaidh*): Pasture
CLOONFAD	RN (*Cluain Fada*): Long pasture, p. 56
CLOONKEAVY	SO (*Cluain Ciabhaigh*): Hazy pasture
CLOONLARA	CE (*Cluain Lára*): Pasture of the mare
CLOONLOUGH	SO (*Cluain Lua*): Lua's pasture
CLOONTIA	MO (*Cluainte*): Meadows
CLOONYMORRIS	G (*Cluain Uí Mhuiris*): Ó Muiris's pasture
CLORHANE	OY (*Clochrán*): Stepping-stones
CLOSKELT	DN (*Cloch Scoilte*): Cleft rock
CLOUGH	DN (*Cloch*): Stone castle, p. 55
CLOUGHJORDAN	TY (*Cloch Shiurdáin*): Jordan's stone castle
CLOUGHMORE	DN (*Cloch Mór*): Big stone, p. 55
CLOUGHOGE	AH (*Clochóg*): Little stone, p. 55

CLOYFIN	DY (*Cloch Fionn*): White stone, p. 55
CLOYNE	C (*Cluain*): Pasture, p. 56
Cnoc Gréine	p. 128
Cnoc Áine	p. 128
COA	FH (*Cuach*): Hollow
COAGH	TE (*Cuach*): Hollow
COAN	KK (*Cuan*): Recess
COBH	C (*Cóbh*): Cove
COLERAINE	DY (*Cúil Rathain*): Nook of the ferns, pp 66, 132
COLLINAMUCK	G (*Caladh na Muc*): Riverside meadow of the pigs
COLLON	LH (*Cuilleann*): Steep slope
COLLOONEY	SO (*Cúil Mhuine*): Nook of the thicket, p. 66
COMBER	DN (*Comar*): Confluence, p. 59
COMMEEN	DL (*Coimín*): Common land
CONAIR	KY (*Conair*): Path
CONEY ISLAND	CE & DN (*Coiní* + Island): Rabbits + island
CONG	MO (*Conga*): Narrow stretch of water between two larger stretches
CONLIG	DN (*Coinleac*): Hound-stone
CONVOY	DL (*Conmhá*): Hound-plain
CONWAL	DL & LM (*Congbháil*): Cloister, p. 60
COOLANEY	SO (*Cúil Mhaine*): Nook of the thicket
COOLATTIN	L, WW & WX (*Cúl Aitinn*): Hill of gorse, p. 14
COOLBAUN	KK (*Cúl Bán*): White hill, p. 66
COOLBAUN	TY (*Cúil Bhán*): White nook, p. 66
COOLBOY	DL & WW (*Cúl Buí*): Yellow hill, p. 66
COOLCARRIGAN	KE (*Cúil Charraigín*): Nook of the little rock
COOLCOR	OY (*Cúil Chorr*): Nook of the hills
COOLCULLEN	KK (*Cúl an Chuillinn*): Back of the steep slope, p. 66
COOLDERRY	MN & OY (*Cúl Doire*): Back of the oakwood, p. 66
COOLE	WH (*Cúil*): Nook, p. 65
COOLEA	C (*Cúil Aodha*): Aodh's nook
COOLEY POINT	LH (*Cuailnge* + Point): Point of Cooley
COOLGRANGE	KK (*Cúil Ghráinseach*): Nook of the monastic farm
COOLGREANY	WX (*Cúil Ghréine*): Nook of the sun, p. 66
COOLIGRAIN	LM (*Cúl le Gréin*): Nook of the sun
COOLKEERAGH	DY (*Cúil Chaorach*): Nook of the sheep
COOLKENNO	WW (*Cúil Uí Chionaoith*): Nook of the Ó Cionath
COOLMEEN	CE (*Cúil Mhín*): Smooth nook, p. 66
COOLMORE	DL (*Cúl Mór*): Big hill, p. 66

COOLOCK	D (*Cúlóg*): Little corner
COOLRAIN	LS (*Cúil Ruáin*): Nook of the red ground, p. 66
COOLSALLAGH	DN (*Cúl Salach*): Dirty hill
COOMATLOUKANE	KY (*Com an tSleabcáin*): Hollow of the edible seaweed, p. 59
COOMNAGOPPUL	KY (*Com na gCapall*): Hollow of the horses, p. 59
COON	KK (*Cuan*): Harbour/haven, p. 65
COONEEN	FH (*Cúinnín*): Little corner
COORACLARE	CE (*Cuar an Chláir*): Curve of the plain
COPPEEN	C (*Caipín*): Cap, p. 39
CORBALLA	SO (*Corrbhaile*): Odd homestead
CORBALLY	CE (*Corrbhaile*): Odd homestead
CORBET	DN (*Carbad*): Jaw
CORBO	TE (*Corr Bhó*): Snout of the cow
CORCLOGH	MO (*Corr Cloch*): Snout of the stone
CORCREAGHY	LH (*Corr Chríochach*): Snout of the boundary
CORGLASS	LM (*Corr Ghlas*): Grey/green hill
CORK	C (*Corcaigh*): Swamp, p. 60
CORKEY	AM (*Corcaigh*): Swamp, p. 60
CORLEAD	LD (*Corr Liath*): Grey rounded hill
CORLESMORE	CN (*Corrlios Mór*): Big rounded hill of the fort
CORNAFANOG	FH (*Corr na bhFeannóg*): Pointed hill of the crow, p. 61
CORNAFEAN	CN (*Corr na Féinne*): Hill of the Fianna
CORNAFULLA	RN (*Corr na Fola*): Hill of the blood, p. 61
CORNAMONA	G (*Corr na Móna*): Hill of the bog, p. 61
CORNDARRAGH	OY (*Carn Darach*): Heap of the oak-tree(s)
COROFIN	CE (*Cora Finne*): Weir of the white (water), p. 60
CORRACULLIN	OY & WH (*Corr an Chuillinn*): Hill of the steep slope
CORRANDULLA	G (*Corr an Dola*): Hill of the loop
CORRANNY	FH (*Corr Eanaigh*): Hill of the bog
CORRAUN	MO (*Corrán*): Crescent-shaped place, p. 62
CORRAWALLAN	LM (*Corr an Mhailín*):
CORRIB LOUGH	G (*Loch Coirib*): Lake of Oirbse
CORRIGA	LM (*Carraigeach*): Abounding in rocks
CORRIGEENROE	RN (*Carraigín Rua*): Little red rock
CORROFIN	CE & G (*Cora Finne*): Weir of the white (water), p. 60
CORRY	LM (*Cora*): Weir, p. 60
CORTOWN	MH (*Baile Cor*): Homestead of the twist
CORTUBBER	MN (*Corr Tobair*): Hill of the well
CORVALLY	MN (*Cor an Bhealaigh*): Twist of the pass

COURTMACSHERRY	C (*Cúirt Mhic Sheafraidh*): Mansion of Mac Seafraidh
CRAANFORD	WX (*Áth an Chorráin*): Ford of the crescent
CRAGGAGH	CE (*Creagach*): Abounding in rocks or crags
CRAIGATUKE	TE (*Creag an tSeabhaic*): Crag of the hawk, p. 64
CRAIGAVAD	DN (*Creag an Bháda*): Rock of the boat, pp 20, 64
CRAIGBAN	AM (*Creag Bán*): White crag, p. 64
CRAIGBANE	DY (*Creag Bán*): White crag, p. 64
CRAIGBOY	G (*Creag Buí*): Yellow crag, p. 64
CRAIGBRACK	DY (*Creag Breac*): Speckled crag, p. 64
CRAIGDOO	DL (*Creag Dubh*): Black crag, p. 64
CRAIGLEA	DY (*Creag Liath*): Grey crag, p. 64
CRAIGMORE	DY & AM (*Creag Mór*): Big crag, p. 64
CRAIGNAGAT	AM (*Creag na gCat*): Crag of the cats, p. 64
CRAIGS	AM (*Creaga*): Crags, p. 64
CRAN	CN & FH (*Crann*): Tree, p. 62
CRANA RIVER	DL (*Crannach* + River): Abounding in trees + river, p. 62
CRANAGH	TE (*Crannach*): Place abounding in trees, p. 62
CRANCAM	RN (*Crann cam*): Crooked tree, p. 62
CRANFORD	DL (*Creamhghort*): Garlic field
CRANMORE	MO (*Crann Mór*): Big tree, p. 62
CRANN	AH (*Crann*): Tree, p. 62
CRANNAGH	G, MO, LS, RN & TY (*Crannach*): Place abounding in trees, p. 62
CRANNOGUE BOY	DL (*Crannóg Buí*): Yellow artificial island, p. 62
CRANNOGUE	TE (*Crannóg*): Artificial island, p. 62
CRANNY	CE, DY, DL & TE (*Crannach*): Place abounding in trees, p. 62
CRATLOE	CE (*Creatalach*): Place of frames
CRAUGHWELL	G (*Creachmhaoil*): Garlic wood
CREAGH	FH (*Creach*): Plunder
CRECORA	L (*Craobh Chórtha*): Palace of the sign
CREEGH	CE (*Críoch*): Boundary
CREENAGH	AM (*Críonach*): Things dry and rotten with age
CREESLOUGH	DL (*Crioslach*): Gullet lake
CREEVAGH	CE, DL, G, MO, OY, etc. (*Craobhach*): Place of sacred trees, p. 63
CREEVE	AM, AH, DL, DN, LD, MN, MO, etc. (*Craobh*): Sacred tree, p. 62

CREEVELEA	LM (*Craobh Liath*): Grey sacred tree
CREEVEROE	AH (*Craobh Ruadh*): Red branch, p. 63
CREEVES	L (*Craobha*): Sacred trees
CREGAGH	DN (*Creagach*): Abounding in rocks or crags, p. 64
CREGBOY	G (*Creag Buí*): Yellow crag, p. 64
CREGDUFF	MO (*Creag Dubh*): Black crag, p. 64
CREGG	SO (*Creag*): Crag, p. 64
CREGGAN	AH, DY & WH (*Creagán*): Little crag, p. 64
CREGGANBAUN	MO (*Creagán Bán*): White rocky place, p. 27
CREGGS	G & RN (*Creaga*): Rocks
CREW HILL	TE (*Craobh* + Hill): Sacred tree + hill, p. 63
CREW	AM, TE, & DY (*Craobh*): Sacred tree, p. 63
CRILLY	TE (*Crithleach*): Trembling place
CRINKLE	OY (*Críonchoill*): Withered wood
CROAGH PATRICK	MO (*Cruach Phádraig*): Pádraig's rick, p. 65
CROAGH	DL & L (*Cruach*): Rick
CROAGHAN	DL (*Cruachán*): Little rick
CROAGHANMOIRA	WW (*Cruach na Machaire*): Rick of the plain
CROAGHBEG	DL (*Cruach Beag*): Little rick, p. 65
CROCKNAGAPPLE	DL (*Cnoc na gCapall*): Hill of the horses, p. 58
CROGHAN	OY, RN & WW (*Cruachán*): Little rick, p. 65
CROHANE	KY (*Cruachán*): Little rick
CROM	FH (*Crom*): Bend
CROMANE	KY (*Cromán*): Hip
CROMKILL	AM (*Cromchoill*): Bent wood
CROOKHAVEN	C (*Cruachán*): (Haven of) the little rick
CROOM	L (*Cromadh*): Crooked ford
CRORY	WX (*Cruaire*): Hard land
CROSS	CE & MO (*Crois*): Cross, p. 65
CROSSABEG	WX (*Crosa Beaga*): Small crosses, p. 65
CROSSAKEEL	MH (*Crosa Caoil*): Crosses of Caol
CROSSBARRY	C (*Crois an Bharraigh*): Cross of the Barries
CROSSDONEY	CN (*Cros Domhnaigh*): Cross of the church
CROSSERLOUGH	CN (*Crois ar Loch*): Cross on the lake
CROSSGAR	DN (*Crois Ghearr*): Short cross, p. 65
CROSSMAGLEN	AH (*Crois Mhic Lionnáin*): Mac Lionnáin's cross
CROSSMOLINA	MO (*Crois Mhaoilíona*): Maolíona's cross
CROSSOOHA	G (*Crois Uathaidh*): Single cross
CROSSPATRICK	KK & WW (*Crois Phádraig*): Pádraig's cross, p. 65
CROSSREAGH	CN (*Crois Riabhach*): Grey/striped cross

CROWBANE	DL (*Cruach Bán*): White rick, p. 65
CRUIT	DL (*Cruit*): Hump
CRUMLIN	AM & D (*Croimlinn*): Crooked valley
CRUSHEEN	CE (*Croisín*): Little cross
CUILMORE	MO (*Coill Mhóir*): Big wood
CULCRUM	AM (*Coill Chrom*): Bent wood
CULDAFF	DL (*Cúil Daibhche*): Nook of the sandhills
CULFADDA	SO (*Coill Fhada*): Long wood
CULKEENY	DL (*Cúil Chaonaigh*): Wood of the moss
CULKEY	FH (*Cuilceach*): Abounding in reeds
CULLAHILL	LS (*Cúlchoill*): Back of the wood
CULLEENS	MO (*Coillíní*): Small hazelwoods
CULLEN	C & TY (*Cuilleann*): Steep slope, p. 66
CULLENTRA	TE (*Cuilleann Trá*): Steep slope of the strand
CULLION	TE (*Cuilleann*): Steep slope, p. 66
CULLOVILLE	AH (*Baile Mhic Cullach*): Mac Cullach's homestead
CULLYBACKEY	AM (*Coill na Baice*): Wood of the angle, p. 59
CULLYHANNA	AH (*Coilleach Eanach*): Woody place of the swamp
CULMORE	DY (*Cúil Mhór*): Big nook, p. 66
CULMORE	MO (*Coill Mhór*): Big wood
CULNADY	DY (*Cúil Chnáidí*): Nook of annoyance
CULVIN	WH (*Cúl Bhinn*): Back of the peak, p. 66
CUMMER	G (*Comar*): Confluence
CUNARD	D (*Cionn Ard*): High head
CURLEW MOUNTAINS	RN & SO (*Corrsliabh* + Mountains): Pointed mountains (mountains), p. 61
CURR	TE (*Corr*): Pointed hill, p. 61
CURRABEHA	C (*Currach Beithe*): Marsh of the birch, p. 61
CURRACLOE	WX (*Currach Cló*): Marsh of the impression
CURRAGH	KE (*Currach*): Race-track, p. 62
CURRAGH	WD (*Currach*): Marsh, p. 61
CURRAGHBOY	RN (*Currach Buí*): Yellow marsh, p. 61
CURRAGHLAWN	WX (*Currach Leathan*): Broad marsh, p. 61
CURRAGHMORE	WD (*Currach Mór*): Big marsh, p. 61
CURRAGHROE	RN (*Currach Rua*): Red marsh, p. 61
CURRAGLASS	C (*Cora Ghlas*): Green weir
CURRAGLASS	C (*Currach Glas*): Grey/green marsh
CURRAN	AM & DY (*Corrán*): Crescent-shaped place, p. 62
CURRANDRUM	G (*Corr an Droma*): Pointed hill of the ridge, p. 61
CURRANE	MO (*Corrán*): Crescent-shaped place, p. 62

CURRANS	KY (*Corráin*): Crescent-shaped places
CURREENY	TY (*Coiriní*): Little pointed hills, p. 61
CURROW	KY (*Corra*): Round hills, p. 61
CURRY	SO (*Cora*): Weir
CURRYGLASS	C (*Currach Glas*): Grey/green marsh
CUSH	L (*Cois*): Foot
CUSHENDALL	AM (*Cois Abhann Dalla*): Foot of the river Dall
CUSHENDUN	AM (*Cois Abhann Duinne*): Foot of the river Dun
CUSHINA	OY (*Cois Eidhní*): Beside the ivy (river)

D

DAAR RIVER	L (*Abhainn na Darach*): River of the oak
DAARS	KE (*Dairghe*): Oaks
DAINGEAN	OY (*Daingean*): Fortress, pp 16, 67
DALKEY	D (*Deilginis*): Thorn island
DALUA RIVER	C (*Abhainn dá Lua*): River of two waters
DAMMA	KY (*Dá Mhagh*): Two plains, p. 119
DARRAGH	CE (*Darach*): Oak, p. 67
DARRARAGH	MO (*Dairbhre*): Oakwood, p. 67
DARRERY	C, G & L (*Dairbhre*): Oakwood, p. 67
DARRYNANE	KY (*Doire Fhíonáin*): Fíonán's oakwood
DAWROS HEAD	DL (*Damh Ros* + Head): Headland of the oxen (head)
DEEHOMMED	DN (*Deagh Choimead*): Good observation-post
DEEL RIVER	L, MO & WH (*Daoil* + River): Black + river
DEELE RIVER	DL (*Daoil* + River): Black + river
DEENISH ISLAND	KY (*Duibhinis*): Black island (island)
DELGANY	WW (*Deilgne*): Thorny place
DELVIN	WH (*Dealbhna*): (Territory of the) descendants of Dealbaeth
DERG LOUGH	CE, DL, G & TY (*Loch Deirg*): Lake of the red hole
DERG RIVER	TE (*Dearg* + River): Red + river, p. 68
DERNAGREE	C (*Doire na Graí*): Oak-grove of the stud of horses
DERNISH	CE, FH & SO (*Dair Inis*): Oak island
DERRAD	WH (*Doire Fhada*): Long oak-grove
DERRADA	LM (*Doire Fhada*): Long oakwood, p. 85
DERRAGH	C, LD & MO (*Darach*): Oak
DERRANE	RN (*Doireán*): Little oak-grove
DERRAVARAGH LOUGH	WH (*Loch Dairbhreach*): Lake of the abundance of oaks, p. 68
DERREEN RIVER	CW (*Doirín* + River): River of the little oak-grove
DERREEN	G (*Doirín*): Oak-grove
DERREENACARRIN	C (*Doire an Chairn*): Oak-grove of the cairn
DERREENACLAURIG	KY (*Doirín an Chláraigh*): Oak-grove of the planking
DERREENAFOYLE	KY (*Doirín an Phoill*): Oak-grove of the pool
DERREENAVURRIG	KY (*Doirín an Mhuirigh*): Oak-grove of the mariner
DERREENDRISLAGH	KY (*Doirín Drisleach*): Brambly oak-grove

DERREENNAMUCKLAGH	KY (*Doirín na Muclach*): Oak-grove of swine-herds
DERREENSILLAGH	KY (*Doirín Saileach*): Oak-grove of willows
DERRIES	OY (*Doirí*): Oakwoods
DERRINLAUR	WD (*Doire an Láir*): Middle oak-grove
DERRY	DY (*Doire* + *Calgaich/Doire* + *Cholm Cille*): Oak-grove of Calgach/Colm Cille, p. 70
DERRY	DN (*Doire an Bhile*): Oak-grove
DERRYADD	AH (*Doire Fhada*): Long oak-grove, p. 84
DERRYANVILLE	AH (*Doire an Bhile*): Oak-grove of the sacred tree, p. 70
DERRYBAWN	WW (*Doire Bán*): White oak-grove
DERRYBEG	DL (*Doirí Beaga*): Small oak-groves
DERRYBOY	DN (*Doire Buí*): Yellow oak-grove
DERRYCAW	AH (*Doire an Chatha*): Oakwood of the battle
DERRYCHRIER	DY (*Doire an Chriathair*): Oak-tree of the soft bog
DERRYCOFFEY	OY (*Doire Uí Chofaigh*): Oakwood of Ó Cofaigh
DERRYCOOGH	TY (*Doire Cuach*): Oak-grove of the cuckoos
DERRYCOOLY	OY (*Doire Cúile*): Oakwood of the nook
DERRYDAMPH	CN (*Doire Damh*): Oak-grove of the oxen
DERRYFUBBLE	TE (*Doire an Phobail*): Oakwood of the people
DERRYGARRANE NORTH	KY (*Doire an Ghearráin Thuaidh*): Oakwood of the horse, North, p. 150
DERRYGARRANE SOUTH	KY (*Doire an Ghearráin Theas*): Oakwood of the horse, South, p. 150
DERRYGARRANE	KY (*Doire an Ghearráin*): Oakwood of the gelding
DERRYGOOLAN	WH (*Doire an Ghabhláin*): Oak-grove of the fork, p. 89
DERRYGONNELLY	FH (*Doire Ó gConaíle*): Oakwood of Uí Chonaíle
DERRYGOLAN	WH (*Doire an Ghabhláin*): Oak-grove of the fork, p. 70
DERRYGRATH	TY (*Deargráth*): Red fort
DERRYGROGAN	OY (*Doire Grógáin*): Oakwood of the little heap
DERRYHARNEY	FH (*Doire Uí Chearnaigh*): Ó Cearnaigh's oakwood
DERRYHAW	AH (*Doire an Chatha*): Oakwood of the battle
DERRYHOWLAGHT	FH (*Doire Thaimleacht*): Oak-grove of the plague grave
DERRYKEEVAN	AH (*Doire Chaomháin*): Caomhán's oak-grove
DERRYKEIGHAN	AM (*Doire Chaechain*): Caechan's oak-grove
DERRYLAHARD	C (*Doire Leath Ard*): Oak-grove of the half (i.e. gentle) height
DERRYLANE	CN (*Doire Leathan*): Broad oakwood
DERRYLANEY	FH (*Doire Léana*): Oak-grove of the meadow

DERRYLARD	AH (*Doire Leath Ard*): Oak-grove of the half (i.e. gentle) height
DERRYLEAGH	KY (*Doire Liath*): Grey oakwood
DERRYLESTER	FH (*Doire an Leastair*): Oakwood of the small boat
DERRYLICKA	KY (*Doire Lice*): Oakwood of the flagstone
DERRYLIN	FH (*Doire Fhlainn*): Oak-grove of Flann
DERRYMIHIN	C (*Doire Mheithean*): Oak-grove of saplings
DERRYMORE	AH (*Doire Mór*): Large oakwood
DERRYNABLAHA	KY (*Doire na Blátha*): Oakwood of flowers
DERRYNACAHERAGH	C (*Doire na Catharach*): Oak-grove of the stone fort
DERRYNACLEIGH	G (*Doire na Cloiche*): Oak-grove of the stone
DERRYNAFEANA	KY (*Doire na bhFiann*): Oak-grove of the Fianna
DERRYNAFUNSHA	KY (*Doire na Fuinse*): Oakwood of the ash
DERRYNAGREE	KY (*Doire na Graí*): Oakwood of the stud
DERRYNANAFF	MO (*Doire na nDamh*): Oak-grove of the oxen
DERRYNASAGGART MOUNTAINS	KY (*Sléibhte Dhoire na Sagart*): Mountains of the oak-grove of the priests, p. 142
DERRYNASHALOGE	TE (*Doire na Sealg*): Oak-grove of the hunt
DERRYNESS	DL (*Doirinis*): Oak island
DERRYRUSH	G (*Doire Iorrais*): Oak-grove of the headland
DERRYTRASNA	AH (*Doire Trasna*): Oak-grove across
DERRYVEAGH MOUNTAINS	DL (*Sléibhte Dhoire Bheitheach*): Mountains of the oak-grove of the birches
DERRYVOHY	MO (*Doire Bhoithe*): Oak-grove of the hut
DERRYWILLOW	LM (*Doire Bhaile*): Oak-grove of the homestead
DERRYWINNY	CN (*Doire Bhainne*): Oak-grove of the milk
DERVOCK	AM (*Dearbhóg*): Touchstone
DESERT	MN (*Díseart*): Hermitage, pp 69, 70
DESERTCREAT	TE (*Díseart dá Chríoch*): Hermitage of two territories, p. 70
DESERTEGNY	DL (*Díseart Éignigh*): Éigneach's hermitage, p. 69
DESERTMARTIN	DY (*Díseart Mhártain*): Mártan's hermitage
DESERTOGHILL	DY (*Díseart Uí Thuathail*): Ó Tuathal's hermitage, p. 69
DEVENISH	FH (*Daimh Inis*): Island of oxen, p. 100
DEVLIN	DL, MO & MN (*Duibh Linn*): Black pool
DIAN	MN & TE (*Daingean*): Fortress
DIFFREEN	LM (*Dubh Thrian*): Black third
DINGIN	CN (*Daingean*): Fortress

DINGLE	KY (*Daingean*): Fortress, p. 67
DINIS	C (*Duibhinis*): Black island
DISERT	DL (*Díseart*): Hermitage, p. 69
DOAGH ISLE	DL (*Dumhachoileán*): Sandhill island
DOAGH	AM (*Dumhach*): Sandbank
DOAGHBEG	DL (*Dumhaigh Bhig*): Little sandbank
DOE CASTLE	DL (*Caisleán na dTuath*): Castle of the territories, p. 158
DOLLA	TY (*Dolla*): Loops
DONABATE	D (*Dún an Bháid*): Fort of the boat, p. 20
DONACARNEY	MH (*Domhnach Cearnaigh*): Cearnach's church
DONADEA	KE (*Domhnach Dheá*): Church of Deadha
DONAGH	FH (*Domhnach*): Church
DONAGHADEE	DN (*Domhnach Daoi*): Church of the rampart
DONAGHANIE	TE (*Domhnach an Eich*): Church of the steed
DONAGHCLONEY	DN (*Domhnach Cluana*): Church of the field
DONAGHEDY	TE (*Domhnach Caoide*): Caoide's church, p. 72
DONAGHEY	TE (*Dún Eachaidh*): Eachaidh's fort
DONAGHMORE	LS, MH & TY (*Domhnach Mór*): Big church, p. 72
DONAGHMOYNE	MN (*Domhnach Maighean*): Church of the little plain
DONAGHPATRICK	MH (*Domhnach Phádraig*): Pádraig's church
DONAGHRISK	TE (*Domhnach Riascadh*): Church of the marsh, p. 72
DONAMON	RN (*Dún Iomain*): Ioman's fort
DONARD	WW & WX (*Dún Ard*): High fort
DONASKEAGH	TY (*Dún na Sciath*): Fort of the shields
DONEGAL	DL (*Dún na nGall*): Fort of the foreigners, p. 77
DONERAILE	C (*Dún ar Aill*): Fort on the cliff, p. 13
DONNYBROOK	D (*Domhnach Broc*): Broc's church, p. 72
DONNYCARNEY	D (*Domhnach Cearnaigh*): Cearnach's church
DONOHILL	TY (*Dún Eochaille*): Fort of the yew-wood
DONORE	MH (*Dún Uabhair*): Fort of pride
DONOUGHMORE	C (*Domhnach Mór*): Big church
DOO LOUGH	CE & MO (*Dubh Loch*): Black lake
DOOAGH	MO (*Dú Acha*): Mound of the field
DOOCASTLE	MO (*Caisleán an Dumha*): Mound castle
DOOCHARY	DL (*Dúchoraidh*): Black weir
DOOCREGGAUN	MO (*Dubh Creagán*): Little black crag, p. 64
DOOGARRY	CN (*Dúgharraí*): Garden mound
DOOGHBEG	MO (*Dumha Beag*): Small mound
DOOGORT	MO (*Du Gort*): Salty mound
DOOHAMLET	MN (*Dúthamhlacht*): Black plague burial

DOOHAT	MN (*Dútháite*): Black site
DOOHOMA	MO (*Dú Thuama*): Black mound
DOOISH	DL & TE (*Dubhais*): Black ridge
DOOLEEG	MO (*Dú Liag*): Black flag
DOOLIN	CE (*Dúlinn*): Black pool
DOON	G & L (*Dún*): Fort
DOONAHA	CE (*Dún Átha*): Fort of the ford
DOONALLY	SO (*Dún Aille*): Fort of the cliff
DOONBEG	CE (*Dún Beag*): Small fort, pp 27, 78
DOONFEENY	MO (*Dún Fine*): Fine's fort
DOORAHEEN	WH (*Dubhrathain*): Black ferny ground
DORSEY	AH (*Dorsa*): Gates
DOUGLAS	C & LS (*Dúglas*): Black stream
DOVEA	TY (*Dubhfhéith*): Black bog
DOWNINGS	DL (*Dúnaibh*): Forts, p. 78
DOWNPATRICK	DN (*Dún Pádraig*): Pádraig's fort, p. 78
DOWRA	CN & LM (*Damhshraith*): Ox-holm
DREHID	KE (*Droichead*): Bridge, p. 74
DRIMFRIES	DL (*Droim Fraoigh*): Heather-ridge
DRIMINIDY	C (*Droim Inide*): Ridge of Shrove
DRIMNAGH	D (*Droimneach*): Ridged land
DRIMOLEAGUE	C (*Drom dhá Liag*): Ridge of two stones
DRINAGH	C & WX (*Draighneach*): Abounding in blackthorns, p. 74
DRINAN	D (*Draighnen*): Place producing blackthorn
DROGHED	DY (*Droichead*): Bridge, p. 74
DROGHEDA	LH (*Droichead Átha*): Bridge of the ford, p. 74
DROICHEAD NUA	KE (*Droichead Nua*): New bridge
DROIMLAMPH	DY (*Droim Leamh*): Elm-ridge
DROM	KY & TY (*Drom*): Ridge
DROMACOMER	L (*Drom an Chomair*): Ridge of the confluence
DROMADA	L & MO (*Droim Fhada*): Long ridge, p. 85
DROMAHAIR	LM (*Drom dhá Eithiar*): Ridge of two demons
DROMALIVAUN	KY (*Drom Leamháin*): Elm-ridge, p. 107
DROMARA	DN (*Droim Bearach*): Pointed ridge
DROMARD	SO (*Droim Ard*): High ridge, p. 16
DROMBANE	TY (*Drom Bán*): White ridge
DROMBOFINNY	C (*Droim Bó Finne*): Ridge of the white cow, p. 31
DROMCOLLIHER	L (*Drom Collachair*): Ridge of the hazelwood
DROMIN	L & LH (*Droim Ing*): Little ridge

DROMINA	C (*Droimneach*): Ridged land
DROMINDOORA	CE (*Drom an Dúdhoire*): Ridge of the dark oak-grove
DROMINEER	TY (*Drom Inbhir*): Ridge of the estuary
DROMISKIN	LH (*Droim Ineasclainn*): Ridge of the torrent
DROMKEEN	L (*Drom Caoin*): Beautiful ridge
DROMLUSK	KY (*Droim Loiscthe*): Burnt ridge
DROMMAHANE	C (*Drom Átháin*): Ridge of the little ford
DROMOD	LM (*Dromad*): Ridge
DROMORE	C, DN, TE, etc. (*Droim Mór*): Big ridge
DRUM	MN (*Droim*): Ridge
DRUMACRIB	MN (*Droim Mhic Roib*): Mac Rob's ridge
DRUMADRIHID	CE (*Droim an Droichid*): Ridge of the bridge
DRUMAHOE	DY (*Droim na hUamha*): Ridge of the cave, p. 160
DRUMAKILL	MN (*Droim na Coille*): Ridge of the wood
DRUMANEE	DY (*Droim an Fhiaidh*): Ridge of the deer
DRUMANESPIC	CN (*Droim an Easpaig*): Ridge of the bishop
DRUMANESS	DN (*Droim an Easa*): Ridge of the waterfall
DRUMANEY	TE (*Droim Eanaigh*): Ridge of the bog
DRUMANNON	AH (*Droim Meannáin*): Ridge of the pinnacle
DRUMANTEE	AH (*Dromainn Tí*): Ridge of the marking
DRUMAROAD	DN (*Droim an Róid*): Ridge of the route
DRUMARRAGHT	FH (*Droim Arracht*): Ridge of the apparition
DRUMATOBER	G (*Droim an Tobair*): Ridge of the well
DRUMBANE	TY (*Drom Bán*): White ridge
DRUMBO	DN (*Droim Both*): Ridge of the hut, p. 270
DRUMBOY	DL (*Drom Buí*): Yellow ridge
DRUMBRUGHAS	CN & FH (*Droim Brughas*): Ridge of the mansion
DRUMCAR	LH (*Droim Chora*): Ridge of the weir, p. 60
DRUMCLIFF	SO (*Droim Cliabh*): Ridge of the baskets
DRUMCOLLOGHER	L (*Drum Collachair*): Ridge of the hazelwood
DRUMCONDRA	D & MH (*Droim Conrach*): Ridge of the path
DRUMCONRATH	MH (*Droim Conrach*): Ridge of the path
DRUMCOSE	FH (*Droim Cuas*): Ridge of the hollow
DRUMCREE	WH (*Droim Cria*): Ridge of the clay
DRUMCROONE	DY (*Droim Cruithen*): Ridge of the Cruithin
DRUMCULLEN	OY (*Droim Cuilinn*): Holly-ridge
DRUMDEEVIN	DL (*Droim Diomhaoin*): Idle ridge
DRUMDERAOWN	C (*Droim 'ir dhá Abhainn*): Ridge between two rivers, p. 12
DRUMENNY	TE (*Droim Eanaigh*): Ridge of the marsh

DRUMFAD	DL, DN, SO & TE (*Droim Fhada*): Long ridge, p. 84
DRUMFADDA	C & KY (*Droim Fhada*): Long ridge, p. 84
DRUMFEA	CW (*Droim Féich*): Ridge of the raven
DRUMFIN	SO (*Droim Fionn*): White ridge
DRUMFREE	DL (*Droim Fraoigh*): Ridge of the heather
DRUMGATH	DN (*Droim Ga*): Ridge of the spear
DRUMGOOSE	AH, MN & TE (*Droim gCaas*): Ridge of the cave
DRUMHAWAN	MN (*Droim Shamhuin*): Ridge of the winter festival
DRUMHUSKERT	MO (*Droim Thuaisceart*): Northern ridge
DRUMKEEN	DL (*Droim Caoin*): Smooth ridge
DRUMKEERAN	LM (*Droim Caorthainn*): Ridge of the rowans, p. 75
DRUMLANE	CN (*Droim Leathan*): Wide ridge
DRUMLEA	TE (*Droim Liath*): Grey ridge
DRUMLEE	DN (*Droim Laegh*): Ridge of the calf
DRUMLEEVAN	LM (*Droim Leamháin*): Elm-ridge, p. 107
DRUMLEGAGH	TE (*Droim Liagach*): Ridge of the boulder
DRUMLISH	LD (*Droim Lis*): Ridge of the fort
DRUMLOOSE	WH (*Droim Lus*): Ridge of herbs
DRUMMIN	MO (*Dromainn*): Little ridge
DRUMMOHER	L (*Droim Mothar*): Ridge of the ruined fort
DRUMMOND	LS (*Dromainn*): Ridge
DRUMMULLIN	RN (*Droim an Mhuilinn*): Ridge of the mill
DRUMNACARRA	LH (*Droim na Chairthe*): Ridge of the pillar-stone
DRUMNAFINNAGLE	DL (*Droim na Fionghal*): Ridge of the fratricide
DRUMNAFINNILA	LM (*Droim na Fionghal*): Ridge of the fratricide
DRUMNAHEARK	DL (*Droim na hAdhairce*): Ridge of the horn
DRUMNAHOE	AM & TE (*Droim na hUamha*): Ridge of the cave, p. 160
DRUMNAKILLY	TE (*Droim na Coille*): Ridge of the wood
DRUMNANALIV	MN (*Droim na nDealbh*): Ridge of the phantoms
DRUMNASHALOGE	TE (*Droim na Sealg*): Ridge of the hunt
DRUMQUIN	TE (*Droim Caoin*): Smooth ridge
DRUMRAGH	TE (*Droim Rátha*): Ridge of the ring-fort
DRUMRALLA	FH (*Droim Rálach*): Ridge of oak
DRUMRANEY	WH (*Droim Raithne*): Ridge of ferns, pp 75, 132
DRUMREE	MH (*Droim Rí*): Ridge of the king
DRUMSHANBO	LM (*Droim Sean-bhó*): Ridge of the old cow, p. 31
DRUMSKINNY	FH (*Droim Scine*): Ridge of the knife
DRUMSNA	LM (*Droim ar Snámh*): Floating ridge
DRUMSRU	KE (*Droim Sruth*): Ridge of the streams
DRUMSURN	DY (*Droim Sorn*): Ridge of the furnaces

DRUNG	CN (*Drong*): Folk
DUAGH	KY (*Dubháth*): Black ford
DUARRIGLE	C (*Dubh Aireagal*): Black oratory
DUBLIN	D (*Dubh Linn*): Black pool, p. 75
DUGORT	MO (*Dú Goirt*): Black field
DUHALLOW	C (*Duthaigh Ealla*): District of the (river) Ealla
DULANE	MH (*Tulán*): Little hill
DULEEK	MH (*Damhliag*): Stone church, p.xxx
DUN LAOGHAIRE	D (*Dún Laoghaire*): Laoghaire's fort
DUNAFF	DL (*Dún Damh*): Fort of oxen
Dún Ailinne	KE, p. 76
DUNANY	LH (*Dún Áine*): Áine's fort
DUNBEG	G (*Dún Beag*): Small fort, p. 77
DUNBELL	KK (*Dún Bile*): Fort of the tree
Dún Bhalor	DL: Balor's fort, p. 76
Dún Bhinne	KY: Fort of the cliff, p. 76
DUNBOYNE	MH (*Dún Bóinne*): Fort of the white cow goddess
DUNCANNON	WX (*Dún Canann*): Canainn's fort
Dún Cermna	C, p. 76
DUNCORMICK	WX (*Dún Chormaic*): Cormac's fort
DUNCRUN	DY (*Dún Cruithen*): Fort of the Cruithin, p. 23
Dún dá Lethglas	p. 109
DUNDALK	LH (*Dún Dealgan*): Dealga's fort, p. 25
DUNDAREIRKE	C (*Dún dá Radharc*): Fort of two prospects
DUNDARYARK	KK (*Dún dá Rhadharc*): Fort of two prospects
DUNDERRY	MH (*Dún Doire*): Fort of the oak-grove, p. 70
DUNDONALD	DN (*Dún Dónaill*): Dónall's fort, p. 77
DUNDROD	AM (*Dún dTrod*): Fort of the fights
DUNDRUM	D, DN, LS & TY (*Dún Droma*): Fort of the ridge, pp 75, 77
DUNEANE	AM (*Dún dá Éan*): Fort of two birds, p. 67
DUNEEL	WH (*Dún Aoil*): Lime fort
DUNEIGHT	DN (*Dún Echdach*): Eochaid's fort, p. 77
DUNFANAGHY	DL (*Dún Fionnachaidh*): Fort of the white field
DUNFORE	SO (*Dún Fuar*): Cold fort, p. 77
DUNGALL	AM (*Dún Gall*): Fort of the strangers, p. 77
DUNGANNON	TE (*Dún Geanainn*): Geanann's fort
DUNGANSTOWN	WX (*Baile Uí Dhonnagáin*): Homestead of Donnagán
DUNGARVAN	KK & WD (*Dún Garbháin*): Garbhán's fort
DUNGIVEN	DY (*Dún Geimhin*): Geimhean's fort

DUNGLOW	DL (Dún Cloiche): Fort of the stone
DUNGOURNEY	C (Dún Guairne): Guairne's fort
DUNHILL	WD (Dún Aill): Fort-cliff, p. 13
DUNINENY	AM (Dún an Aonaigh): Fort of the assembly, p. 17
DUNIRY	G (Dún Doighre): Fort of the blast
DUNKERRIN	OY (Dún Cairin): Caire's fort
DUNKERRON	KY (Dún Ciaráin): Ciarán's fort
DUNKINEELY	DL (Dún Cionnfhaolaidh): Cionnfhaoladh's fort
DUNLAVIN	WW (Dún Luáin): Luán's fort
DUNLEER	LH (Dún Léire): Léire's fort
Dún Lethglaise	p. 109
DUNLEWY	DL (Dún Lúiche): Lughaidh's fort
DUNLOY	AM (Dún Lathaí): Fort of the mire
DUNLUCE	AM (Dún Lios): Fort of the fort
DUNMANUS	C (Dún Mánais): Mánas's fort
DUNMOON	WD (Dún Móin): Món's fort
DUNMORE	DL, G & WD (Dún Mór): Big fort, p. 77
DUNMOYLE	TE (Dún Maol): Bald fort
DUNMURRY	AM (Dún Muirí): Muireadhach's fort, p. 77
DUNNALONG	DY (Dún na Long): Fortress of the ships
DUNNAMAGGAN	KE & KK (Dún na mBogán): Fort of the soft ground
DUNNAMANAGH	TE (Dún na Manach): Fort of the monks, p. 78
DUNNAMARK	KY (Dún na mBarc): Fort of the boats
DUNNAMORE	TE (Domhnach Mór): Big church, p. 72
DUNQUIN	KY (Dún Chaoin): Smooth fort
DUNRAYMOND	MN (Dún Réamainn): Réamann's fort
DUNREE	DL (Dún Riabhach): Striped fort
DUNSALLAGH	CE (Dún Salach): Dirty fort
DUNSEVERICK	AM (Dún Sobhairce): Sobhairce's fort, pp 76, 133
DUNSHAUGHLIN	MH (Domhnach Seachlainn): Seachnall's church, p. 72
DUNTINNY	DL (Dún Teine): Fort of the fire
DURROW	LS (Darú): Oak-plain
DURRUS	C (Dú-ros): Black grove
DURSEY	C (Dóirse): Gates
DYAN	TE (Daingean): Stronghold
DYSART	RN & WH (Díseart): Hermitage, p. 70
DYSERT	CE (Díseart): Hermitage, p. 70

Eachlann	Horseland, p. 104
EASKY	SO (*Iascach*): Abounding in fish
EDEN	AM (*Éadan*): Brow, p. 80
EDENDERRY	AM & OY (*Éadan Doire*): Brow of the oakwood, p. 80
EDENDORK	TE (*Éadan na dTorc*): Brow of the hogs, p. 80
EDENTRILLICK	DN (*Éadan Trilic*): Brow of the three stones, p. 80
EDERNEY	FH (*Eadarnaigh*): Ambush
EDGEWORTHSTOWN	LD, p. 83
EGLISH	TE (*Eaglais*): Church, p. 100
EIGHTER	CN (*Íochtar*): Lower (place), p. 100
EIGHTERCUA	KY (*Íochtar Cua*): Lower hollow, p. 100
EIRK	KY (*Adharc*): Peak
ELPHIN	RN (*Ail Finn*): Fionn's stone
EMLAGH	MO (*Imleach*): Borderland, p. 99
EMLAGHFAD	SO (*Imleach Fada*): Long borderland, p. 99
EMLAGHMORE	KY (*Imleach Mór*): Large borderland, p. 99
EMLY	TY (*Imleach*): Borderland, p. 99
EMO	LS (*Íoma*): Image
ENNELL LOUGH	WH (*Loch Ainnínne*): Lough of Ainneann
ENNIS	CE (*Inis*): Island, p. 99
ENNISKEAN	C (*Inis Céin*): Cian's island
ENNISKERRY	WW (*Áth na Sceire*): Ford of the rocky place
ENNISKILLEN	FH (*Inis Ceithleann*): Ceithle's island
ENNISTIMMON	CE (*Inis Díomáin*): Díomán's island
ERRIGAL KEEROGUE	TE (*Earagail Do Chiaróg*): Do Chiaróg's oratory, p. 82
ERRIGAL MOUNTAIN	DL (*Earagail* + Mountain): Oratory + mountain, p. 82
ERRIS HEAD	MO (*Iorras* + Head): Promontory + head, p. 101
ERRISLANNAN	G (*Iorras Fhlannáin*): Flannan's head, p. 101
ESHNADEELADA	FH (*Ais na Diallaite*): Ridge of the saddle
ESKE LOUGH	DL (*Loch Iasc*): Abounding in fish lake
ESKER	D & LD (*Eiscir*): Gravel-ridge, p. 83
ESKERRIDGE	TE (*Eiscir* + Ridge): Gravel-ridge (ridge), p. 83
ESKINE	KY (*Eisc Dhoimnin*): Deep fissure
ESKRA	TE (*Eiscreach*): Place of gravel-ridges, p. 83
ESNADARRA	FH (*Ais na Darach*): Side of the place abounding in oaks

F

<table>
<tr><td>FAD LOUGH</td><td>DL (Loch Fada): Long lake</td></tr>
<tr><td>FAES</td><td>L (Feá): Wood</td></tr>
<tr><td>FAHA</td><td>K & WD (Faiche): Green, p. 85</td></tr>
<tr><td>FAHAMORE</td><td>KY (Faiche Mhór): Big green, p. 85</td></tr>
<tr><td>FAHAN</td><td>DL (Fathain): Burial-place</td></tr>
<tr><td>FAHANASOODRY</td><td>L (Faiche na Súdaire): Green of the tanners</td></tr>
<tr><td>FAHEERAN</td><td>OY (Faiche Chiaráin): Ciarán's green</td></tr>
<tr><td>FAHY</td><td>OY (Faiche): Green, p. 85</td></tr>
<tr><td>FAIAFLANNAN</td><td>DL (Faiche Flannáin): Flannan's green</td></tr>
<tr><td>Faill Dhubh</td><td>KY: Black cliff, p. 85</td></tr>
<tr><td>Faill Fhada</td><td>KY: Long cliff, p. 85</td></tr>
<tr><td>FALCARRAGH</td><td>DL (Fál Carrach): Scabby fence</td></tr>
<tr><td>FALLAGLOON</td><td>DY (Folach Glún): Hidden rise</td></tr>
<tr><td>FALLEENADATHA</td><td>L (Faillín an Deatha): Little cliff of the smoke</td></tr>
<tr><td>FARDRUM</td><td>WH (Fordhroim): Ridge-top</td></tr>
<tr><td>FARGRIM</td><td>FH & LM (Fordhroim): Ridge-top</td></tr>
<tr><td>FARNAGH</td><td>WH (Farnocht): Bare hill</td></tr>
<tr><td>FARNAGHT</td><td>LM (Farnocht): Bare hill</td></tr>
<tr><td>FARNALORE</td><td>WH (Fearann an Lobhair): Land of the leper</td></tr>
<tr><td>FARNANES</td><td>C (Fearnáin): Place producing alders</td></tr>
<tr><td>FARNAUGHT</td><td>SO (Farnocht): Bare hill</td></tr>
<tr><td>FARNEY</td><td>MN (Fearnmagh): Alder plain</td></tr>
<tr><td>FARRA</td><td>AH (Farrach): Meeting-place</td></tr>
<tr><td>FARRAGH</td><td>CN (Farrach): Meeting-place</td></tr>
<tr><td>FARRAGHROE</td><td>WH (Farracha Ruadha): Red meeting-places</td></tr>
<tr><td>FARRAN</td><td>C, KY & WH (Fearann): Territory, p. 87</td></tr>
<tr><td>FARRANBOLEY</td><td>D (Fearann Buaile): Territory of the milking-place, p. 87</td></tr>
<tr><td>FARRANFADDA</td><td>C (Fearann Fada): Long territory, p. 87</td></tr>
<tr><td>FARRANFORE</td><td>KY (Fearann Fuar): Cold land, p. 87</td></tr>
<tr><td>FARRANMACBRIDE</td><td>DL (Fearann Mhic Bhríde): Mac Bride's land</td></tr>
<tr><td>FARSETMORE</td><td>DL (Fearsad Mór): Large sandbank</td></tr>
<tr><td>FARSID</td><td>C (Fearsad): Sandbank</td></tr>
<tr><td>FARTA</td><td>G (Fearta): Graves, p. 87</td></tr>
<tr><td>FARTAGH</td><td>CN & FH (Feartach): Place of graves, p. 87</td></tr>
<tr><td>FEAGARRID</td><td>WD (Féith Ghairid): Short stream</td></tr>
</table>

FEAKLE	CE (*Fiacall*): Tooth
FEALE RIVER	KY & L (*Feil* + River): Fial's river
FEARN HILL	DL (*Fearn* + Hill): Alder hill
FEDAMORE	L (*Feadamair*): Place of streams
FEDANY	DN (*Feadanach*): Place of streams
FEEBANE	MN (*Fioda Bán*): White wood, p. 87
FEENAGH	L (*Fiodhnach*): Wooded place, p. 88
FEENISH	CE (*Fiodh-Inis*): Woody island
FEENY	DY (*Fineadha*): Woods
FELTRIM	DN (*Fealdruim*): Wolf-ridge
FENAGH	LM (*Fiodhnach*): Wooded place, p. 88
FENIT	KY (*Fianait*): Wild place
FENNAGH	CW (*Fionnmhach*): White plain, p. 88
FENNOR	WD (*Fionnúr*): Place by white water
FEOHANAGH	L (*Feothanach*): Windy place
FERBANE	OY (*Féar Bán*): White grass, p. 27
FERMOY	C ([*Mainistir*] *Fhear Maighe*): (Monastery of the district of) Fir Mhaí
FERMOYLE	KY (*Formael*): Round hill
FERN LOUGH	DL (*Loch Fearna*): Lake of the alders, p. 87
FERNS	WX (*Fearna*): Place of alder-trees, p. 87
FERTA	KY (*Fearta*): Graves, p. 87
FERTAGH	LM & MH (*Feartach*): Place of graves, p. 87
FETHARD	TY & WX (*Fiodh Ard*): High wood, p. 87
FEWS	AH & WD (*Feá*): Woods, p. 88
FIDDOWN	KK (*Fiodh Dúin*): Wood of the fort, p. 88
FIERIES	KY (*Foidhrí*): Slopes
FIGILE RIVER	OY (*Abhainn Fhiodh Gaibhle*): River of the wood of the fork, p. 88
FIN LOUGH	CE (*Loch Fionn*): White lake
FINAGHY	AM (*Fionnachadh*): White field, p. 88
FINDRUM	DL & TE (*Fionn Droim*): White ridge
FINEA	WH (*Fiodh an Átha*): Wood of the ford, p. 88
FINGLAS	D (*Fionnghlas*): Bright stream, pp 19, 88
FINISK	WD (*Fionnuisce*): White water
FINN LOUGH	DL (*Loch Finne*): White lake
FINNEA	CN & WH (*Fiodh an Átha*): Wood of the ford, pp 19, 88
FINNY	MO (*Fionnáithe*): White kiln
FINTONA	TE (*Fionntamhnach*): Bright clearing
FINTOWN	DL (*Baile na Finne*): Homestead of the (river) Finn

FINTRA	CE (*Fionn Traigh*): White strand
FINTRAGH	DL (*Fionn Traigh*): White strand
FINVOY	AM (*Fionnbhoth*): White hut, p. 88
FOFANNYBANE	DN (*Fofannaigh Bhán*): White thistle land
FOFANNYREAGH	DN (*Fofannaigh Riabhach*): Striped thistle land
FOILNAMAN	TY (*Faill na mBan*): Cliff of the women, p. 85
FORE	WH ([*Baile*] *Fhobhair*): (Homestead of the) spring
FORMAL	MH (*Formael*): Round hill
FORMIL	TE (*Formael*): Round hill
FORMWEEL	G (*Formael*): Round hill
FOYFIN	DL (*Faiche Fionn*): Fair green, p. 85
FOYLE LOUGH	DL (*Loch Feabhail*): Lough of Feabhal
FOYNES	L (*Faing*): Raven
FREAGHDUFF	TY (*Fraech Dubh*): Black heathery place
FREAGHMORE	WH (*Fraech Mór*): Large heathery place
FREEDUFF	AH & CN (*Fraech Dubh*): Black heathery place
FRESHFORD	KK (*Achadh Úr*): Fresh field, p. 156
FROGHANSTOWN	WH (*Baile Fraocháin*): Homestead of the bilberries
FUERTY	RN (*Fiodharta*): Wooded place
FUNSHION RIVER	C & L (*Fuinseann* + River): Ash-producing + river
FURRALEIGH	WD (*Foradh Liath*): Grey mound
FYBAGH	KY (*Fadhbach*): Lumpy place
FYFIN	TE (*Faiche Fionn*): Fair green, p. 85

G

G

GAGGIN	C (*Géagán*): Arm
GALBALLY	L, TE, WX, etc. (*Gallbhaile*): Foreigner's homestead
GALBOOLY	TY (*Gallbhuaile*): Milking-place of the foreigner
GALLAN	TE (*Gallán*): Standing stone, p. 89
GALLANE	C (*Gallán*): Standing stone, p. 89
GALLEN	MO (*Gailenga*): (Territory of) the descendants of Gaileng
GALLIAGH	DY ([*Baile na*] *gCailleach*): (Settlement of the) nuns
GALMOY	TY (*Gabhal Mhaí*): Fork of the plain, p. 89
GALTRIM	MH (*Cala Truim*): Holm of the elder
GALWAY	G (*Gaillimh*): Stony (river)
GALWOLIE	DL (*Gallbhuaile*): Milking-place of the foreigner
GARA LOUGH	SO (*Loch Uí Gadhra*): Ó Gadhra's lake
GARBALLY	G (*Gearrbhaile*): Short homestead
GARDICE	LM (*Garbhros*): Rough copse
GARDRUM	FH & TE (*Gearrdroim*): Short ridge
GARNAVILLA	TY (*Garrán an Bhile*): Grove of the sacred tree, p. 90
GARNISH	C (*Gar-inis*): Rough island
GARRANAMANAGH	KY (*Garrán na Manach*): Grove of the monks, p. 90
GARRANARD	MO (*Garrán Ard*): High grove, p. 90
GARRANE	TY (*Garrán*): Grove, p. 90
GARRANLAHAN	RN (*Garrán Leathan*): Broad grove, p. 90
GARRAUN	CE & G (*Garrán*): Grove, p. 90
GARRISKIL	WH (*Garascal*): Rough nook
GARRON POINT	AM (*Gearrán* + Point): Horse point
GARRY	AM (*Garraí*): Garden, p. 91
GARRYDUFF	C (*Garraí Dubh*): Black garden, p. 91
GARRYHILL	CW (*Gharbhchoill*): Rough wood, p. 90
GARRYNAFELA	WH (*Garraí na Féile*): Garden of the hospitality
GARRYOWEN	L (*Garraí Eoghain*): Eoghan's garden, p. 91
GARRYSPILLANE	L (*Garraí Uí Spealán*): Ó Spealán's garden, p. 9
GARVAGH	DY (*Garbhachadh*): Rough field, pp 13, 90
GARVAGHEY	TE (*Garbhachadh*): Rough field, p. 90
GARVAGHY	DN (*Garbhachadh*): Rough field, p. 90
GARVERY	FH (*Garbhaire*): Rough land
GATHABAWN	KY (*Geata Bán*): White gate, p. 27

GAY ISLAND	FH (*Inis na nGédh*): Goose island
GEARHA	KY (*Gaortha*): Wooded valley, p. 89
GEARHAMEEN	KY (*Gaortha Mín*): Smooth wooded valley, p. 89
GEARHASALLAGH	KY (*Gaortha Sailech*): Wooded valley of willows, p. 89
GILL LOUGH	KY, LM & SO (*Loch Gile*): Lake of brightness
GLANARUDDERY MOUNTAINS	KY (*Sléibhte Ghleann an Ridire*): Valley of the knight mountains, pp 93, 142
GLANDORE	C (*Gleann Dor*): Valley of the doors
GLANMIRE	C (*Gleann Maghair*): Valley of the plain, p. 92
GLANMORE	KY (*Gleann Mór*): Big valley, p. 92
GLANTANE	C (*Gleanntán*): Little valley, p. 93
GLANWORTH	C (*Gleann Iubhair*): Valley of the yew
GLASCARN	WH (*Glascharn*): Green cairn
GLASDRUMMAN	DN (*Glasdromainn*): Grey/green ridge, p. 91
GLASHABOY	C (*Glaise Buí*): Yellow stream, p. 91
GLASLOUGH	MN (*Glasloch*): Grey/green lake, p. 91
GLASNEVIN	D (*Glas Naíon*): Stream of the child, p. 91
GLASSAN	WH (*Glasán*): Little stream, p. 91
GLASSAVULLAUN	D (*Glas an Mhulláin*): Streamlet of the small summit, p. 124
GLASSLECK	LH (*Glasleac*): Grey/green flag
GLASTHULE	D (*Glas Tuathail*): Tuathal's streamlet, p. 91
GLASTRY	DN (*Glasrach*): Green grassy place
GLEN	CN, KK & WD (*Gleann*): Valley, p. 92
GLENADE	SO (*Gleann Éada*): Éada's valley
GLENAGEARY	D (*Gleann na gCaorach*): Valley of the sheep
GLENAGOWR	L (*Gleann na nGabhar*): Valley of the goats
GLENAMADDY	RN (*Gleann na Madadh*): Valley of the dogs, p. 92
GLENAMOY	MO (*Gleann na Muaidhe*): Valley of the clouds
GLENANNE	AH (*Gleann Anna*): Anna's valley
GLENARD	AM (*Gleann Ard*): High valley, p. 92
GLENARM	AM (*Gleann Arma*): Valley of arms
GLENASMOLE	D (*Gleann na Smól*): Valley of the thrushes
GLENAVY	AM (*Lann Abhaigh*): Church of the dwarf, pp 7, 93, 104
GLENBEG	C (*Gleann Beag*): Small valley, p. 92
GLENBEIGH	KY (*Gleann Beithe*): Valley of the birch, p. 92
GLENBOY	SO (*Gleann Buí*): Yellow valley, p. 92
GLENBRYAN	WX (*Gleann Bhriain*): Brian's valley
GLENBUSH	AM (*Gleann na Buaise*): Valley of the (river) Bush

GLENCAIRN	WD (*Gleann an Chairn*): Valley of the cairn, p. 92
GLENCAR	KY & SO (*Gleann an Chairthe*): Valley of the standing stone
GLENCOLUMBKILLE	DL (*Gleann Cholm Cille*): Valley of Colm Cille, p. 93
GLENCOVET	DL (*Gleann Coimheada*): Valley of the observation-post
GLENCULLEN	D (*Gleann Cuilinn*): Valley of holly
GLENDALOUGH	WW (*Gleann dá Locha*): Valley of two lakes, pp 67, 92
GLENDAVAGH	TE (*Gleann dá Mhaighe*): Valley of two plains
GLENDERRY	KY (*Gleann Doire*): Valley of the oak-grove
GLENDOWAN	DL (*Gleann Domhain*): Deep valley, p. 92
GLENDUFF	C (*Gleann Dubh*): Black valley, p. 92
GLENDUN	AM (*Gleann Dun*): Valley of the (river) Dun
GLENEANY	DL (*Gleann Eidneach*): Valley of the river abounding in ivy
GLENEASK	SO (*Gleann Iasc*): Fish valley
GLENEELY	DL (*Gleann Daoile*): Valley of the (river) Daol
GLENFARNE	LM & SO (*Gleann Fearna*): Valley of the alders, pp 87, 92
GLENFLESK	KY (*Gleann Fleisce*): Valley of the hoop
GLENGARRIFF	C (*Gleann Garbh*): Rough valley, p. 90
GLENGESH	DL (*Gleann Geis*): Valley of the taboo
GLENGEVLIN	CN (*Gleann Gaibhle*): Gaibhle's valley
GLENHULL	TE (*Gleann Choill*): Valley of the wood
GLENMALURE	WW (*Gleann Maolúra*): Maolúra's valley, p. 93
GLENMORE	KK & KY (*Gleann Mór*): Big valley, p. 92
GLENNAGERAGH	TE (*Gleann na gCaorach*): Valley of the sheep
GLENNAMADDY	G (*Gleann na Madadh*): Valley of the dogs, p. 92
GLENNASCAUL	G (*Gleann an Scáil*): Valley of the phantom, p. 93
GLENNAVADDOGE	G (*Gleann na bhfeadóg*): Glen of the plovers
GLENNAWOO	SO (*Gleann na bhFuath*): Valley of the spectres
GLENOE	AM (*Gleann Eo*): Valley of the yew, p. 92
GLEN OF IMAIL	WW (*Gleann Ó Maoil*): Valley of Uí Maoil
GLENONE	DY (*Cluain Eoghain*): Eoghan's pasture, p. 93
GLENQUIN	L (*Gleann an Chuin*): Valley of the hollow
GLENROE	L (*Gleann Rua*): Red valley
GLENSMOIL	DL (*Gleann an Smóil*): Valley of the thrush
GLENSOOSKA	KY (*Gleann Samhaisce*): Valley of the heifer
GLENTANE	G (*Gleanntán*): Little valley, p. 93
GLENTIES	DL (*Gleannta*): Valleys, p. 93
GLENTOGHER	DL (*Gleann Tóchair*): Valley of the causeway, p. 93

GLENVAR	DL (*Gleann an Bhairr*): Valley of the top
GLENWHERRY	AM (*Gleann an Choire*): Valley of the cauldron (river)
GLIN	L (*Gleann*): Valley, p. 92
GLOUNTHAUNE	C (*Gleanntán*): Small valley
GLYNN	AM, CW & WX (*Gleann*): Valley, p. 92
GNEEVGULLIAGH	KY (*Gníomh go Leith*): A gneeve and a half
GOLA	DL (*Gabhla*): Forks, p. 89
GOLDEN	TY (*Gabhailín*): Little fork, p. 89
GOLEEN	C (*Góilín*): Inlet, p. 93
GOREY	WX (*Guaire*): Sandbank
GORT	G (*Gort*): Tilled field, p. 93
GORTACLARE	TE (*Gort an Chláir*): Tilled field of the plain, p. 94
GORTAHILL	CN (*Gort an Choill*): Tilled field of the wood, p. 94
GORTAMULLIN	KY (*Gort an Mhuilinn*): Tilled field of the mill, p. 94
GORTANEAR	WH (*Gort an Fhéir*): Garden of the grass
GORTAREVAN	OY (*Gort an Riabháin*): Tilled field of the little stripe
GORTATLEA	KY (*Gort an tSléibhe*): Tilled field of the mountain, p. 94
GORTAVALLA	L (*Gort an Bhaile*): Tilled field of the homestead
GORTAVILLY	TE (*Gort an Bhile*): Tilled field of the ritual tree
GORTAVOY	TE (*Gort an Mhaí*): Tilled field of the plain, p. 94
GORTEEN	G, SO, WD, etc. (*Goirtín*): Little tilled field, p. 94
GORTEENY	G (*Goirtíní*): Little tilled fields, p. 94
GORTICASTLE	TE (*Gort an Chaisil*): Tilled field of the stone fort, p. 94
GORTIN	TE (*Goirtín*): Little tilled field, p. 94
GORTINAGIN	TE (*Goirtín na gCeann*): Tilled field of the heads
GORTINURE	DY (*Gort an Iuir*): Field of the yew, p. 101
GORTMORE	TY (*Gort Mhór*): Large tilled field
GORTNAGAPPUL	C & KY (*Gort na gCapaill*): Field of the horse
GORTNAGOYNE	G & RN (*Gort na gCadhan*): Field of the ducks
GORTNAGROUR	L (*Gort na gCreabhar*): Field of the woodcock
GORTNAHAHA	CE & TY (*Gort na hÁithe*): Field of the kiln, p. 94
GORTNAHOE	TY (*Gort na hUamha*): Tilled field of the cave, p. 94
GORTNAHOIMNA	C (*Gort na hOmna*): Field of the oak
GORTNAHOO	TY (*Gort na hUamha*): Tilled field of the cave, p. 94
GORTNANANNY	G (*Gort an Eanaigh*): Field of the marsh
GORTNAVEA	G (*Gort na bhFiadh*): Field of the deer
GORTNAVEIGH	TY (*Gort na bhFiadh*): Field of the deer
GORTREAGH	TE (*Gort Riabhach*): Striped field, p. 136
GORVAGH	SO (*Garbhach*): Rough place
GOUGANE BARRA	C (*Guagán Barra*): Mountain recess of Barra

GOWLANE	KY (*Gabhlán*): Fork, p. 89
GOWLAUN	G (*Gabhlán*): Fork, p. 89
GOWNA LOUGH	CN (*Loch Gamhna*): Lake of the calf
GOWRAN	KY (*Gabhrán*): (Pass of) Gobhrán
GRAGEEN	WX (*Gráigín*): Little hamlet, p. 94
GRAIG	C, L, G & TY (*Gráig*): Hamlet, p. 94
GRAIGEEN	L (*Gráigín*): Little hamlet, p. 94
GRAIGNAGOWER	KY (*Gráig na nGabhar*): Hamlet of the goats, p. 95
GRAIGUE	C, G, SO & TY (*Gráig*): Hamlet, p. 95
GRAIGUECULLEN	CW (*Gráig Chuillinn*): Hamlet of the steep slope
GRAIGUENAMANAGH	KY (*Gráig na Manach*): Hamlet of the monks, p. 95
GRANAGH	L (*Greanach*): Gravelly place, p. 96
GRANEY	KE (*Greanach*): Gravelly place, p. 96
Grange of	
Muckamore	p. 96
GRANGE	C, D, G, etc. (*Gráinseach*): Monastic grange, p. 95
GRANGECON	WW (*Gráinseach Choinn*): Conn's grange
GRANGICAM	DN (*Gráinseach Cam*): Crooked grange, p. 96
GRANSHA	DL, DN, etc. (*Gráinseach*): Monastic grange, pp. 96, 115
GREENAN	DL, AM, FH, etc. (*Grianán*): Sunny/important place, p. 97
GREENANE	KY & WW (*Grianán*): Sunny/important place, p. 97
GREENANS	DL (*Grianáin*): Sunny/important places
GREENANSTOWN	MH (*Baile Uí Ghríanáin*): Homestead of Ó Gríanáin
GREENAUN	LM & CE (*Grianán*): Sunny/important place, p. 97
GREENORE	LH & WX (*Grianphort*): Sunny port
GRENAGH	C (*Greanach*): Gravelly place, p. 96
GRIANAN	DL (*Grianán*): Important place
GROGAN	LS (*Grógán*): Little heap
GROOMSPORT	DN (*Port an Ghiolla Ghruama*): Port of the doleful fellow
GUBAVEENY	LH (*Gob an Mhianaigh*): Mouth of the mine, p. 93
GUBBACROCK	FH (*Gob dhá Chnoc*): Beak of two hills, p. 93
GUILEEN	C (*Gaibhlín*): Little fork, p. 89
GULLADOO	LM (*Guala Dhubh*): Black shoulder, p. 98
GULLADUFF	DY (*Guala Dhubh*): Black shoulder, pp 75, 98
GURRANEBRAHER	C (*Garrán na mBráthar*): Grove of the brothers
GURTEEN	G & SO (*Goirtín*): Little tilled field, p. 94
GURTEENY	G (*Goirtíní*): Small tilled fields

GURTNAHOE	TY (*Gort na hUamha*): Tilled field of the caves, p. 94
GURTYMADDEN	G (*Gort Uí Mhadaín*): Ó Madaín's tilled field, p. 94
GUSSERANE	WX (*Ráth na gCosarán*): Fort of the trampling
GWEEBARRA	DL (*Gaoth Beara*): Inlet of the water
GWEEDORE	DL (*Gaoth Dobhair*): Inlet of the water, p. 90
GWEESALIA	MO (*Gaoth Sáile*): Inlet of the sea, p. 90
GYLEEN	C (*Gaibhlín*): Little fork, p. 89

HELVICK	WD: See NORSE NAMES, p. 125
Holy Cross	p. 106
HOWTH	D: See NORSE NAMES, p. 125

I

IDA	KK (*Uí Deaghaigh*): Descendants of Deaghadh
ILEN RIVER	C (*Abhainn Eibhlinn*): Sparkling river
ILLANFAD	DL (*Oileán Fada*): Long island, p. 127
ILLAUNFADDA	G (*Oileán Fada*): Long island, p. 127
ILLAUNMORE	TY (*Oileán Mór*): Large island, p. 127
ILLAUNSLEA	KY (*Oileán Shléibhe*): Island of the mountain
ILLAUNTANNIG	KY (*Oileán tSeanaigh*): Seanach's island, p. 127
IMAILE	WW (*Uí Mail*): Descendants of Mal
INAGH	CE (*Eidhneach*): Ivied
INAN	MH (*Eidhneán*): Ivy, p. 82
INANE	C & TY (*Eidhneán*): Ivy, p. 82
INCH	C, DN, KY & WX (*Inis*): Island/water-meadow, p. 99
INCHAGOILL	G (*Inis an Ghoill*): Island of the foreigners
INCHEE	KY (*Insí*): Water-meadows
INCHENNY	TE (*Inis Eanaigh*): Island of the marsh
INCHFARRANNAGLERAGH	KY (*Inse Fhearann na gCléireach*): Water-meadow of the land of the clerics
INCHICORE	D (*Inse Chór*): Island of the snout
INCHICRONAN	CE (*Inse Cronáin*): Cronán's island
INCHIDERAILLE	C (*Inis Idir dá Fhaill*): Island between two cliffs
INCHIGEELAGH	C (*Inse Geimhleach*): Island of the prisoner
INCHINALEEGA	KY (*Inse na Léige*): Water-meadow of the stone
INCHINGLANNA	KY (*Inse an Ghleanna*): Water-meadow of the glen
INCHIQUIN LOUGH	C & CE (*Loch Inse Uí Choinn*): Lake of Ó Coinn's island
INCHNAMUCK	TY (*Inse na Muc*): Island/holm of the pigs, p. 100
INISHANNON	C (*Inis Eonáin*): Eonán's island
INISHBARRA	G (*Inis Bearacháin*): Island of the heifers
INISHBIGGLE	MO (*Inis Bigil*): Island of the fasting
INISHBOFIN	DL & G (*Inis Bó Finne*): Island of the white cow, pp 31, 100
INISHCARRA	C (*Inis Cara*): Island of the leg
INISHCRONE	SO (*Inis Crabhann*): Island of the gravel-ridge of the river
INISHDADROUM	CE (*Inis dá Drom*): Island of two backs
INISHDOOEY	DL (*Inis Dubhthaigh*): Island of the sandhill
INISHEER	G (*Inis Oirthir*): Eastern island, p. 100
INISHFREE	DL (*Inis Fraoigh*): Island of the heather, p. 100

INISHIRRER	DL (*Inis Oirthir*). Eastern island, p. 100
INISHKEEN	L & MN (*Inis Caoin*): Beautiful island, p. 99
INISHKEERAGH	DL (*Inis Chaorach*): Island of sheep, p. 100
INISHLACKAN	G (*Inis Leacan*): Island of the hillside
INISHMAAN	G (*Inis Meáin*): Middle island, p. 100
INISHMACOWNEY	CE (*Inis Mhic Uaithne*): Mac Uaithne's island
INISHMEANE	DL (*Inis Meáin*): Middle island, p. 100
INISHMORE	G (*Inis Mór*): Big island
INISHMURRAY	SO (*Inis Muirí*): Muireadhach's island, p. 100
INISHNAGOR	DL & SO (*Inis na gCorr*): Island of the cranes
INISHOWEN	DL (*Inis Eoghain*): Eoghan's island, p. 100
INISHSHARK	G (*Inis Airc*): Island of hardship
INISHSIRRER	DL (*Inis Oirthir*): Eastern island
INISHTOOSKERT	KY (*Inis Tuaisceart*): Northern island, p. 100
INISHTURK	G (*Inis Toirc*): Island of the boar
INISHVICKILLANE	KY (*Inis Mhicileáin*): Micileán's island
INISTIOGE	KK (*Inis Tíog*): Tíog's island, p. 100
INNISFALLEN	KY (*Inis Faithlenn*): Fathlenn's island
INNISKEEN	LH (*Inis Caoin*): Beautiful island, p. 99
INVER	DL (*Inbhear Náile*): Estuary (of Náile), p. 99
INVERAN	G (*Indreabhán*): Little estuary, p. 99
INVEREELA	WW (*Inbhear Daeile*): Estuary of the (river) Deel
ISERTKELLY	KK (*Díseart Cheallaigh*): Ceallach's hermitage
ISLAND	C & MO (*Oileán*): Island, p. 127
ISLANDMOYLE	DN (*Oileán Maol*): Bare island, p. 127
ISLANDREAGH	AM (*Oileán Riabhach*): Grey/striped island, p. 127

K

KANTURK	C (*Ceann Toirc*): Head of the boar, p. 47
KEADEEN	WW (*Céidín*): Little hill, p. 49
KEADEW	RN (*Céideadh*): Hill
KEADY	AH (*Céide*): Hill, p. 49
KEADYDRINAGH	SO (*Céide Draigneach*): Flat-topped hill of the blackthorns, p. 49
KEALARIDDIG	KY (*Caol an Roidigh*): Marshy stream of the red mire, p. 42
KEALKILL	C (*Caolchoill*): Narrow wood, p. 42
KEASH	SO (*Céis*): Wicker causeway
KEAVA	RN (*Céibh*): Long grass
KEAVE	G (*Céibh*): Long grass
KEEL	MO (*Caol*): Narrow/marshy stream, p. 42
KEELOGES	LM (*Caológa*): Strips, p. 43
KEENAGH	LD (*Caonach*): Moss, p. 43
KEENAGHBEG	MO (*Caonach Beag*): Small moss, p. 43
KEERAGH ISLANDS	WX (*Oileáin na gCaorach*): Islands of the sheep
KEERAUNNAGARK	G (*Caorán na gCearc*): Moor of the hens
KEIMANEIGH	C (*Céim an Fhia*): Gap of the deer, p. 49
KELLS	AM, KY & KK (*Cealla*): Churches
KELLS	MH (*Ceanannas*): Great residence
KENAGH	LD (*Caonach*): Moss, p. 43
KENMARE	KY (*Ceann Mara*): Head of the sea, p. 47
KERRYKEEL	DL (*Ceathrú Chaol*): Narrow quarter, p. 42
KESH	FH & SO (*Ceis*): Wicker causeway, p. 49
KESHCARRIGAN	LM (*Ceis Charraigín*): Wicker causeway of the little rock, p. 49
KEY LOUGH	RN (*Loch Cé*): Loch of the quay
KIELDUFF	KY (*Cill Dubh*): Black church
KILANERIN	WX (*Coill an Iarainn*): Wood of the iron
KILBAHA	CE (*Cill Bheatach*): Church of the birches
KILBALLYPORTER	MH (*Coill an Bhealaigh* + Porter): Wood of the pass (of Porter)
KILBANE	CE (*Cill Bhán*): White church
KILBARRACK	D (*Cill Bharróg*): Church of little Barra
KILBARRON	DL (*Cill Bharfionn*): Barfionn's church

KILBARRY	C (*Cill Barra*): Barra's church
KILBEGGAN	WH (*Cill Bheagáin*): Beagán's church
KILBEHENY	L (*Coill Bheithne*): Wood of birches
KILBENNAN	G (*Cill Bheanáin*): Beanán's church
KILBERRY	MH & KE (*Cill Bhearaigh*): Church of Bearach
KILBRICKAN	G (*Cill Bhreacáin*): Church of Breacán
KILBRICKEN	LS (*Cill Bhriocáin*): Church of Briocán
KILBRIDE	DN, CW & WW (*Cill Bhríde*): Church of Bríd, p. 50
KILBRIEN	WD (*Cill Bhriain*): Church of Brian
KILBRIN	C (*Cill Bhrain*): Church of Bran
KILBRITTAIN	C (*Cill Briotáin*): Church of Briotán
KILBROGAN	C (*Cill Brógáin*): Brogan's church
KILCAIMIN	G (*Cill Chaimín*): Church of Caimín
KILCAR	DL (*Cill Charthaigh*): Carthach's church
KILCARN	MH (*Cill an Chairn*): Church of the cairn
KILCASH	TY (*Cill Chais*): Church of Cas
KILCAVAN	LS (*Cill Chaomháin*): Church of Caomhán
KILCHREEST	G (*Cill Chríost*): Church of Christ
KILCLARE	LM (*Coill an Chláir*): Wood of the plain, p. 54
KILCLIEF	DN (*Cill Cléithe*): Church of the hurdle, p. 54
KILCLOHER	CE (*Cill Chloichir*): Church of the stony place
KILCLONE	MH (*Coill Chluana*): Church of the meadow
KILCLONFERT	OY (*Cill Chluana Fearta*): Church of the pasture of the grave
KILCLOONEY	DL (*Cill Chluana*): Church of the pasture
KILCOCK	KE (*Cill Choca*): Church of Coca
KILCOGY	CN (*Cill Chóige*): Cóig's church
KILCOLGAN	G & OY (*Cill Cholgan*): Church of Colga
KILCOLMAN	C & L (*Cill Cholmáin*): Church of Colmán
KILCOMIN	OY (*Cill Chuimín*): Church of Cuimín
KILCOMMON	TY (*Cill Chuimín*): Church of Cuimín
KILCONLY	G (*Cill Chonla*): Conla's church
KILCONNELL	G (*Cill Chonaill*): Church of Conall
KILCOO	DN (*Cill Chua*): Cua's church, p. 50
KILCOOLE	WW (*Cill Chomhghaill*): Church of Comhghall
KILCOOLEY	TY (*Cill Cúile*): Church of the nook
KILCORMAC	OY (*Cill Chormaic*): Church of Cormac
KILCORNAN	L (*Cill Chornáin*): Church of Cornán
KILCORNEY	C (*Cill Coirne*): Church of Coirne
KILCOTTY	WX (*Cill Chota*): Church of Cota

KILCROHANE	C (*Cill Crócháin*): Church of Cróchán
KILCULLEN	KE (*Cill Chuillinn*): Church of the steep slope, pp 53, 66
KILCUMMIN	KY (*Cill Chuimín*): Church of Cuimín
KILCURRY	LH (*Cill an Churraigh*): Church of the marsh, pp 61, 62
KILDALKEY	MH (*Cill Dealga*): Church of the thorn
KILDANGAN	KE (*Cill Daingin*): Church of the fortress, p. 58
KILDANGAN	OY (*Coill an Daingin*): Wood of the fortress, p. 58
KILDARE	KE (*Cill Dara*): Church of the oak-tree, pp 53, 67
KILDAVIN	CW (*Cill Damháin*): Church of Damhán
KILDERMODY	WD (*Cill Dhiarmada*): Church of Diarmaid
KILDIMO	L (*Cill Díoma*): Díoma's church
KILDOROUGH	CN (*Coill Dorcha*): Dusky wood
KILDORRERY	C (*Cill Dairbhre*): Church of the place of oaks
KILDREENAGH	CW (*Cill Draigneach*): Church of blackthorns
KILDRUM	DL (*Coill Droma*): Wood of the ridge
KILDYSART	CE (*Cill an Dísirt*): Church of the hermitage
KILFEAGHAN	DN (*Cill Fhéichín*): Féichín's church, p. 51
KILFEAKLE	TY (*Cill Fiacal*): Church of the teeth
KILFEARAGH	CE (*Cill Fhiachrach*): Church of Fiachra
KILFENORA	CE (*Cill Fhionnúrach*): Church of Fionnúir
KILFINANE	L (*Cill Fhionáin*): Church of Fionán
KILFINNY	L (*Cill na Fiodhnaí*): Church of the wooded place
KILFLYNN	KY (*Cill Flainn*): Church of Flann
KILFREE	SO (*Cill Fraoich*): Church of the heather
KILFULLERT	DN (*Coill Fulachta*): Wood of the cooking-place
KILGARVAN	KY (*Cill Gharbháin*): Church of Garbhán
KILGLASS	G & SO (*Coill Ghlas*): Green wood, pp 59, 92
KILGLASS	RN & SO (*Cill Ghlas*): Green church, p. 92
KILGOBNET	KY & WD (*Cill Ghobnait*): Church of Gobnait
KILGOWAN	KE (*Coill Ghabhann*): Wood of the smith
KILKEA	KE (*Cill Chathaig*): Church of Cathach
KILKEASY	KE (*Cill Chéise*): Church of Céis
KILKEE	CE (*Cill Chaoidhe*): Church of Caoi
KILKEEL	DN (*Cill an Chaoil*): Church of the narrow, p. 42
KILKELLY	MO (*Cill Cheallaigh*): Church of Ceallach
KILKENNY	KK (*Cill Chainnigh*): Church of Cainneach
KILKERIN	CE (*Cill Chéirín*): Church of Céirín
KILKERRIN	G (*Cill Chiaráin*): Ciarán's church
KILKERRIN	G (*Cill Choirín*): Church of the little turn

KILKIERAN	G & KK (*Cill Chiaráin*): Church of Ciarán
KILKINLEA	L (*Cill Chinn Sléibhe*): Church of the head of the mountain
KILKISHEN	CE (*Cill Chisín*): Church of the wicker causeway
KILL	CN, KE & WD (*Cill*): Church
KILLACHONNA	WH (*Cill Dachonna*): Church of Dachonna
KILLACOLLA	L (*Cill an Coille*): Church of the wood
KILLADANGAN	MO (*Coill an Daingin*): Wood of the fortress
KILLADEAS	FH (*Cill Chéile Dé*): Church of the Céle Dé
KILLADOON	MO (*Coill an Dúin*): Wood of the fort
KILLADREENAN	WW (*Cill Achaidh Draighnigh*): Church of the field of the blackthorns, p. 74
KILLADYSERT	CE (*Cill an Dísirt*): Church of the hermitage
KILLAG	WX (*Cill Laig*): Church of the hollow
KILLAGAN	AM (*Cill Lagáin*): Church of the small hollow, p. 51
KILLALA	MO (*Cill Ala*): Church of Ala
KILLALOE	CE (*Cill Dalua*): Church of Dalua
KILLALOO	DY (*Coill an Lao*): Wood of the calf
KILLAMERY	KK (*Cill Lamhraí*): Church of Lamhrach
KILLANE	OY (*Cill Anna*): Church of Anna
KILLANN	WX (*Cill Anna*): Church of Anna
KILLANNUMMERY	LM (*Cill an Iomaire*): Church of the ridge, p. 101
KILLANS	AM (*Coillíní*): Little round hills
KILLARAGHT	SO (*Cill Adrochtae*): Adrochta's church, p. 53
KILLARD POINT	DN (*Aird na Cille* + Point): Point of the church (point)
KILLARE	WH (*Cill Air*): Church of slaughter
KILLARGA	LM (*Cill Fhearga*): Church of Fearga
KILLARNEY	KY (*Cill Airne*): Church of the sloes, p. 14
KILLARY	G & MO (*Caolaire*): Narrow sea
KILLASHANDRA	CN (*Cill na Seanrátha*): Church of the old fort, p. 51
KILLASHEE	LD (*Cill Úsaill*): Church of Úsaile, p. 52
KILLASSER	MO (*Cill Lasrach*): Lasrach's church
KILLATEEAUN	MO (*Coill an tSiáin*): Wood of the fairy hill
KILLAVALLY	MO (*Coill an Bhaile*): Wood of the homestead
KILLAVALLY	WH (*Coill an Bhealaigh*): Wood of the pass
KILLAVIL	SO (*Cill Abhaill*): Church of the apple-tree
KILLAVULLEN	C (*Cill an Mhuilinn*): Church of the mill
KILLEA	TY & WD (*Cill Aodha*): Church of Aodh
KILLEAGH	C (*Cill Ia*): Church of Ia
KILLEANY	G (*Cill Éinne*): Church of Éanna

KILLEAVAN	MN (*Cill Laobháin*): Church of Laobhán
KILLEAVY	AH (*Cill Shléibhe*): Church of the mountain, p. 143
KILLEDMOND	CW (*Cill Éamainn*): Church of Éamonn
KILLEEDY	L (*Cill Íde*): Church of Íde
KILLEEN	TY (*Cillín*): Little church
KILLEENADEEMA	G (*Cillín a Díoma*): Díoma's little church
KILLEENDUFF	OY (*Cillín Dubh*): Little black church
KILLEESHILL	TE (*Cill Íseal*): Low church, p. 51
KILLEGAR	L (*Coill an Ghairr*): Wood of the offal
KILLEIGH	OY (*Cill Achaidh*): Church of the field
KILLEN	TE (*Cillín*): Little church
KILLENAGH	WD (*Cill Eanach*): Church of the marsh
KILLENAULE	TY (*Cill Náile*): Church of Náile
KILLERIG	CW (*Cill Dheirge*): Church of the red ground
KILLESHIL	OY (*Cill Íseal*): Low church, p. 51
KILLETER	TE (*Coill Íochtair*): Lower wood
KILLIMER	CE (*Cill Íomar*): Church of Íomar
KILLIMOR	G (*Cill Íomair*): Church of Íomar
KILLINABOY	CE (*Cill Iníne Baoith*): Church of the daughter of Baoth
KILLINARDRISH	C (*Cill an Ard-Dorais*): Church of the high door
KILLINASPICK	KK (*Cill an Easpaig*): Church of the bishop
KILLINCHY	DN (*Cill Duinsí*): Church of Duinseach
KILLINCOOLY	WX (*Cillín Cúile*): Little church of the nook, p. 66
KILLINEY	D (*Cill Iníon Léinín*): Church of the daughters of Léinín
KILLINEY	KY (*Cill Éinne*): Church of Éanna
KILLINICK	WX (*Cill Fhionnóg*): Church of Fionnóg
KILLINIERIN	WX (*Coill an Iarainn*): Wood of the iron
KILLINKERE	CN (*Cillín Céir*): Little church of the wax candles
KILLISKY	WW (*Cill Uisce*): Church of the water, p. 160
KILLOE	LD (*Cill Eo*): Church of the yew, p. 84
KILLOGEENAGHAN	WH (*Coill Ó gCuinneagáin*): Wood of Uí Cuinneagáin
KILLONE	CE (*Cill Eoghain*): Eoghan's church
KILLONEEN	OY (*Cill Eoghanín*): Little Eoghan's church
KILLORAN	G (*Cill Odhráin*): Oran's church
KILLORGLIN	KY (*Cill Orglan*): Church of Forgla
KILLOSCULLY	TY (*Cill Ó Scolaí*): Ó Scolaí's church
KILLOUGH	DN (*Cill Locha*): Church of the lake
KILLOUR	MO (*Cill Iúir*): Church of the tower
KILLOWEN	DN (*Cill Eoin*): Eoin's church
KILLOWNY	OY (*Cill Uaithne*): Church of Uaithne

KILLUCAN	WH (*Cill Liúcainne*): Liúcain's church
KILLURIN	WX (*Cill Liobhráin*): Church of Liobhrán
KILLUSTY	TY (*Cill Loiscthe*): Burnt church
KILLYBEGS	DL (*Cealla Beaga*): Little churches, p. 27
KILLYBRONE	MN (*Coillidh Brón*): Sad woodland
KILLYCOLPEY	TE (*Coill an Cholpa*): Wood of the bullock
KILLYCOMAIN	AH (*Coill Mhic Giolla Mhaoil*): Mac Giolla Maol's wood
KILLYGARN	AM (*Coill na gCarn*): Wood of the cairn
KILLYGARVAN	CE (*Cill Gharbháin*): Church of Garbhán
KILLYGLEN	AM (*Cill Ghlinne*): Church of the glen, p. 51
KILLYKERGAN	DY (*Coill Uí Chiaragáin*): Ó Ciaragáin's wood
KILLYLEA	AH (*Coillidh Liath*): Grey woodland, p. 59, 110
KILLYLEAGH	DN (*Cill Ó Laoch*): Church of Uí Laoch
KILLYMAN	TE (*Cill na mBan*): Church of the women
KILLYON	OY (*Cill Liain*): Church of Lian
KILMACANOGE	WW (*Cill Mocheanóg*): Mocheanóg's church
KILMACDUAGH	CE (*Cill Mhic Duach*): Mac Duach's church
KILMACOW	KK (*Cill Mhic Bhúith*): Church of Mac Búith
KILMACRENAN	DL (*Cill Mhic Réanáin*): Church of Mac Réanán
KILMACTHOMAS	WD (*Coill Mhic Thomáisín*): Wood of Mac Thomáisín
KILMACTRANNY	SO (*Cill Mhic Treana*): Church of Mac Treana
KILMAINE	MO (*Cill Mheáin*): Middle church
KILMAINHAM	D & MH (*Cill Mhaighneann*): Church of Maighne
KILMALEY	CE (*Cill Mháille*): Máille's church
KILMALIN	WW (*Cill Moling*): Church of Moling
KILMALLOCK	L (*Cill Mocheallóg*): Church of Mocheallóg
KILMANAGH	KK (*Cill Mhanach*): Church of the monks
KILMANAHAN	WD (*Cill Mainchín*): Manchan's church
KILMEAD	KE (*Cill Míde*): Middle church
KILMEADEN	WD (*Cill Mhiadáin*): Church of Miadán
KILMEAGUE	KE (*Cill Maodhóg*): Church of Maodhóg
KILMEEDY	L (*Cill Míde*): Church of Íde
KILMESSAN	MH (*Cill Measáin*): Church of Measán
KILMICHAEL	C & WX (*Cill Mhichil*): Church of Micheál
KILMIHIL	CE (*Cill Mhichíl*): Church of Micheál
KILMOGANNY	KK (*Cill Mogeanna*): Mogeanna's church
KILMORE	CE, RN & WX (*Cill Mhór*): Big church
KILMOREMOY	MO (*Cellola Maghna Muaide*): Big church of the plain, p. 52
KILMORONY	LS (*Cill Maolrunaidh*): Church of Maolrunaidh

KILMOVEE	MO (*Cill Mobhí*): Church of Mobhí
KILMOYLE	AM (*Cill Maol*): Bald/dilapidated church
KILMOYLEY	KY (*Cill Mhaoile*): Church of the bald person
KILMURRY	C & CE (*Cill Mhuire*): Mary's church
KILMURVY	G (*Cill Mhuirbhigh*): Church of the beach
KILMYSHALL	WX (*Cill Mísil*): Church of the low central place
KILNABOY	CE (*Cill Iníne Baoith*): Church of the daughters of Baoth
KILNACLOGHY	RN (*Coill na Cloiche*): Wood of the stone, p. 55
KILNAGROSS	LM (*Coill na gCros*): Wood of the crosses
KILNALAG	G (*Coill na Lag*): Wood of the hollow
KILNALECK	CN (*Coill na Leice*): Wood of the flagstones
KILNAMANAGH	TY (*Coill na Manach*): Wood of the monks, p. 58
KILNAMONA	CE (*Cill na Móna*): Church of the bog
KILPEDDER	WW (*Cill Pheadair*): Peadar's church
KILQUIGGAN	WW (*Cill Chomhgáin*): Comhgán's church
KILRAINE	DL (*Cill Riáin*): Rián's church
KILRANELAGH	WW (*Cill Rannaireach*): Church of the verses
KILRAUGHTS	AM (*Cill Reachtais*): Church of the legislation
KILREA	DY (*Cill Ria*): Grey church
KILREEKILL	G (*Cill Ricill*): Ricill's church
KILRONAN	G (*Cill Rónáin*): Rónán's church
KILROOSKEY	RN (*Coill na Rúscaí*): Wood of the crusts
KILROOT	AM (*Cill Ruaidh*): Church of the red soil, pp 54, 138
KILROSS	DL (*Cill Rois*): Church of the grove
KILROSS	TY (*Cill Ros*): Church of the promontory
KILRUSH	CE (*Cill Rois*): Church of the grove
KILSALLAGH	G & MO (*Coill Salach*): Dirty wood
KILSALLAGHAN	D (*Cill Shalcáin*): Church of the willows
KILSARAN	LH (*Cill Saráin*): Sarán's church
KILSHANCHOE	KE (*Cill Seanchua*): Church of the old hollow
KILSHANNY	CE (*Cill Sheanaigh*): Seanach's church
KILSHEELAN	TY (*Cill Síoláin*): Síolán's church
KILSKEER	MH (*Cill Scíre*): Scíre's church
KILSKEERY	TE (*Cill Scíre*): Scíre's church
KILSKYRE	MH (*Cill Scíre*): Scíre's church
KILTAMAGH	MO (*Coillte Mach*): Woods of the plain
KILTEALY	WX (*Cill Tíle*): Tíl's church
KILTEEL	KE (*Cill tSíle*): Síle's church
KILTEELY	L (*Cill Tíle*): Tíl's church

KILTEGAN	WW (*Cill Téagáin*): Téagán's church
KILTERNAN	D (*Cill Thiarnáin*): Tiarnán's church
KILTOBER	WH (*Coill Tobair*): Wood of the well
KILTOOM	RN (*Cill Tuama*): Church of the burial mound
KILTORMER	G (*Cill Tormóir*): Tormór's church
KILTULLAGH	G (*Cill Tulach*): Church of the hills
KILTURK	FH (*Coill Torc*): Boar wood
KILTYCLOGHER	LM (*Coillte Clochair*): Woods of the stony place, p. 59
KILVERGAN	AH (*Cill Uí Mhuireagáin*): Church of Ó Muireagán, p. 51
KILWAUGHTER	AM (*Cill Uachtar*): Upper church, pp 51, 160
KILWORTH	C (*Cill Úird*): Church of the ritual
KINAWLEY	FH (*Cill Náile*): Náile's church
KINCASSLAGH	DL (*Ceann Caslach*): Weak head
KINCORA	CE (*Cionn Coradh*): Head of the weir, p. 60
KINCUN	MO (*Cionn Con*): Head of the dog, p. 47
KINDRUM	DL (*Ceann Droma*): Head of the ridge, p. 47
KINEIGH	KY (*Cionn Ech*): Head of the horse, p. 47
KINGARROW	DL (*Ceann Garbh*): Rough head, p. 47
KINLOUGH	LM (*Cionn Locha*): Head of the lake, p. 47
KINNEA	CN & DL (*Cionn Ech*): Head of the horse, p. 47
KINNEGAD	WH (*Ceann Átha Gad*): Head of the ford of the withies, p. 47
KINNITY	OY (*Ceann Eitigh*): Eiteach's head
KINSALE	C (*Cionn tSáile*): Head of the salt water, p. 47
KINSALEBEG	WD (*Cionn tSáile Beag*): Little head of the salt water, p. 47
KINSALEY	D (*Cionn tSáile*): Head of the salt water
KINVARRA	G (*Cinn Mhara*): Head of the sea, p. 47
KIPPURE	WW (*Cipiúr*) Big place of mountain-grass
KIRCUBBIN	DN (*Cill Ghobáin*): Gobán's church
KISHKEAM	C (*Coiscéim [na Caillí]*): Footstep (of the hag)
KNAPPAGH	MO (*Cnapach*): Bumpy area
KNOCK	CE, DN & MO (*Cnoc*): Hill, p. 57
KNOCKADERRY	L (*Cnoc an Doire*): Hill of the oakwood, p. 57
KNOCKADOON	C (*Cnoc an Dúin*): Hill of the fort, p. 57
KNOCKAINY	L (*Cnoc Áine*): Áine's hill, p. 57
KNOCKALOUGH	CE & TY (*Cnoc an Locha*): Hill of the lough
KNOCKAN ILLAUN	MO (*Cnoc an Oileáin*): Hill of the island
KNOCKANANNA	WW (*Cnoc an Eanaigh*): Hill of the marsh
KNOCKANARRIGAN	WW (*Cnoc an Aragain*): Hill of the conflicts

KNOCKANEVIN	C (*Cnocán Aoibhinn*): Pleasant small hill, p. 58
KNOCKANORAN	LS & C (*Cnoc an Uaráin*): Hill of the spring, p. 160
KNOCKANORE	WD (*Cnoc an Óir*): Hill of gold
KNOCKATALLON	MN (*Cnoc an tSalainn*): Hill of the salt
KNOCKAUNNAGLASHY	KY (*Cnocán na Glaise*): Small hill of the stream
KNOCKBOY	C, KY & WD (*Cnoc Buí*): Yellow hill, p. 57
KNOCKBRACK	DL (*Cnoc Breac*): Speckled hill
KNOCKCLOGHRIM	DY (*Cnoc Clochdhroma*): Hill of the stony ridge
KNOCKCROGHERY	RN (*Cnoc an Chrocaire*): Hill of the hangman, p. 57
KNOCKDRIN	WH (*Cnoc Droinne*): Humpy hill
KNOCKEEN	KY (*Cnoicín*): Little hill
KNOCKERRY	CE (*Cnoc Doire*): Hill of the oakwood
KNOCKGRAFFON	CY (*Cnoc Rafann*): Rafainn's hill
KNOCKLAYD	AM (*Cnoc Leithid*): Broad hill
KNOCKLONG	L (*Cnoc Loinge*): Hill of the ship
KNOCKLOUGHRIM	DY (*Cnoc Clochdroma*): Hill of the stony ridge, p. 57
KNOCKMEALDOWN	TY & WD (*Cnoc Mhaoldhomhnigh*): Maoldomhnach's hill, p. 57
KNOCKMORE	MO (*Cnoc Mór*): Big hill, p. 57
KNOCKMOYLE	G & TE (*Cnoc Maol*): Bald hill, p. 57
KNOCKNACARRY	AM (*Cnoc na Cora*): Hill of the weir
KNOCKNAGASHEL	KY (*Cnoc na gCaiseal*): Hill of the stone forts
KNOCKNAGREE	C (*Cnoc na Groighe*): Hill of the horse-stud
KNOCKNAHORN	TE (*Cnoc na hEorna*): Hill of the barley
KNOCKNAMUCKLEY	AH (*Cnoc na Muclaí*): Hill of the drove of swine
KNOCKRAHA	C (*Cnoc Rátha*): Hill of the fort
KNOCKRATH	WW (*Cnoc Rátha*): Hill of the fort
KNOCKTOPHER	KK (*Cnoc an Tóchair*): Hill of the causeway, p. 155
KNOCKVICAR	RN (*Cnoc an Bhiocáire*): Vicar's hill
KYLEBRACK	G (*Coill Bhreac*): Speckled wood
KYLEMORE	G (*Coill Mhór*): Big wood

L

LABASHEEDA	CE (*Leaba Shíoda*): Grave of Síoda
LABBACALLEE	C (*Leaba Caillighe*): Hag's bed
LABBAMOLAGA	C (*Leaba Molaga*): Molaga's bed
LABBY	DY, DL & SO (*Leaba*): Grave, p. 106
LABBYFIRMORE	MN (*Leaba an Fhir Mhóir*): Grave of the big man, p. 106
LACHTCARN	TY (*Leacht Chairn*): Grave of the cairn, p. 107
LACK	FH (*Leac*): Flagstone, p. 106
LACKAGH	KE (*Leacach*): Abounding in flagstones
LACKAMORE	TY (*Leaca Mhór*): Big hillside, p. 107
LACKAN	WW (*Leacain*): Hillside, p. 107
LACKAROE	C & OY (*Leaca Rua*): Red hillside, p. 107
Lag an Aonaigh	MH, p. 16
LAGAN RIVER	AM & DN (*Lagán* + River): Little hollow/lake + river, p. 103
LAGAN	DL (*Lagán*): Little hollow/lake, p. 103
LAGHIL	DL (*Leamhchoill*): Elmwood, p. 108
LAGHILE	CE & TY (*Leamhchoill*): Elmwood, p. 108
LAGHT	C (*Leacht*): Grave, p. 107
LAGHTANE	L (*Leachtán*): Little grave, p. 107
LAGHTGEORGE	G (*Leacht Sheoirse*): Seoirse's grave, p. 107
LAGHTNEILL	C (*Leacht Néill*): Néill's grave, p. 107
LAGHY	DL (*Laitigh*): Mire, p. 103
LAGNAMUCK	MO (*Lag na Muc*): Hollow of the pigs, p. 103
LAGORE	M (*Loch Gabhra*): Lake of the goat
LAHARAN	C & KY (*Leath Fhearann*): Half of a measure of land, p. 109
LAHARDAUN	MO (*Leath Ardán*): Side of a plateau, p. 109
LAHESSERAGH	TY (*Leath Sheisreach*): Half ploughland, p. 109
LAHINCH	CE (*Leath Inse*): Peninsula, p. 109
Laighin	p. 4
LAMBEG	AM (*Lann Bheag*): Small church, p. 104
LAMMY	FH & TE (*Leamhach*): Abounding in elms, p. 108
LANAGLUG	TE (*Lann na gClog*): Church of the bells
LARACOR	MH (*Láithreach Cora*): Site of the weir, p. 104
LARAGH	LD (*Leath Ráth*): Half a ring-fort, p. 109
LARAGH	LS, MN & WW (*Láithreach*): Site, p. 104

LARGAN	MO (*Leargain*): Slope, p. 109
LARGANREAGH	DL (*Leargan Riabhach*): Striped slope, p. 109
LARGY	AM, DY, FH, etc. (*Leargaidh*): Slope, p. 109
LARGYBRACK	DL (*Leargaidh Breac*): Speckled slope, p. 109
LARGYDONNELL	SO (*Learga Uí Dhónaill*): Ó Dónaill's slope, p. 109
LARGYREAGH	DY (*Leargaidh Riabhach*): Striped slope, p. 109
LARNE	AM (*Latharna*): (People of) Latharna
LATAMARD	MN (*Leacht na mBard*): Grave of the bard
LATTERAGH	TY (*Leatracha*): Hill-slopes, p. 110
LATTIN	TY (*Leathtón*): Valley-bottom
LATTOON	MN (*Leathtón*): Valley-bottom
LAUGHIL	G, LD, MO, etc. (*Leamhchoill*): Elmwood, p. 108
LAUGHILL	FH & LS (*Leamhchoill*): Elmwood, p. 108
LAUNE RIVER	KY (*Leamháin* + River): Elm + river, p. 108
LAURAGH	KY (*Láithreach*): Site, p. 104
LAVAGH	DL & SO (*Leamhach*): Abounding in elms, p. 108
LAVALLY	CE, C, G, etc. (*Leth Baile*): Half townland, p. 109
LAVEY	DY & CN (*Leamhach*): Abounding in elms, p. 108
LEABEG	OY (*Liath Beag*): Small grey place
LEAFIN	MH (*Liathmhuine*): Grey thicket, p. 110
LEAFONNY	SO (*Liathmhuine*): Grey thicket, p. 110
LEAHAN	DL (*Leathan*): Broad space
LEAHANMORE	DL (*Leathan Mór*): Big broad space
LEAMLARA	C (*Léim Lára*): Leap of the mare, p. 109
LEAP	C (*Léim*): Leap, p. 109
LEARMORE	TE (*Ladhar Mór*): Large fork, p. 103
LEARMOUNT	TE (*Ladhar* + Mount): Fork + mount, p. 103
Leath Cuinn	p. 108
Leath Mogha	p. 108
LECALE	DN (*Leath Cathail*): Cathal's portion, p. 108
LECARROW	G (*Leithcheathrú*): Half quarter
LECKANVY	MO (*Leacán Mhaigh*): Hillside of the plain
LECKAUN	SO (*Leacán*): Hillside, p. 107
LEE RIVER	C (*Laoi* + River): Water + river
LEEG	MN (*Liag*): Flagstone, p. 110
LEEK	MN (*Liag*): Flagstone, p. 110
LEEKE	AM & DY (*Liag*): Flagstone, p. 110
LEENAUN	G (*Líonán*): Shallow sea-bed
LEFINN	DL (*Liathmhuine*): Grey thicket, p. 110
LEGANANNY	DN (*Lag an Eanaigh*): Hollow of the marsh

LEGGAMADDY	DN (*Lag an Mhadaidh*): Hollow of the dog, p. 103
LEGGS	FH (*Laig*): Hollows
LEGLAND	TE (*Leithghleann*): Side of a valley, p. 110
LEGONIEL	AM (*Lag an Aoil*): Hollow of the lime, p. 2
LEGVOY	RN (*Lec Mhagh*): Flaggy plain
LEHINCH	CE (*Leath Inse*): Peninsula, p. 109
LEIGHLIN	CW (*Leithghleann*): Side of a valley, pp 109, 110
LEIGHMONEY	C (*Liathmhuine*): Grey thicket, p. 110
LEITRIM	DN & LM (*Liathdroim*): Grey ridge, p. 110
LEIXLIP	KE: See NORSE NAMES, p. 125
LEMANAGHAN	OY (*Liath Mancháin*): Grey land of Manchán, p. 110
LEMLARA	C (*Léim Lára*): Leap of the mare, p. 109
LEMYBRIEN	WD (*Léim Uí Bhriain*): Leap of Ó Briain
LENADERG	DN (*Láthreach Dair-Thighe*): Site of the oratory, p. 68
LENADOON POINT	SO (*Léana Dúin* + Point): Meadow of the fort + point
LENAMORE	LD & WH (*Léana Mór*): Great meadow
LENE LOUGH	WH (*Loch Léibhinn*): Léibhinn's lake
LENY	WH (*Léana*): Meadow
LERRIG	KY (*Leirg*): Slope
LETTER	FH & KY (*Leitir*): Hillside, p. 110
LETTERBARROW	DL (*Leitir Barra*): Top hillside
LETTERBREEN	FH (*Leitir Bhruin*): Hillside of the breast
LETTERBRICK	MO (*Leitir Bruic*): Badger hillside, p. 110
LETTERFINNISH	KY (*Leitir Fionnuisce*): Hillside of bright water, p. 110
LETTERGESH	G (*Leitir Geis*): Hillside of the taboo
LETTERKENNY	DL (*Leitir Ceanainn*): Cannanan's hillside
LETTERMACAWARD	DL (*Leitir Mhic an Bhaird*): Mac an Bard's hillside
LETTERMORE	G (*Leitir Móir*): Big hillside, p. 110
LETTERMULLAN	G (*Leitir Mealláin*): Hill-slope of Meallán, p. 110
LETTERNADARRIV	KY (*Leitir na dTarbh*): Hillside of the bulls, p. 110
LEVALLY	G & MO (*Leathbhaile*): Half townland, p. 109
LIAFIN	DL (*Liathmhuine*): Grey thicket, p. 110
LICKEEN	KE (*Licín*): Small flagstone
LICKOWEN	C (*Leic Eoghain*): Eoghan's flagstone
LIFFORD	DL (*Leifear*): Side of the water
LIMAVADY	DY (*Léim an Mhadaidh*): Leap of the dog, p. 109
LIMERICK	L (*Luimneach*): Bare area
LINNS	LH (*Lann*): Church, p. 104
LISACUL	RN (*Lios an Choill*): Fort of the wood

LISBANE	DN & L (*Lios Bán*): White fort, p. 112
LISBEG	G (*Lios Beag*): Little fort, p. 113
LISBELLAW	FH (*Lios Béal Átha*): Fort of the mouth of the ford, p. 114
LISBODUFF	CN (*Lios Bó Dubh*): Fort of the black cow
LISBOY	AM, C, DN, etc. (*Lios Buí*): Yellow fort, p. 112
LISCANNOR	CE (*Lios Ceannúir*): Fort of Ceannúr
LISCARNEY	MO (*Lios Cearnaigh*): Carnach's fort
LISCARROLL	C (*Lios Cearúill*): Fort of Cearúll, p. 115
LISCLOON	TE (*Lios Claon*): Sloping fort
LISCOLMAN	AM (*Lios Cholmáin*): Colman's fort, p. 113
LISDEEN	CE (*Lios Duinn*): Chief's fort
LISDOONVARNA	CE (*Lios Dúin Bhearna*): Fort of the fort of the gap, pp 30, 114
LISDOWNEY	KK (*Lios Dúnadhaigh*): Fort of Dúnadhach
LISDUFF	CN & MO (*Lios Dubh*): Black fort, p. 112
LISGOOLE	FH (*Lios Gabhail*): Fort of the fork
LISLEA	AH & DY (*Lios Liath*): Grey fort, p. 113
LISLEVANE	C (*Lios Leamháin*): Elm fort
LISMACAFFRY	WH (*Lios Mhic Gofraidh*): Fort of Mac Gofraidh
LISMAHON	DN (*Lios Mócháin*): Móchán's fort, p. 115
LISMORE	WD (*Lios Mór*): Big fort, p. 113
LISMOYNEY	WH (*Lios Maighne*): Fort of the precinct
LISNACASK	WH (*Lios na Cásca*): Easter fort
LISNACREE	DN (*Lios na Crí*): Fort of the boundary
LISNADILL	AH (*Lios na Daille*): Fort of the blind man
LISNAGADE	DN (*Lios na gCéad*): Fort of the hundreds, p. 114
LISNAGARVEY	DN (*Lios na gCearrbhach*): Fort of the gamblers, p. 113
LISNAGEER	CN (*Lios na gCaor*): Fort of the berries, p. 113
LISNAGELVIN	DY (*Lios Mhic Ghiolláin*): Mac Giollán's fort
LISNAGRY	L (*Lios na Groighe*): Fort of the stud
LISNAKILL	WD (*Lios na Cille*): Fort of the church
LISNALINCHY	AM (*Lios Uí Loingsigh*): Fort of Ó Loingseach, p. 114
LISNALONG	MN (*Lios na Long*): Fort of the boat
LISNAMUCK	DY (*Lios na Muc*): Fort of the pigs, p. 113
LISNARRICK	FH (*Lios na nDaróg*): Fort of the oak
LISNASKEA	FH (*Lios na Scéithe*): Fort of the shield
LISNASTREAN	DN (*Lios na Sriain*): Fort of the bridle
LISPOLE	KY (*Lios Póil*): Fort of the pool
Lisrobert	MO, p. 114

LISRODDEN	AM (*Lios Rodáin*): Rodán's fort
LISROE	CE, C, KY, etc. (*Lios Ruadh*): Red fort, p. 113
LISRONAGH	TY (*Lios Rónach*): Seal fort
LISRYAN	LD (*Lios Riáin*): Rián's fort
LISSACREASIG	C (*Lios an Chraosaigh*): Fort of the glutton
LISSALWAY	RN (*Lios Sealbhaigh*): Fort of Sealbhach
LISSAN	TE (*Leasán*): Little fort, p. 113
LISSANISKA	C, KY & L (*Lios an Uisce*): Fort of the water, pp 113, 161
LISSANISKY	C, RN & TY (*Lios an Uisce*): Fort of the water, p. 113
LISSARDA	C (*Lios Ardachaidh*): Fort of the high field
LISSATAVA	MO (*Lios an tSamhaidh*): Fort of the sorrel, p. 113
LISSELTON	KY (*Lios Eiltín*): Fort of the little doe
LISSINAGROAGH	SO (*Lisín na gCruach*): Little fort of the ridge
LISSUE	AM (*Lios Aedha*): Aedh's fort, pp 113, 114
LISSYCASEY	CE (*Lios Uí Chathasaigh*): Ó Cathasaigh's fort
LISTOODER	DN (*Lios an tSúdaire*): Fort of the cobbler
LISTOWEL	KY (*Lios Tuathail*): Fort of Tuathal
Liswilliam	RN, p. 114
LIXNAW	KY (*Leic Snámha*): Floating island
Loch Garman	WX, p. 15
LOGHILL	L (*Leamhchoill*): Elmwood, p. 108
LONGFORD	LD (*Longphort*): Fortified house, pp 117, 130
LOOP HEAD	CE (*Léim* + Head): Head of the leap, p. 109
LOSKERAN	WD (*Loiscreán*): Burnt ground
LOSSET	CN (*Losad*): Well-laid-out field
LOUGHAN	MH (*Lochán*): Little lake, p. 116
LOUGHANAVALLY	WH (*Lochán an Bhealaigh*): Little lake of the valley, p. 116
LOUGHANURE	DL (*Loch an Iúir*): Lake of the yew, p. 116
LOUGHBRICKLAND	DN (*Loch Bricreann*): Lake of Bricriu, p. 116
LOUGH DERRAVARAGH	WH (*Loch Dairbhreach*): Lake of the abundance of oaks, p. 68
LOUGHDUFF	CN (*Lathaigh Dhubh*): Black mire, p. 103
LOUGH ENNELL	WH (*Loch Ainninne*): Lake of great fairness
LOUGHER	KY (*Luachair*): Rushy place, pp 116, 117
LOUGHERMORE	DY (*Luachair Mhór*): Big rushy place, p. 117
LOUGH ERNE	FH (*Loch Éirne*): Éirne's lake
LOUGH ESKE	DL (*Loch Iasc*): Fish lake, p. 116
LOUGHGALL	AH (*Loch gCál*): Cabbage lake

LOUGHGLINN	RN (*Loch Glinn*): Lake of the valley
LOUGHGUILE	AM (*Loch Caol*): Lough of the narrows
LOUGHIL	L (*Leamchoill*): Elmwood
LOUGHINISLAND	DN (*Loch an Oileáin*): Lake of the island
LOUGH LENE	WH (*Loch Léibhinn*): Léibhinn's lake
LOUGHLINSTOWN	D (*Baile Uí Lachnáin*): Homestead of Ó Lachnán
LOUGHMACRORY	TE (*Loch Mhic Ruairí*): Mac Ruairí's lake, p. 116
LOUGH NEAGH	AH, AM, DN, DY & TE: (*Loch nEchach*): Eochaid's lake
LOUGHREA	G (*Loch Ria*): Grey lake, pp 116, 136
LOUGHROS	DL (*Luachras*): Rushy place
LOUP	DY (*Lúb*): Bend
LOUTH	LH (*Lugh*): Hollow
LOWERY	DL & FH (*Leamhraidhe*): Place of elms, p. 108
LUCAN	D (*Leamhcán*): Place of elms, p. 108
LUGACAHA	WH (*Log an Chatha*): Hollow of the battle
LUGGACURREN	LS (*Log an Churraigh*): Hollow of the marsh, p. 103
LUGNAQUILLA	WW (*Log na Coille*): Hollow of the wood, p. 103
LURGA	MO (*Lorgain*): Shank/ridge, p. 117
LURGAN	AH, DL & WH (*Lorgain*): Shank/ridge, p. 117
LURGANGREEN	LH (*Lorgain* + Green): Shank/ridge + green
LURGANREAGH	DN (*Lorgan Riabhach*): Striped ridge, p. 117
LUSK	D (*Lusca*): Meaning uncertain
LYNALLY	OY (*Lann Eala*): Church of (Colmán) Eala, p. 104
LYNN	WH (*Lann*): Church, p. 104
LYRACRUMPANE	KY (*Ladhar an Chrompáin*): Fork of the river valley
LYRE	C (*Ladhar*): Fork, p. 103
LYRENAGEEHA	C (*Ladhar na Gaoithe*): Fork of the wind, p. 103
LYRENAGREENA	L (*Ladhar na Gréine*): Fork of the sun, p. 103

MAAM	G (*Mám*): Mountain-pass
MAAS	DL (*Más*): Buttock, p. 120
MABRISTA	WH (*Má Briste*): Broken plain
MACE	G & MO (*Más*): Buttock, p. 120
MACGILLYCUDDY'S REEKS	KY (*Cruacha Dubha*): Black ricks
MACNEAN LOUGH	CN, FH & LM (*Loch Mac nÉan*): Mac Nean's lake
MACOSQUIN	DY (*Má Choscáin*): Coscán's plain
MACROOM	C (*Má Chromtha*): Plain of the crooked ford, p. 118
MADABAWN	CN (*Maide Bán*): White wood
MADDADOO	WH (*Maide Dubh*): Black wood
MAGHAREE ISLANDS	KY (*Machairí* + Islands): Flat places + islands
MAGHERA	DN (*Machaire*): Plain, p. 118
MAGHERA	DY (*Machaire Rátha*): Plain of the fort, p. 118
MAGHERABEG	DL (*Machaire Beag*): Small plain, pp 27, 118
MAGHERABOY	MO (*Machaire Buí*): Yellow plain, p. 118
MAGHERACLOONE	MN (*Machaire Cluana*): Plain of the pasture, p. 118
MAGHERADERNAN	WH (*Machaire Ua dTighearnáin*): Plain of Uí Tighearnáin
MAGHERAFELT	DY (*Machaire Theach Fíolta*): Plain of the house of Fioghalta, p. 118
MAGHERAGALL	AM (*Machaire na gCeall*): Plain of the church
MAGHERALIN	DN (*Machaire Lainne*): Plain of the church, p. 118
MAGHERAMORNE	AM (*Machaire Morna*): Plain of the Morna
MAGHERANERLA	WH (*Machaire an Iarla*): Earl's field
MAGHERANAGEERAGH	FH & TE (*Machaire na gCaorach*): Plain of the sheep
MAGHEREE ISLANDS	KY (*Machairí* + Islands): Flat places + islands
MAGHERY	DL (*Machaire*): Plain, p. 118
MAGILLIGAN	DY ([Aird] *Mhic Ghiollagáin*): (Point of) Mac Giollagán
MAHOONAGH	L (*Má Thamhnach*): Plain of the clearings
MAIGUE RIVER	L (*Maigh* + River): River of the plain
MAIN RIVER	AM (*Maighin* + River): River of the plain
MAINE RIVER	KY (*Maighin* + River): River of the plain
MALAHIDE	D (*Mullach Íde*): Íde's summit

MALIN	DL (*Malainn*): Brow or brae
MALINBEG	DL (*Malainn Bhig*): Small brow or brae
MALINMORE	DL (*Malainn Mhóir*): Large brow or brae
MALLARANNY	MO (*Mala Raithní*): Brow of the ferns
MALLOW	C (*Mala*): Plain of the rock
MALLUSK	AM (*Má Bhloisce*): Plain of the noise
MANISTER	L (*Mainistir*): Monastery, p. 119
MANTUA	RN (*Móinteach*): Moorland
Marino	D, p. 84
Maryborough	LS, p. 84
MASTERGEEHY	KY (*Maistir Gaoithe*): Churning wind
MATEHY	C (*Má Teithe*): Smooth plain
MAULAGALLANE	KY (*Meall an Ghalláin*): Knoll of the standing stone, pp 89, 120
MAULNAGOWER	KY (*Meall na nGabhar*): Knoll of the goats, p. 120
MAULNAHORNA	KY (*Meall na hOrna*): Knoll of the barley, p. 120
MAULYNEILL	KY (*Meall Uí Néill*): Ó Néill's knoll, p. 120
MAUMAKEOGH	MO (*Mám an Cheo*): Pass of the mist
MAUMTRASNA	MO (*Mám Trasna*): Mountain-pass
MAUMTURK	G (*Mám Tuirc*): Pass of the boar
MAUSREVAGH	G (*Más Riabhach*): Striped thigh, pp 120, 136
MAUSROWER	KY (*Más Ramhar*): Fat thigh, p. 120
MAYGLASS	WX (*Magh Glas*): Green plain
MAYNOOTH	KE (*Magh Nuad*): Plain of Nuadha
MAYO	MO (*Maigh Eo*): Plain of the yews, p. 84
MAYOGALL	DY (*Má Ghuala*): Plain of the shoulder
MAZE	DN (*Má*): Plain
MEALAGHANS	OY (*Maelachán*): Little bare hills
MEELDRUM	WH (*Maoldruim*): Bald ridge
MEELIN	C (*Maolinn*): Hillock
MEENACLADY	DL (*Mín an Chladaigh*): Smooth place of the shore
MEENACROSS	DL (*Mín na Croise*): Smooth place of the cross
MEENAGORP	TE (*Mín na gCorp*): Smooth place of the dead bodies, p. 122
MEENANEARY	DL (*Mín an Aoire*): Smooth place of the satirist
MEENAVEAN	DL (*Mín na bhFiann*): Gentle place of the Fianna, p. 122
MEENISKA	WH (*Meadhón Uisge*): Middle water
MEIGH	AH (*Maigh*): Plain
MELLIFONT	LH: See LATIN NAMES, p. 105
MELMORE	DL (*Meall Mór*): Big lump

MELVIN LOUGH	FH (*Loch Meilbhe*): Lake of Meilbhe
MENLOUGH	G (*Mionlach*): Small place
MENLOUGH	G (*Mionloch*): Small lake
MINE HEAD	WD (*Mionn Ard*): High crown + head
MOATE	WH (*Móta*): Mound
MODELLIGO	WD (*Má Deilge*): Plain of the thorn
MODREENY	TY (*Má Dreimhne*): Plain of fury
MOGEELY	C (*Mágh Ile*): Ile's plain
MOGLASS	TY (*Má Ghlas*): Grey/green plain
MOHILL	LM (*Maothail*): Soft place
MOIRA	DN (*Má Ráth*): Plain of the ring-fort
MONAGHAN	MN (*Muineachán*): Place of thickets
MONAMOLIN	WX (*Muine Moling*): Thicket of Moling, p. 124
MONARD	TY (*Móin Ard*): High bog, p. 123
MONASEED	WX (*Moin na Saighead*): Bog of the arrows
MONASTER	L (*Mainistir*): Monastery, p. 119
MONASTERADEN	SO (*Mainistir Aodáin*): Aodán's monastery
MONASTERANENAGH	L (*Mainistir an Aonaigh*): Monastery of the assembly, p. 17
MONASTERBOICE	LH (*Mainistir Bhuithe*): Buite's monastery, p. 119
MONASTEREVIN	KE (*Mainistir Eimhín*): Monastery of Eimhín, p. 119
MONASTERLEIGH	DN (*Mainistir Liath*): Grey abbey, p. 119
MONAVULLAGH	WD (*Móin an Mhullaigh*): Bog of the summit, p. 123
MONEA	FH (*Má Niadh*): Plain of the champion
MONEYFLUGH	KY (*Muine Fliuch*): Wet thicket
MONEYGALL	OY (*Muine Gall*): Thicket of the stones, p. 124
MONEYGASHEL	CN (*Muine na gCaiseal*): Thicket of the stone forts, p. 124
MONEYGLASS	AM (*Muine Glas*): Grey/green thicket, p. 124
MONEYLEA	WH (*Muine Liath*): Grey thicket, p. 110
MONEYMORE	DY (*Muine Mór*): Big thicket, p. 124
MONEYNEANY	DY (*Móin na nIonadh*): Bog of wonders
MONEYNICK	AM (*Muine Chnoic*): Thicket of the hill, p. 124
MONEYREAGH	DN (*Monadh Riabhach*): Striped bog, p. 123
MONEYSTOWN	WW (*Muine* + Town): Thicket town
MONIVEA	G (*Muine Mheá*): Thicket of the mead, p. 124
MONROE	WH (*Móin Ruadh*): Red bog
MOONCOIN	KE (*Móin Choinn*): Conn's bog, p. 123
MOONE	KE (*Maoin*): Gift
MORENANE	L (*Boirneán*): Little stony place

MORNINGTON	MH (*Baile Uí Mhornáin*): Ó Mornán's town
MOROE	L (*Má Rua*): Red plain
MOTHEL	WD (*Maothail*): Soft place
MOUNTBOLUS	OY (*Cnocán Bhólais*): Hill of Bolas
MOUNTMELLICK	LS (*Móinteach Mílic*): Moor of the wet ground
MOUNTRATH	LS (*Móin Rátha*): Bog of the fort, p. 123
MOURNE MOUNTAINS	DN (*Mughdhorna* + Mountains): Mountains of the Mughdhorna tribe
MOVEEN	CE (*Má Mhín*): Smooth plain, pp 118, 120
MOVILLA	DN (*Má Bhile*): Plain of the sacred tree, p. 30
MOVILLE	DL (*Má Bhile*): Plain of the sacred tree, pp 30, 118
MOWHAN	AH (*Má Bhán*): White plain, p. 118
MOY RIVER	MO & SO (*Muaidh* + River): Stately + river
MOY	TE (*Máo*): Plain, p. 118
MOYALLEN	DN (*Má Almhain*): Almhan's plain
MOYARD	G (*Maigh Ard*): High plain, p. 118
MOYARGET	AM (*Má Airgid*): Silver plain, p. 119
MOYASTA	CE (*Má Sheasta*): Upright plain
MOYCARKY	L (*Má Chairce*): Plain of oats, p. 118
MOYCASHEL	WH (*Magh Chaisil*): Plain of the stone fort
MOYCULLEN	G (*Magh Cuilinn*): Plain of holly, p. 118
MOYDOW	LD (*Má Dumha*): Plain of the mound, p. 119
MOYDRUM	WH (*Magh Droma*): Plain of the ridge
MOYGASHEL	TE (*Má gCaisil*): Plain of the stone fort, pp 40, 119
MOYGLASS	G (*Maigh Ghlas*): Grey/green plain
MOYLE	TY (*Mael*): Hill
MOYLOUGH	G (*Maigh Locha*): Plain of the lake
MOYMORE	CE (*Má Mhór*): Big plain, p. 118
MOYNALTY	MH (*Má nEalta*): Plain of the bird-flocks
MOYNE	MO & TY (*Maighin*): Little plain
MOYNE	MO, TY & WW (*Maighean*): Precinct
MOYOLA RIVER	DY (*Magh nÉola* + River): Éola's plain + river
MOYVALLY	KE (*Magh Bhealaigh*): Plain of the pass, p. 118
MOYVANE	KY (*Maigh Mheáin*): Middle plain
MOYVORE	WH (*Magh Mhora*): Mora's plain
MOYVOUGHLY	WH (*Má Bhachla*): Plain of the crosier, p. 119
MUCKAMORE	AM (*Má Chomair*): Plain of the confluence, p. 118
MUCKISH	DL (*Mucais*): Pig-ridge
MUCKNO LOUGH	MN (*Loch Muc Shnámh*): Lake of the pigs'

	swimming-place
MUCKROS	DL (*Mucros*): Pig promontory
MUCKROSS	KY (*Mucros*): Pig grove
Muclann	p. 104
MUFF	DL (*Magh*): Plain, p. 118
MUINE BHEAG	CW: Small thicket
MULDONAGH	DY (*Maol Domhnaigh*): Small hill of the church
MULLAGH	CN, G & MH (*Mullach*): Summit, p. 124
MULLAGHANATTIN	KY (*Mullach an Aitinn*): Summit of the gorse
MULLAGHAREIRK	C & L (*Mullach an Radhairc*): Summit of the vista, p. 124
MULLAGHBAWN	AH (*Mullach Bán*): White summit, p. 124
MULLAGHCARN	TE (*Mullach an Chairn*): Summit of the cairn
MULLAGHCLEEVAUN	WW (*Mullach Cliabháin*): Summit of the cradle, p. 124
MULLAGHMORE	DY & SO (*Mullach Mór*): Big summit, p. 124
MULLAN	MN (*Muileann*): Mill, p. 123
MULLAN	TE (*Mullán*): Small hill, p. 124
MULLENAKILL	KK (*Muileann na Cille*): Mill of the church, p. 123
MULLINACUFF	WW (*Muileann Mhic Dhuibh*): Mill of Mac Duibh, p. 123
MULLINAHONE	TY (*Muileann na hUamhan*): Mill of the cave, pp 123, 160
MULLINAVAT	KK (*Muileann an Bhata*): Mill of the stick
MULLINGAR	WH (*Muileann Cearr*): Crooked mill, p. 123
MULLINORAN	WH (*Muileann an Fhuaráin*): Mill of the spring
MULRANY	MO (*Mala Raithne*): Ferny brae
MULROY BAY	DL (*Maol Rua* + Bay): Bay of the small red hill
MULTYFARNHAM	WH (*Mullach Tighe Farannáin*): Summit of Farannán's house
Mumu	p. 4
MUNLOUGH	CN (*Móin Loch*): Bog-lake
MUNTERBURN	TE (*Muintir Bhirn*): Family of Birn
MUNTERLONEY	TE (*Muintir Luinigh*): Family of Luinigh
MURLOUGH	DN (*Murbholg*): Sea-swell
MURRAGH	C (*Murbhach*): Salt-marsh
MURREAGH	KY (*Muiríoch*): Beach
MURROE	L (*Magh Rua*): Red plain
MURROOGH	CE (*Murúch*): Beach
MWEELAHORNA	WD (*Maol na hEorna*): Hill of the barley
MWEELREA	MO (*Maol Ria*): Grey hill
MYROE	DY (*Má Rua*): Red plain
MYSHALL	CW (*Míseal*): Low central place

N

NAAS	KE (*Nás*): Assembly
NACUNG LOUGH	DL (*Loch na Cuinge*): Lake of the yoke
NAD	C (*Nead |an Iolair|*): (Eagle's) nest, p. 125
NARRAGHMORE	KE (*An Fhorrach Mhór*): The big forrach (= area of land)
NART	MN (*An Fheart*): The grave
NAUL	D (*An Aill*): The cliff, pp 13, 16
NAVAN	AH (*An Eamhain*): Uncertain, p. 16
NAVAN	MH (*An Uaimh*): The cave, p. 16
NEAGH LOUGH	AM, DY & TE (*Loch nEathach*): Eochaid's lake
NEALE	MO (*An Éill*): The bird-flock, p. 16
NED	CN, FH & DY (*Nead*): Nest, p. 125
NEDDANS	TY (*Na Feadáin*): The streamlets
NEDEEN	C & KY (*Neadín*): Little nest, p. 125
NENAGH	TY (*An Aonach*): The assembly, p. 16
NENDRUM	DN (*Naendruim*): Nine ridges
NEWCASTLELYONS	D (*Nuachaisleán Liamhna*), p. 126
NEWRY	DN (*An tIúr*): The yew-tree, p. 101
Newtown Forbes	LD, p. 83
Newtown Stewart	TE, p. 83
NEWTOWNARDS	DN (*Baile Nua na hAirde*): New town of the promontory, p. 83
NEWTOWNBREDA	DN (*Baile Nua na Bréadaí*): New town of Breda
NIER RIVER	WD (*An Uidhir*): The dun-coloured river
NINCH	MH (*An Inse*): The island
NOBBER	MH (*An Obair*): The construction, p. 16
NOUGHAVAL	C (*Nuachabháil*): New cloister, pp 60, 126
NORE RIVER	LS & TY (*An Fheoir* + River): River Feoir
NURE	WH (*An Iubhar*): The yew-tree
NURNEY	CW & KE (*An Urnaí*): The oratory, p. 16

O

OGHIL	G (*Eochaill*): Yew-wood, p. 84
OGONNELLOE	CE (|*Tuath*| Ó *gConaíle*): (Territory) of Uí Chonaíle
OMAGH	TE (*Ómaigh*): Sacred plain
OMEATH	LH (Ó *Méith*): (People) of Uí Méith
OMEY ISLAND	G (*Iomaidh*): Bed (of Feichín) island
ONAGHT	G (*Eoghanacht*): (Place of) descendants of Eoghan
OOLA	L (*Ubhla*): Apple-trees, p. 12
ORAN	RN (*Uarán*): Spring, p. 160
ORANMORE	G (*Órán Mór*): Big spring, p. 160
ORLAR	MO (*Urlár*): Valley floor
Ormeau	DN, p. 84
OUGHTER LOUGH	CN (*Loch Uachtar*): Upper lake
OUGHTERARD	G & KE (*Uachtar Ard*): High upper place, p. 160
OULART	WX (*Abhallort*): Orchard, p. 11
OUNAGEERAGH	C (*Abh na gCaorach*): River of the sheep
OURNA LOUGH	TY (*Loch Odharna*): Dun-coloured lake
OVENS	C (*Uamhanna*): Caves
OW RIVER	WW (*Abh* + River): River (river)
OWBEG	(*Abh Beag*): Little river
OWEL LOUGH	WH (*Loch Uair*): Uair's lake
OWENASS RIVER	LS (*Abhainn Easa* + River): River of the waterfall (river)
OWENAVORRAGH RIVER	WX (*Abhainn an Bhorraidh* + River): River liable to flood (river)
OWENBEG	SO (*Abhainn Bheag*): Small river, p. 11
OWENBOY	C (*Abhainn Bhuí*): Yellow river, p. 36
OWENDALULLEEGH RIVER	G (*Abhainn dá Loilíoch* + River): River of two milch cows (river)
OWENDUFF RIVER	MO (*Abhainn Dhubh* + River): Black river (river)
OWENEA RIVER	DL (*Abhainn an Fia* + River): River of the deer (river)
OWENGLIN RIVER	G (*Abhainn Ghlinne* + River): River of the valley (river)
OWENINY RIVER	MO (*Abhainn Eidhneach* + River): Ivied river (river)
OWENKILLEW RIVER	TE (*Abhainn Choille* + River): River of the wood (river)

OWENMORE RIVER	C, MO & SO (*Abhainn Mór* + River): Big river (river), p. 11
OWENNACURRA RIVER	C (*Abhainn na Cora* + River): River of the weir (river)
OWENREA BURN	TE (*Abhainn Riabhach* + Burn): Grey river + burn
OWENTOCKER RIVER	DL (*Abhainn Tacair* + River): River of the pickings (river)
OWENUR RIVER	RN (*Abhainn Fhuar* + River): Cold river (river)
OWENWEE	DL (*Abhainn Bhuí* + River): Yellow river (river), p. 36
OWER	G (*Odhar*): Dun-coloured place
OWEY ISLAND	DL (*Uaigh*): Cave
OWVANE RIVER	C (*Abh Bhán* + River): White river (river)

P

Portballintrae

PORTBALLINTRAE	AM (*Port Bhaile an Trá*): Port of the homestead of the beach, pp 130, 156
PORTGLENONE	AM (*Port Chluain Eoghain*): Port of Eoghan's meadow
PORTLAOISE	LS (*Port Laoise*): Port of the tribe of Laeighis
PORTLAW	WD (*Port Lách*): Port of the hill
PORTLOMAN	WH (*Port Lomáin*): Lomán's port
PORTMARNOCK	D (*Port Mearnóg*): Mearnóg's port
PORTNABLAGH	DL (*Port na Bláiche*): Port of the flowers
PORTNOO	DL (*Port Nua*): New port, p. 130
Portobello	D, p. 84
PORTROE	TY (*Port Rua*): Red port
PORTRUSH	AM (*Port Rois*): Port of the promontory, p. 130
PORTSALON	DL (*Port an tSalainn*): Port of the salt
PORTUMNA	G (*Port Omna*): Bank of the tree-trunk, p. 130
POTTIAGHAN	WH (*Poiteacháin*): Bad ground
POULAPHUCA	D (*Poll an Phúca*): Pool of the sprite, p. 130
POULARGID	C (*Poll an Airgid*): Silver pool, p. 130
POULNAGAT	WH (*Poll na gCat*): Hole of the cats
PREBAUN	WH (*Preabán*): Patch
PUCKAUN	TY (*Pocán*): Small heap

Q

QUERRIN	CE (*Cuibhreann*): Tilled field
QUILLY	DN, DY & WD (*Coillidh*): Woodland
QUILTY	CE (*Coillte*): Woods, p. 59
QUIN	CE (*Cúinne*): Nook
QUOILE RIVER	DN (*Caol* + River): Narrow river

R

RADEMON	DN (*Ráth Deamáin*): Deamán's fort, p. 134
RAHAN	OY (*Raithean*): Ferny place, p. 132
RAHARA	RN (*Ráth Aradh*): Noble fort
RAHARNEY	WH (*Ráth Fhearna*): Fort of the alder
RAHEEN	C, WH & WX (*Ráithín*): Little fort, p. 134
RAHEENS	MO (*Ráithíní*): Little forts
RAHENY	D (*Ráth Eanaigh*): Fort of the marsh, p. 81
RAHOLP	DN (*Ráth Cholpa*): Fort of the bullock, p. 134
RAHUGH	WH (*Ráth Aodha*): Aodh's fort, p. 134
RAMELTON	DL (*Ráth Mealtain*): Mealtan's fort
RAMORE	AM (*Ráth Mór*): Big fort
RANDALSTOWN	AM (*Baile Raghnaill*): Raghnal's town
RANELAGH	D (*Raghnallach*): Raghnal's place
RANNAFAST	DL (*Rann na Feirste*): Point of the sandbank
RAPHOE	DL (*Ráth Bhoth*): Fort of the hut, pp 32, 134
RASHARKIN	AM (*Ros Earcáin*): Earcán's grove
RATH LOIRC	C (*Ráth Loirc*): Fort of the murder
Ráth Ailinne	KE, p. 76
RATH	OY & WD (*Ráth*): Fort, p. 134
RATHANGAN	KE (*Ráth Iomgháin*): Fort of Iomghán
RATHBEG	AM (*Ráth Beag*): Little fort, p. 27
RATHCABBAN	TY (*Ráth Cabáin*): Fort of the cabin, p. 39
RATHCARRA	WH (*Ráth Charrach*): Rocky fort
RATHCLITTAGH	WH (*Ráth Cleiteach*): Fort of the feathers
RATHCOGUE	WH (*Ráth Cogaidh*): Fort of the war
RATHCONRATH	WH (*Ráth Conarta*): Fort of the houndpack
RATHCOOL	C (*Ráth Cúil*): Fort of the hill, p. 134
RATHCOOLE	D (*Ráth Cúil*): Fort of the hill
RATHCORE	MH (*Ráth Cuair*): Fort of Cuar
RATHCORMACK	C (*Ráth Chormaic*): Cormac's fort
RATHDANGAN	WW (*Ráth Daingin*): Fort of the fortress, p. 134
RATHDOWNEY	LS (*Ráth Domhnaigh*): Fort of the church
RATHDRISHOGE	WH (*Ráth Driseog*): Fort of the brambles
RATHDRUM	WW (*Ráth Droma*): Fort of the ridge
RATHFARNHAM	D (*Ráth Fearnáin*): Fort of the alder
RATHFEIGH	MH (*Ráth Faiche*): Fort of the green

RATHFIELD	KY (*Páirc na Rátha*): Field of the ring-fort, p. 129
RATHFRAN	MO (*Ráth Bhrain*): Bran's fort, p. 134
RATHFRILAND	DN (*Ráth Fraoileann*): Fraoileann's fort
RATHFYLANE	WX (*Ráth Fialáin*): Fialán's fort
RATHGALL	WW (*Ráth Gall*): Fort of the stone
RATHGANNY	WH (*Ráth Ghainmhe*): Sandy fort
RATHGAR	D (*Ráth Garbh*): Rough fort, p. 134
Rathgilbert	LS, p. 134
RATHGORMUCK	WD (*Ráth Ó gCormaic*): Fort of Uí Chormaic
RATHKEALE	L (*Ráth Caola*): Caola's fort
RATHKEEVIN	TY (*Ráth Chaoimhín*): Kevin's fort, p. 134
RATHKENNY	AM & MH (*Ráth Cheannaigh*): Ceannaigh's fort
RATHLACKEN	MO (*Ráth Leacan*): Fort of the hillside, p. 134
RATHLEE	SO (*Ráth Lao*): Fort of the calf
RATHLIN ISLAND	AM (*Reachra* + Island): Reachra + island
RATHLIN O'BIRNE ISLAND	DL (*Reachlainn Uí Bhirn* + Island): Ó Birn's Reachlainn + Island
RATHMAREGA	WH (*Ráth Mharga*): Fort of the market
RATHMORE	AM, KE & KY (*Ráth Mhór*): Large fort, pp 27, 134
RATHMOYLE	KK (*Ráth Mhaol*): Bald fort
RATHMULLAN	DN (*Ráth Mhuilinn*): Fort of the mill, pp 123, 135
RATHMULLEN	SO (*Ráth an Mhuilinn*): Fort of the mill
RATHNAMAGH	MO (*Ráth na Mach*): Fort of the plain
RATHNAMUDDAGH	WH (*Ráth na mBodach*): Fort of the clowns
RATHNEW	WW (*Ráth Naoi*): Noé's fort
RATHNURE	WX (*Ráth an Iúir*): Fort of the yew, p. 134
RATHOWEN	WH (*Ráth Eoghain*): Eoghan's fort, p. 134
RATHRUANE	C (*Ráth Ruáin*): Ruán's fort
RATHTOE	CW (*Ráth Tó*): Tó's fort
RATHTROANE	MH (*Ráth Ruáin*): Ruán's fort
RATHVILLA	OY (*Ráth Bhile*): Fort of the sacred tree, p. 31
RATHVILLY	CW (*Ráth Bhile*): Fort of the sacred tree, p. 31
Rathwalter	TY, p. 134
RATOATH	MH (*Ráth Tó*): Tó's fort
RATTOO	KY (*Ráth Tó*): Tó's fort
RAUBAUN	WH (*Ráth Bán*): White fort
RAY	DL (*Ráith*): Fort
REA LOUGH	G (*Loch Ria*): Grey lake
REACASHLAGH	KY (*Réidchaisleach*): Clearing of the stone forts, p. 136

REANACLOGHEEN	WD (*Réidh na gCloichín*): Clearing of the little stones, p. 136
REANASCREENA	C (*Rae na Scríne*): Level place of the shrine, p. 130
REAR	TY (*Rae*): Level place, p. 132
RECESS	G (*Sraith Salach*): Dirty holm
REE LOUGH	LD, RN, WH (*Loch Rí*): King's lake
REEN	KY (*Rinn*): Point, p. 136
REENASCREENA	C (*Rae na Scríne*): Level place of the shrine
REENS	C (*Roighne*): Choicest part
RELAGHBEG	CN (*Reidhleach Beag*): Small level place
RELICK	WH (*Reilig*): Graveyard
RENANIRREE	C (*Rae na nDoirí*): Level place of the oaks
RENVYLE	G (*Rinn Mhaoile*): Promontory of the bald man
RHODE	OY (*Ród*): Route
Rialto	D, p. 84
RINAWADE	D (*Rinn an Bháid*): Point of the boat, p. 20
RINDOWN	RN (*Rinn Dúin*): Point of the fort, p. 137
RINE	CE (*Rinn*): Point
RINEANNA	CE (*Rinn Eanaigh*): Point of the marsh, p. 137
RINEEN	CE (*Rinnín*): Little point, p. 136
RING	WD (*Rinn*): Point, p. 136
RINGAROGY	C (*Rinn Gearróige*): Point of the small portion
RINGASKIDDY	C (*Rinn an Scídigh*): Scídioch's headland
RINGCURRAN	C (*Rinn Chorráin*): Point of the sickle, p. 136
RINGFAD	DN (*Rinn Fhada*): Long point, p. 136
RINGRONE	C (*Rinn Róin*): Seal point, p. 137
RINGSEND	D (*Rinn*): Point
RINMORE	DL (*Rinn Mhór*): Large point, p. 136
RINN	LD & LM (*Rinn*): Point, p. 136
RINNAFAGHLA	DL (*Rinn na Fochla*): Point of the cave
RINNEEN	G & KY (*Rinnín*): Little point, p. 136
RINVILLE	G (*Rinn Mhíl*): Point of the animal
RINVYLE	G (*Rinn Mhaoile*): Promontory of the bald man
Robinhood	CE & D, p. 84
ROCK OF DUNAMASE	LS (*Dún Masg* + Rock): Rock of the fort of Masg
ROE RIVER	DY (*Rua* + River): Red river
ROSBEG	DL (*Ros Beag*): Little point, p. 137
ROSBERCON	KK (*Ros Ó mBearchon*): Uí Bhearchon's grove
ROSCOMMON	RN (*Ros Comáin*): Comán's grove

ROSCOR	FH (Ros Corr): Beak promontory
ROSCREA	TY (Ros Cré): Cré's point, p. 138
ROSENALLIS	LS (Ros Fhionnghlaise): Grove of the bright stream
ROSGUIL	DL (Ros Goill): Goll's promontory
ROSINVER	LM (Ros Inbhir): Grove of the estuary
ROSLEA	FH (Ros Liath): Grey grove, p. 138
ROSMUCK	G (Ros Muc): Headland of pigs, p. 137
ROSNAKILL	DL (Ros na Cille): Grove of the church
ROSS CARBERY	C (Ros Ó gCairbre): Uí Chairbre's point, p. 138
ROSS LOUGH	AH, G & MN (Loch Rois): Lake of the grove
ROSS	MH (Ros): Grove
ROSSADREHID	TY (Ros an Droichid): Grove of the bridge
ROSSCAHILL	G (Ros Chathail): Cahill's grove
ROSSES	DL (Rosa): Promontories, p. 137
ROSSINAN	KK (Ros Fhionáin): Fionán's grove, p. 138
ROSSLARE	WX (Ros Láir): Middle promontory, p. 138
ROSSMORE	C & G (Ros Mór): Big promontory
ROSTREVOR	DN (Ros Treabhuir): Trevor's promontory
ROSTURK	MO (Ros Toirc): Grove of the boar
ROUGHTY RIVER	KY (Ruachtach + River): Destructive river
ROUNDSTONE	G (Cloch na Rón): Stone of the seals
ROWER	KK (Robhar): Flood
RUBANE	DN (Rubha Bán): White clearing
RUE POINT	AM (Rubha + Point): Point of the clearing
RUSH	D (Ros): Promontory
RUSKEY	RN (Rúscaigh): Morass

S

SAGGART	D (*Teach Sagard*): Sagra's house
ST JOHN'S POINT	DL & DN (*Steach Eoin*): Eoin's house, p. 148
ST MULLIN'S	KK (*Tigh Moling*): Moling's house
SALEEN	C (*Sáilín*): Little (arm of the) sea
SALLAHIG	KY (*Saileáin*): Place of the willows
SALLINS	KE (*Saileáin*): Place of the willows
SALLYNOGGIN	D (*Naigín*): Noggin
SALTEE ISLANDS	WX (*Oileán an tSalainn*): Salt island
SANTRY	D (*Seantrabh*): Old dwelling, p. 140
SAUL	DN (*Sabhall*): Barn
SAVAL	DN (*Sabhall*): Barn
SAWEL MOUNTAIN	TE (*Samhail* + Mountain): Apparition + mountain
SCADDY	DN (*Sceadaigh*): Spotted
SCARDAUNE	MO (*Scardán*): Tiny waterfall
SCARIFF	KY (*Scarbh*): Shallow ford, p. 139
SCARNAGEERAGH	MN (*Scarbh na gCaorach*): Shallow ford of the sheep, p. 139
SCARRIFF	C, CE, G (*Scairbh*): Shallow ford, p. 139
SCARTAGLIN	KY (*Scairteach an Ghlinne*): Thicket of the valley
SCARTEEN	KY (*Scairtín*): Little thicket
SCARVA	DN (*Scarbhach*): Abounding in shallow fords, p. 139
SCATTERY	CE (*Inis Chathaigh*): Cathach's island
SCHULL	C (*Scoil*): School
SCRABO	DN (*Screabach*): Crusted
SCRAGHAN	WH (*Scrathán*): Sward
SCRAHANAGNAVE	KY (*Screathan na gCnámh*): Scree of the bones
SCRAMOGE	RN (*Scramóg*): Meaning uncertain
SCREEB	G (*Scríb*): Furrow
SCREEN	WX (*Scrín*): Shrine, p. 139
SCREGGAN	OY (*Screagán*): Rough place
SCRIBBAGH	FH (*Scriobach*): Bad pasture
SCUR LOUGH	LM (*Loch an Scuir*): Lake of the camp
SEADAVOG	DL (*Suí Dabhóg*): Davog's seat, p. 144
SEEFIN	C, DN, MO & WD (*Suí Finn*): Fionn's seat, p. 144
SELLOO	MN (*Suí Lua*): Lua's seat
SESKANORE	TE (*Seisceann Mhór*): Big marsh, p. 142
SESKILGREEN	TE (*Seisíoch Chill Ghréine*): Plot of the church of the sun

SESKIN	TY (*Seisceann*): Marsh, p. 141
SESKINORE	TE (*Seisceann Mhór*): Big marsh, p. 142
SESKINRYAN	CW (*Seisceann Ríain*): Rían's marsh
SHANAGARRY	C (*Seangharraí*): Old garden, p. 140
SHANAGOLDEN	L (*Seanghualainn*): Old shoulder, p. 140
SHANAHOE	LS (*Seanchua*): Old hollow, p. 140
SHANBALLY	C (*Seanbhaile*): Old homestead, pp 25, 140
SHANBALLYMORE	C (*Seanbhaile Mór*): Large old homestead
SHANCO	MN (*Seanchua*): Old hollow, p. 140
SHANHOE	LS (*Seanchua*): Old hollow, p. 140
SHANKILL	AM & D (*Seanchill*): Old church, pp 51, 140
SHANLARAGH	C (*Seanlárach*): Old ruins
SHANNON RIVER	CE & L: Ancient goddess, p. 137
SHANONAGH	WH (*Sean dDomhnach*): Old church
SHANRAGH	LS (*Seanráth*): Old fort, p. 140
SHANRAHAN	TY (*Seanraithean*): Old ferny place, p. 140
SHANTONAGH	MN (*Seantonnach*): Old quagmire
SHANVAUS	LM (*Seanmhás*): Old plain, p. 140
SHARAVOGUE	OY (*Searbhóg*): Bitter place
SHEEAN	MO (*Sián*): Fairy mound
SHEEFIN	WH (*Suí Finn*): Fionn's seat, p. 144
SHEEFRY HILLS	MO (C*noic Shiofra*): Siofra's hills
SHEELIN LOUGH	CN, MH & WH (*Loch Síleann*): Sileann's lake
SHEHY MOUNTAINS	C (*Seithe*): Hides
SHERCOCK	CN (*Searcóg*): Sweetheart
SHERKIN ISLAND	C (*Inis Arcáin* + Island): Arcán's island (island)
SHESKINATAWY	DL (*Seisceann an tSamhaid*): Swamp of the sorrel, p. 142
SHESKINSHULE	TE (*Seisceann Siúil*): Moving marsh, p. 142
SHILLELAGH	WW (*Síol Éalaigh*): Progeny of Éalach
SHINGLIS	WH (*Seanlios*): Old fort
SHINRONE	OY (*Suí an Róin*): Seat of the seal, p. 144
SHRAHEENS	MO (*Sraithíní*): Little holms
SHRONOWEN	KY (*Srón Abhann*): Snout of the river
SHROUGH	TY (*Sruth*): Stream, p. 143
SHROUGHAN	WW (*Sruthán*): Stream, p. 143
SHROVE	DL (*Srúibh*): Snout
SHRUE	WH (*Sidh Ruadh*): Red fairy hill
SHRULE	MO (*Sruthail*): Stream, p. 143
SINEIRL	AM (*Suí an Iarla*): Seat of the earl, p. 144
SION MILLS	TE (*Muileann an tSiáin*): Mill of the fairy mound

SKAGH	C & L (*Sceach*): Hawthorn, p. 139
SKAHARD	L (*Sceach Ard*): High hawthorn, p. 139
SKEA	FH & TE (*Sceach*): Hawthorn, p. 139
SKEAGH	AM, CN, DL, LS, TY (*Sceach*): Hawthorn, p. 139
SKEAGHMORE	WH (*Sceach Mhór*): Big hawthorn, p. 139
SKEARD	MO (*Scéird*): Bleak hill
SKEGONIEL	AM (*Sceitheog an Iarla*): Bush of the earl
SKENARGET	TE (*Sceach Airgid*): Silver hawthorn, p. 139
SKERRIES	AM & D (*Sceirí*): Reef islands, p. 139
SKIDDERNAGH	MO (*Sciodarnach*): Place of puddles
SKREEN	MH & SO (*Scrín*): Shrine, p. 139
SKULL	C (*Scoil*): School
SLADE	WX (*Slaod*): Fall-away of ground
SLANE	MH ([Baile] *Shláine*): (Homestead of) fullness
SLANEBEG	WH (*Sleamhain Bheag*): Small sleek place
SLANEMORE	WH (*Sleamhain Mhór*): Big sleek place
SLANEY RIVER	CW, WX & WW (*Sléine* + River):
SLAUGHTMANUS	DY (*Leacht Mhánasa*): Mánas's grave, p. 107
SLEAHEAD	KY (*Ceann Sléibhe*): Head of the mountain
SLEATYGRAIGUE	LS (*Gráig Shléibhte*): Hamlet of the mountains
SLEMISH	AM (*Sliabh Mis*): Mountain of Mis
SLIEVADUFF	KY (*Sliabh an Daimh*): Mountain of the ox
SLIEVE ANIERIN	LM (*Sliabh an Iarainn*): Iron mountain
SLIEVE BERNAGH	CE & DN (*Sliabh Bearnach*): Gapped mountain
SLIEVE BINNIAN	DN (*Sliabh Binneáin*): Mountain of the small peak
SLIEVE BLOOM	LS & OY (*Sliabh Bladhma*): Blaze mountain
SLIEVE COMMEDAGH	DN (*Sliabh Coimhéideach*): Guarding mountain
SLIEVE CROOB	DN (*Sliabh Crúibe*): Claw mountain
SLIEVE DONARD	DN (*Sliabh Domhangairt*): Domhangart's mountain, p. 143
SLIEVE GALLION	DY (*Sliabh gCalláinn*): Mountain of noise
SLIEVE GAMPH	MO & SO (*Sliabh Gamh*): Mountain of storms, p. 142
SLIEVE GULLION	MH (*Sliabh gCuillinn*): Mountain of the steep slope
SLIEVE LEAGUE	DL (*Sliabh Liag*): Mountain of flags, pp 111, 142
SLIEVE MISH	KY (*Sliabh Mis*): Mountain of Mis
SLIEVE NA CALLIAGH	MH (*Sliabh na Calliagh*): Mountain of the hag, p. 142
SLIEVE SNAGHT	DL (*Sliabh Sneachta*): Mountain of snow, p. 142
SLIEVEARDAGH	KK & TY (*Sliabh Ardachaidh*): Mountain of the high field, p. 142
SLIEVEAUGHTY	G (*Sliabh Eachtgha*): Eachtgha's mountain

SLIEVECALLAN	CE (*Sliabh Collán*): Hazel mountain
SLIEVEFELIM	L (*Sliabh Eibhlinne*): Eibhlinn's mountain
SLIEVEMORE	TE (*Sliabh Mór*): Big mountain, p. 142
SLIEVENAMON	TY (*Sliabh na mBan*): Mountain of the women, p. 142
SLIEVEROE	KK (*Sliabh Rua*): Red mountain, pp 138, 142
SLIEVETOOEY	DL (*Sliabh Tuaidh*): Mountain of the district
SLIGO	SO (*Sligeach*): Abounding in shells
SMAGHRAN	RN (*Smeachrán*): Stripe of land
SNEEM	KY (*Snaidhm*): Knot
SPEENOGE	DL (*Spionóg*): Spoon
SPIDDAL	G & MH (*Spidéal*): Hospital, p. 143
SPINK	LS (*Spinc*): Pinnacle
SPITTALTOWN	WH (*Baile an Ospidéil*): Town of the hospital, p. 143
SRAH	MO (*Srath*): Holm, p. 143
SRAHMORE	MO (*Sruth Mór*): Big holm, p. 143
SRUE	G (*Sruth*): Stream, p. 143
SRUH	WD (*Sruth*): Stream, p. 143
STACKALLAN	MH (*Steach Colláin*): Collán's house
STAMULLEN	MH (*Steach Maolín*): Maolín's house
STILLORGAN	D (*Steach Lorgan*): Lorcan's house, p. 148
STRABANE	TE (*Srath Bán*): White holm, pp 27, 143
STRADBALLY	KY, LS & WD (*Sráidbhaile*): Street-town, p. 143
STRADONE	CN (*Sraith an Domhain*): Holm of the world
STRAGOLAN	FH (*Srath Gabhláin*): Holm of the fork
STRAHART	WX (*Sraith Airt*): Art's home
STRAID	AM, DL & MO (*Sráid*): Street, p. 143
STRAIDARRAN	DY (*Sráidbhaile Uí Áráin*): Street town of the Uí Áráin
STRALONGFORD	TE (*Srath Longphoirt*): Holm of the fortified house
STRANAGALWILLY	TE (*Srath na Gallbhuaile*): Holm of the foreigner's milking-place
STRANGFORD	DN: See NORSE NAMES, p. 125
STRANMILLIS	AM (*Sruthán Milis*): Sweet stream, p. 144
STRANOCUM	AM (*Sraith Nócam*): Nocam's holm
STRANORLAR	DL (*Srath an Urláir*): Holm of the valley floor, p. 143
STREET	WH (*Sráid*): Street, p. 143
STROAN	AM, CN & KK (*Sruthán*): Stream, p. 143
STRUELL	DN (*Sruthail*): Stream, p. 143
SUIR RIVER	TY & WD (*Siúr* + River): Sister + river
SWATRAGH	DY (*Suaitreach*): Soldier
SWILLY RIVER	DL (*Súileach* + River): Clear-seeing + river
SWORDS	D (*Sord*): Sward

T

TACKER LOUGH	CN (*Loch Tacair*): Artificial lake
TACUMSHIN, LOUGH	WX (*Loch Theach Cuimsin*): Lake of Cuimsin's house
TAGHEEN	MO (*Teach Chaoin*): Pleasant house
TAGHMON	WH & WX (*Teach Munna*): Munna's house
TAGHNAFEARAGH	WH (*Teach na bFiarach*): House of the lea fields
TAGHSHINNY	LD (*Teach Siní*): Sineach's house
TAGOAT	WX (*Teach Gót*): Gót's house
TALLAGHT	D (*Tamhlacht*): Plague burial-place, p. 145
TALLOW	WD (*Tulach*): Hill
Tamlachta Órláim	Órlám's burial-place, p. 145
TAMLAGHT FINLAGAN	DY (*Tamhlacht Fionnlugháin*): Fionnlugh's burial-place, p. 145
TAMLAGHT O'CRILLY	DY (*Tamlacht* + O'Crilly): Burial-place + O'Crilly, p. 145
TAMLAGHT	DY (*Tamhlacht*): Plague burial-place
TAMNAGHBANE	AH (*Tamhnach Bán*): White cultivated spot, p. 147
TAMNEY	DL (*Tamhnaigh*): Cultivated spot, p. 147
TAMNYRANKIN	DY (*Tamhnaigh* + Rankin): Rankin's cultivated spot, p. 147
TANDERAGEE	AH (*Tóin re Gaoith*): Backside to the wind, p. 90
TANG	WH (*Teanga*): Tongue
TARA	MH (*Teamhair*): Conspicuous place
TARBERT	KY (*Tairbeart*): Isthmus
TARELTON	C (*Tír Eiltín*): Eiltín's country
TAUGHMACONNELL	RN (*Teach Mhic Conaill*): Mac Conaill's house
TAUR	C (*Teamhair*): Conspicuous place
TAWIN ISLAND	G (*Rinn Tamhain*): Point of the stump
TAWNAGHLAHAN	DL (*Tamhnach Lahan*): Broad cultivated spot, p. 147
TAWNYEELY	LM (*Tamhnaigh Aelaigh*): Cultivated spot of the lime, p. 147
TAWNYINAH	MO (*Tamhnaigh an Eich*): Clearing of the horse
TAWNYLEA	SO (*Tamhnaigh Liatha*): Grey cultivated spot
TAY LOUGH	WW (*Loch Té*): Lake of tea

TAY RIVER	WD (*Tae* + River): Tay + river
Teampall Chaomháin	Caomhán's church, p. 149
Teampall Mhic Dhuach	Mac Duach's church, p. 149
TEARAGHT ISLAND	KY (*Oileán Tiaracht*): Buttock island
TEDAVNET	MN (*Tigh Damhnata*): Damhnait's house, p. 147
TEELIN	DL (*Teileann*): Dish
TEERMACLANE	CE (*Tír Mhic Calláin*): Mac Callán's country
TEERMORE	WH (*Tír Mór*): Large district
TEERNACREEVE	WH (*Tír dá Craebh*): District of two sacred trees
TEEWORKER	MH (*Taobh Urchair*): Side of the cast
TEMPLEBOY	SO (*Teampall Baoith*): Baoth's church
TEMPLEBRENDAN	MO (*Teampall Brendáin*): Brendan's church, p. 148
TEMPLECRONAN	CE (*Teampall Crónáin*): Cronan's church, p. 148
TEMPLEDERRY	TY (*Teampall Doire*): Church of the oakwood
TEMPLEETNEY	TY (*Teampall Eithne*): Eithne's church
TEMPLEFINN	DN (*Teampall Fionn*): White church, p. 149
TEMPLEGLANTINE	L (*Teampall an Ghleanntáin*): Church of the valley
TEMPLEMARTIN	C & WX (*Teampall Mártan*): Mártan's church, p. 148
TEMPLEMICHAEL	C (*Teampall Mhichil*): Michael's church, p. 148
TEMPLEMORE	TY (*Teampall Mór*): Big church
TEMPLEMOYLE	DN (*Teampall Maol*): Bald church, p. 148
TEMPLENAKILLA	KY (*Teampall na Cille*): Church of the church, p. 148
TEMPLENOE	KY (*Teampall Nua*): New church, p. 126
TEMPLEOGUE	D (*Teach Mealóg*): Mealóg's church
TEMPLEORAN	WH (*Teampall Fhuaráin*): Church of the spring
TEMPLEORUM	KK (*Teampall Fhothram*): Church of Fothram
TEMPLEPATRICK	AM & MO (*Teampall Phádraig*): Patrick's church, p. 148
TEMPLESHAMBO	WX (*Teampall Seanbhoth*): Church of the old huts
TEMPLETOUHY	TY (*Teampall Tuatha*): Church of the territory
TEMPO	FH (*Tiompú [Deiseal]*): (Right-hand) turn
TERENURE	D (*Tír an Iúir*): Territory of the yew, p. 101
TERMON	CN & DL (*Tearmann*): Sanctuary land, p. 150
TERMONAGUIRK	TE (*Tearmann* + Maguirk): Sanctuary + Maguirk, p. 150
TERMONFECKIN	LH (*Tearmann Feichín*): Feichín's sanctuary, p. 150
TERRYGLASS	TY (*Tír dhá Ghlas*): Territory of two streams, p. 152
TEVRIN	WH (*Teamhrín*): Small conspicuous hill
Thomastown	KK, p. 83
THONOGE RIVER	TY (*Tonóg* + River): Little hole + river
THURLES	TY (*Durlas*): Stronghold
TIBOHINE	MO (*Tigh Baoithín*): Baothan's church

TICLOY	AM (*Tigh Cloiche*): House of stone, p. 148
TIERMACLANE	CE (*Tír Mhic Calláin*): Mac Callán's country
TIEVEMORE	DL (*Taobh Mór*): Large side
TIMAHOE	KE & LS (*Tigh Mochua*): Mochua's house, p. 147
TIMOLEAGUE	C (*Tigh Molaige*): Molaga's house, p. 147
TIMOLIN	KE (*Tigh Moling*): Moling's house, p. 147
TINAHELY	WW (*Tigh na hÉille*): House of the latchet
TINNAKILLA	WX (*Tigh na Coille*): House of the wood, p. 148
TINODE	WH (*Tigh an Fhóid*): House of the sod
TIPPERARY	TY (*Tiobraid Árann*): Ára's well, p. 151
Tír Conaill	Conall's territory, p. 152
Tír Gaedheal	Ireland, p. 152
TIRAWLEY	MO (*Tír Amhalghaidh*): Amhalghaidh's territory, p. 152
TIRBOY	G (*Tír Buí*): Yellow territory, p. 152
TIRERAGH	SO (*Tír Fhiachrach*): Fiachra's territory, p. 152
TIRKANE	DY (*Tír Chatháin*): Cathán's country
TIRNAMONA	MN (*Tír na Móna*): Territory of the bog, p. 152
TOAMES	C (*Tuaim*): Mound
Tobar Crócháin	Cróchán's well, p. 154
TOBARMACDUGH	G (*Tobar Mhic Dhuach*): Mac Duach's well, p. 154
TOBER	CN (*Tobar*): Well, p. 153
TOBERAVILLA	KY (*Tobar an Bhile*): Well of the sacred tree, p. 154
TOBERBREEDY	C (*Tobar Bhríde*): Bríd's well, p. 154
TOBERBUNNY	D (*Tobar Bainne*): Well of milk, p. 154
TOBERCURRY	SO (*Tobar an Choire*): Well of the cauldron, p. 154
TOBERDONEY	(*Tobar Domhnaigh*): Sunday's well, pp 74, 154
TOBERMOGUE	WH (*Tobar Mhodóg*): Modóg's well, p. 154
TOBERMORE	DY (*Tobar Mór*): Big well, p. 153
TOEM	TY (*Tuaim*): Mound, p. 157
TOGHBLANE	DN (*Teach Bhláin*): Bláin's house
TOGHER	C, LH & OY (*Tóchar*): Causeway, p. 154
TOGHERBANE	KY (*Tóchar Bán*): White causeway, p. 155
TOGHERBEG	G & WW (*Tóchar Beag*): Little causeway, p. 155
TOMHAGGARD	WX (*Teach Moshagard*): Moshagra's house
TON	MN (*Tóin*): Bottom
TONDUFF	DL (*Tóin Dubh*): Black bottom
TONRAGEE	MO (*Tóin re Gaoith*): Backside to the wind
TOOM	TY (*Tuaim*): Mound, p. 157
TOOMARD	G (*Tuaim Ard*): High mound, p. 157
TOOMBEOLA	G (*Tuaim Beola*): Beola's mound

TOOME	AM (*Tuaim*): Burial mound, p. 157
TOOMEBRIDGE	AM (*Droichead Thuama*): Bridge of the mound
TOOMYVARA	TY (*Tuaim Uí Mheára*): Ó Meára's mound, p. 157
TOOR	L (*Tuar*): Bleach-green, p. 158
TOORAREE	L (*Tuar an Fraoigh*): Bleach-green of the heather, p. 158
TOOREEN	MO (*Tuairín*): Little bleach-green, p. 158
TOOREENNAFERSHA	KY (*Tuairín na Feirste*): Little bleach-green of the sandbank, p. 158
TOOREENNAHONE	KY (*Tuairín na hÓn*): Little bleach-green of the hole, p. 158
TOOREVAGH	WH (*Tuar Riabhach*): Striped bleach-green
TOORMORE	C (*Tuar Mór*): Big bleach-green, p. 158
TORY ISLAND	DL (*Toraigh*): Island abounding in towers
TOUR	L (*Tuar*): Bleach-green, p. 158
TOURLESTRANE	SO (*Tuar Loistreáin*): Loistreán's bleach-green
TOURMAKEADY	MO (*Tuar Mhic Éadaigh*): Mac Éadaigh's bleach-green, p. 158
TOURNAFULLA	L (*Tuar na Fola*): Bleach-green of substance
TOYE	DN (*Tuaith*): Territory
TRAFRASK	C (*Trá Phraisce*): Strand of the kale, p. 154
TRALEE	KY (*Tráigh Lí*): Strand of the (river) Lí, p. 154
TRAMORE	WD (*Trá Mhór*): Big strand, p. 156
TRANAROSSAN	DL (*Trá na Rosán*): Strand of the Rosses, p. 154
TRAWMORE	MO (*Trá Mhór*): Big strand, p. 156
TRIEN	MO (*Trian*): Third or good portion
TRILLICK	TE (*Treileac*): Three stones
TRIM	MH ([*Baile Átha*] *Troim*): (Town of the ford of) the elder-tree, pp 18, 57
TROMMAN	MH (*Tromán*): Little place where elders grow, p. 157
TROMMAUN	RN (*Tromán*): Little place where elders grow, p. 157
TROSTAN	AM (*Trostán*): Pole
TUAM	G (*Tuaim*): Mound, p. 157
TUAMGRANEY	CE (*Tuaim Gréine*): Grian's mound, p. 157
TUBBER	G (*Tobar*): Well, p. 153
TUBBRID	KK & TY (*Tiobraid*): Well, p. 151
TULLA	CE (*Tulach*): Hill, p. 158
TULLAGH	DL (*Tulach*): Hill, p. 159
TULLAGHAN	LM & SO (*Tulachán*): Little hill, p. 159
TULLAGHANMORE	WH (*Tulachán Mór*): Big hillock, p. 159
TULLAGHER	KK (*Tulachar*): Hilly place

TULLAHERIN	KK (*Tulach Thirim*): Dry hill, p. 159
TULLAKEEL	KY (*Tulach Chaoil*): Narrow hill, p. 159
TULLAMORE	KY & OY (*Tulach Mhór*): Big hill, p. 159
TULLOW	CW (*Tulach*): Hill, p. 159
TULLROAN	KK (*Tulach Ruáin*): Ruán's hill
TULLY	G (*Tulach*): Hill, p. 159
TULLYALLEN	LH (*Tulach Álainn*): Lovely hill, p. 159
TULLYCO	CN (*Tulaigh Chuach*): Cuckoo hill
TULLYCRINE	L (*Tulach an Chrainn*): Hill of the tree, p. 159
TULLYLISH	DN (*Tulach lis*): Hill of the fort
TULLYRONE	AH (*Tulach Ruáin*): Ruán's hill
TULLYVIN	CN (*Tulach Bhinn*): Hill of the peak
TULRAHAN	MO (*Tulach Shrutháin*): Hill of the stream, p. 159
TUNNYDUFF	CN (*Tonnach Dhubh*): Black quagmire
TUOSIST	KY (*Tuath Ó Síosta*): Territory of the Uí Síosta, p. 158
TURE	DL (*An tlúr*): The yew-tree
TURLOUGH	MO (*Turlach*): Fen, p. 159
TURLOUGHMORE	G (*Turlach Mór*): Large fen, p. 159
TURREAGH	AM (*Torr Riabhach*): Grey heap
TYFARNHAM	WH (*Teach Farannáin*): Farannán's house
TYNAGH	G (*Tuíneach*): Watercourse
TYNAN	AH (*Tuínéan*): Watercourse
TYRELLA	DN (*Teach Riala*): Riail's house, p. 147
TYRONE	(*Tír Eoghain*): Territory of Eoghan, p. 152

ULLARD	KK (*Ulaidh Ard*): High penitential station
ULLAUNS	KK (*Ulán*): Penitential station
UMMAMORE	WH (*Iomaidh*): Contention
UMMERABOY	C (*Iomaire Buí*): Yellow ridge
UMMERACAM	AH (*Iomaire Cam*): Crooked ridge, p. 101
UMRYCAM	DL & DY (*Iomaire Cam*): Crooked ridge, p. 101
URBALREAGH	DY (*Earball Riabhach*): Striped end-piece
URLINGFORD	KK (*Áth na nUrlainn*): Ford of the shafts
URRIN RIVER	WX (*Urrainn* + River): Division + river

V

VALENCIA KY (*Béal Inse*): Mouth of the island
VENTRY KY (*Fionntrá*): White strand

W

WATERESK DN (*Uachtar Easc*): Upper channel
WATERFORD WD: See NORSE NAMES, p. 125
WEXFORD WX: See NORSE NAMES, p. 125
WHIDDY ISLAND C (*Oileán Faoide*): Bad weather island
WICKLOW WW: See NORSE NAMES, p. 125
WITTER DN (*Uachtar*): Upper place

Y

YOUGHAL C & TY (*Eochaill*): Yew-wood, p. 84

BIBLIOGRAPHY OF THE PUBLISHED WORKS OF DEIRDRE FLANAGAN

AS DEIRDRE MORTON:

1952–53   'County Antrim Ordnance Survey Name-Book' (with J.B. Arthurs), *Bull. Ulster Place-Name Soc.*, I (1st series)

1954   'Documentary Sources for County Antrim Place-Names', *Bull. Ulster Place-Name Soc.*, II (1st series)

'Some Early Maps of County Antrim', *Bull. Ulster Place-Name Soc.*, II (1st series)

1955   'Stranmillis, Derryvolgie, Falls and the Cinament' (with J.B. Arthurs), *Bull. Ulster Place-Name Soc.*, III (1st series)

'Some County Down Place-Names of the de Courcy period', *Bull. Ulster Place-Name Soc.*, III (1st series)

1956   'Tuath-Divisions in the Baronies of Belfast and Massereene', *Bull. Ulster Place-Name Soc.*, IV (1st series)

'*Saol Cultúrtha Bhéal Feirste roimh 1850*', *Fearsaid*

1957   'The Church of Shankill and the Chapel of the Ford', *Bull. Ulster Place-Name Soc.*, V (1st series)

'Former Townland Names in Tuath Cinament', *Bull. Ulster Place-Name Soc.*, V (1st series)

1959   'Some Notes on Minor Place-Names in the Glenlark District', *Ulster Folklife*, 5

'Quilting in Glenlark, Co. Tyrone', *Ulster Folklife*, 5

Bibliography

AS DEIRDRE FLANAGAN:

1966   'The Excavation of a Court Cairn at Bavan, Co. Donegal' (with L.N.W. Flanagan), Ulster J. Archaeol., 29 (3rd series)

1969   'Rathbeg, Co. Antrim: the Historical Background', Ulster J. Archaeol., 32 (3rd series)

         'Ecclesiastical Nomenclature in Irish Texts and Place-Names: a comparison', Proc. 10th Internat. Congress Onomastic Sciences, (Vienna)

1970   'Craeb Telcha: Crew, Co. Antrim', Dinnseanchas, V,3

1971   'The Names of Downpatrick', Dinnseanchas, IV, 4

1972/73   'Settlement Terms in Irish Place-Names', Onoma (Leuven), XVII

1973   'Three Settlement Names in County Down: the Turtars of Inishargy; Dunsfort; Tullumgrange', Dinnseanchas, V, 3

1975   'Place-Names as Historical Source-Material', Part 1, Ulster Local Stud., I

1976   'Place-Names as Historical Source-Material', Part 2, Ulster Local Stud., II

         'Exemplary Guide to the Study of a Place-Name: Glenavy td, Co. Antrim', Ulster Local Stud., II

1978   'Place-Names: a Matter of Identity', Bull. Ulster Place-Name Soc., I (2nd series)

         'Common Elements in Irish Place-Names', Bull. Ulster Place-Name Soc., I (2nd series)

         'Transferred Population or Sept-Names: Ulaidh (a quo Ulster)', Bull. Ulster Place-Name Soc., I (2nd series)

         'Places and their Names: Quoile; British', Bull. Ulster Place-Name Soc., I (2nd series)

'Seventeenth-Century Salmon Fishing in Co. Down (River-Name Documentation)', *Bull. Ulster Place-Name Soc.*, I (2nd series)

'In Memoriam: Éamonn de hÓir', *Bull. Ulster Place-Name Soc.*, I (2nd series)

'Corrigenda and Addenda: Ballysugagh and Downpatrick', *Bull. Ulster Place-Name Soc.*, I (2nd series)

1979   'Review of *Toponomia Hiberniae I: Baruntach Dhún Ciaraáin Thuaidh*', *Bull. Ulster Place-Name Soc.*, II (2nd series)

'Review of "The Meaning of Irish Place-Names"', *Bull. Ulster Place-Name Soc.*, II (2nd series)

'The Ulster Place-Name Society', *Onoma*, 23, 1

'Common Elements in Irish Place-Names: *Ceall, Cill*', *Bull. Ulster Place-Name Soc.*, II (2nd series)

'Transferred Population or Sept-Names: *Lathairne/Latharna*', *Bull. Ulster Place-Name Soc.*, II (2nd series)

'Places and their Names: Kilroot', *Bull. Ulster Place-Name Soc.*, II (2nd series)

'Corrigenda and Addenda: Legoneill; Carryduff', *Bull. Ulster Place-Name Soc.*, II (2nd series)

1980   'Review of "The Meaning of Irish Place-Names"', *Ulster Local Studies*, 5, 2

'Place-Names in Early Irish Documentation: Structure and Composition', *Nomina*, 4

1980/81 'Common Elements in Irish Place-Names: *Dún, Ráth, Lios*', *Bull. Ulster Place-Name Soc.*, III (2nd series)

'A Reappraisal of DA in Irish Place-Names', *Bull. Ulster Place-Name Soc.*, III (2nd series)

1981/82 'In Memoriam: Brendan Adams', *Bull. Ulster Place-Name Soc.*, IV (2nd series)

Bibliography

'Some Guidelines to the Use of Joyce's *Irish Names of Places*, Vol. I', *Bull. Ulster Place-Name Soc.*, IV (2nd series)

'A Summary Guide to the More Commonly Attested Ecclesiastical Elements in Place-Names', *Bull. Ulster Place-Name Soc.*, IV (2nd series)

1983   'Some Less Frequently Attested Irish Place-Name Elements of Archaeological Interest', *Nomina*, 7

1984   'The Christian Impact on Early Ireland: Place-Name Evidence', in P. Ní Chatháin and M. Richter (eds), *Ireland and Europe: The Early Church*, (Stuttgart)

AS DEIRDRE UÍ FHLANNAGÁIN

1969   'Lann', *An tUltach*, XLVI

'Iaarsmaina Pagantachta' *An tUltach*, XLVI

'Mireanna Normancha sna Logainmneacha', *An tUltach*, XLVI

'Logainmneacha Normanach in Aird Uladh', *An tUltach*, XLVI

'"Dún" sna Logainmneacha', *An tUltach*, XLVI

1970   '"Ráth" sna Logainmneacha' *An tUltach*, XLVII

'"Lios" sna Logainmneacha', *An tUltach*, XLVII

'Logainmneacha: an Sean agus an Nua' *An tUltach*, XLVII

'"Caiseal" agus "Cathair" sna Logainmneacha', *An tUltach*, XLVII

'"Scoti" agus "Ulster-Scots"', *An tUltach*, XLVII

'An Choill Ultach agus Coillte Eile', XLVII

'"Both" sna Logainmneacha', *An tUltach*, XLVII

'Latharna', *An tUltach*, XLVII

'Teach Eoin agus "tithe" eile', *An tUltach*, XLVII

'Mionainmneacha ar Thuamai Mora', *An Ultach*, XLVII

'Bothar na bhFal, Maigh Lon, An tSeanchill agus Baile na mBrathar', *An tUltach*, XLVII

1971   'Sraidainmneacha', An tUltach, XLVII

1974   'Logainmneacha mar Fhoinse Staire', Dinnseanchas, VI, 1

1976   'Mainistir na hInse, Co. an Dúin', An tUltach, LIII, 8

            'Mainistir an Dúin', An tUltach, LIII, 11
1979   'Review of Atlas a Dó Scoileanna na hÉireann', An tUltach,
            LVI

1982   'Brendan Adams: Scoláire Ilcheardach (Appreciation)', An
            tUltach, LIX

            'Béal Feirste agus Áitainmneacha Laistigh', in (ed. B.S. Mac
            Aodha) Topothesia: Aistí in onóir T.S. Ó Máille (Galway)

FOR FURTHER READING

JOYCE, Patrick W.: *The Origin and History of Irish Names of Places* (Dublin, 1869–1913). Despite being first published at a time when few of the major resources available to students of Irish place-names today existed, this remains the only comprehensive work on the subject. While many of the interpretations advanced by Joyce have been superseded as the result of modern scholarship, it is estimated that, where the criteria of modern toponymy have been applied, 30 per cent of his interpretations are incorrect. This book may most helpfully be used after consulting 'Some Guidelines to the Use of Joyce's *Irish Names of Places*, Vol. I' by Deirdre Flanagan in *Bulletin of the Ulster Place-Name Society*, IV (2nd series) (1981/2).

COUNTY SURVEYS

Ó CÍOBHÁIN, Breandán: *Toponomia Hiberniae* (*Place-Names of Ireland*) (Dublin, 1978–). An ambitious and courageous undertaking, initially dealing with the place-names of County Kerry, with special emphasis on minor names, and consequently with a greater dependence on oral sources in an Irish-speaking area than on the existing documentary evidence. It constitutes an exemplary contribution to place-name studies and can be consulted usefully with reference to names outside County Kerry.

STOCMAN, Gerard et al.: *Place-Names of Northern Ireland* (Belfast, 1992–). Also an ambitious project, but with official backing and financing, and with a team of researchers, based in the Department of Celtic, Queen's University, Belfast. The first county to be studied is County Down and it is treated systematically civil parish by civil parish. The main emphasis is on townland names and full documentation has been assembled for each name. It is a model of the proper approach to and treatment of place-name studies.

Ó MAOLFABHAIL, Art: *Logainmneacha na hÉireann: Contae Luimnigh* (Dublin, 1990).

Ó MURAILE, Nollaig: *Mayo Places: their Names and Origins* (Dublin, 1985).

PRICE, Liam: *The Place-Names of County Wicklow* (Dublin, 1945–67). A pioneering work on the systematic study of the place-names of a single county.

WALSH, Paul: *The Place-Names of Westmeath* (Dublin, 1957).

OTHER PUBLICATIONS

In addition to publications by the Place-Names Office of the Ordnance Survey of Ireland, such as *Gasaitéar na hÉireann/Gazetteer of Ireland* (Dublin, 1989), important articles on Irish place-names may be found in the journals dedicated to the study of names, such as *Bulletin of the Ulster Place-Name Society* (Belfast, 1952–7, 1st series; 1978–82, 2nd series); *Dinnseanchas* (Dublin, 1964–); *Ainm* (Belfast, 1986–), as well as in many of the journals devoted to Irish history, archaeology, linguistics and folklore, such as *Celtica*, *Proceedings of the Royal Irish Academy*, *Ulster Folk-Life*, etc.

SOURCES

(This is not intended to constitute an exhaustive summary of the primary sources of information about Irish place-names; rather, it indicates the type of information that may be gleaned from sources of different kinds. A complete and meaningful list would be impossible to compile briefly.)

The sources of information about the Irish forms of place-names are various. The most useful, in many ways, are those in Irish documentation: first and foremost among these are the various Annals. Here, one of the problems which arises is that a name mentioned, more or less in isolation, cannot be identified with an extant, perhaps badly distorted, modern place-name. Sometimes, however, clues are given as to location; for example, in *Annals of the Four Masters*, under the year 1557, Henry O'Neill is described as arriving at a place called *Tearmonn Uí Moain* ('Church-land of Ó Moain'), where he purchased a horse from Ó Moain. Without the added information that he reached this place after swimming the rivers Deel, Finn and Derg, it would be fairly difficult to identify this place as Termonamongan, Co. Tyrone, where, indeed, the Ó Moain family were hereditary *erenaghs*, or keepers, of the church. Similarly in *Miscellaneous Annals from Mac Carthaigh's Book*, under the year 1130, a hosting by Conchobhar with the Cineál Eoghain and others to *Druim Both* ('Ridge of the hut') is revealed, by its location in *Ulaidh*, to be Drumbo, Co. Down, which is confirmed by the fact that the pillaging included the round tower, oratory and books.

Another valuable Irish source is the martyrologies, such as the *Martyrology of Donegal*. Here a reference under 17 September establishes that a Saint Riaghail, of *Tech Riaghla* in Lecale, gave his name to modern Tyrella, while another under 25 October confirms that a Saint Caoide of *Domhnach Caoide* gave his name to Donaghedy, Co. Tyrone. Other Irish ecclesiastical sources include various lives of saints.

Medieval Latin documentation also contributes to the solution of several potential mysteries. The *Ecclesiastical Taxation of the Dioceses of Down, Connor and Dromore*, for example, otherwise known as *The Pope Nicholas Taxation*, reveals, with assistance from the position of the place in the lists, that *Ecclesia de Rathcolpa*, valued at four marks, is *Rath Colpa* ('Church of the bullock's fort'), and is now represented by Raholp, Co. Down, while *Capella de Baliath*, valued at twenty marks, is *Baile Átha* ('Homestead of the ford'), now Ballee, Co. Down. Other useful medieval sources are the Registers, Visitations and Grants.

Later documentation of value includes further ecclesiastical Visitations made in the seventeenth century as well as the enormous quantity of state records, such as the *Patent Rolls*, *Inquisitions* (both Chancery and Exchequer), *Hearth Money Rolls, Crown and Quit Rent Rolls* and a mass of other documentation, both printed after the original manuscripts and still available only in manuscript. In some, identification of the place in question is facilitated by its position in a list of the lands contained in a parish or barony, though often the names are so badly corrupt that it can be difficult even to recognise the name or names. A schedule of lands allotted to the London Livery Companies, compiled in 1613, lists lands given to the Company of Mercers in the vicinity of Swatragh, Co. Derry. It is really only from the cumulative evidence of their contiguity that it is possible to identify them. Swatragh itself appears as 'Soatrah', Moneysharvan as 'Mone Sharnan', Knockoneill as 'Knock Neale' and Slaghtneill as 'Slot Neale'; none of these forms would be of much benefit in establishing original Irish forms. From the seventeenth century, maps – as tools essential to the process of confiscation – began to appear, including the well-known *Maps of the Downe Survey*, compiled by William Petty in the period 1655–8.